COACHING

FOOTBALL

COACHING FOOTBALL

FROM YOUTH LEAGUES TO THE PROS

TOM FLORES AND BOB O'CONNOR

McGraw·Hill

New York   Chicago   San Francisco   Lisbon   London   Madrid   Mexico City
Milan   New Delhi   San Juan   Seoul   Singapore   Sydney   Toronto

The McGraw·Hill Companies

Library of Congress Cataloging-in-Publication Data

Flores, Tom.
    Coaching football/Tom Flores and Bob O'Connor.—2nd ed.
      p.   cm.
    Includes index.
    ISBN 0-07-143914-5 (alk. paper)
    1. Football—Coaching.   I. O'Connor, Robert, 1932–   II. Title.

  GV954.4.F56   2006
  796.332'07'7—dc22   2005029691

1 2 3 4 5 6 7 8 9 0   CUS/CUS   0 9 8 7 6 5

ISBN 0-07-143914-5

Interior illustrations by Randy Miyake

McGraw-Hill books are available at special quantity discounts to use as premiums and sales promotions, or for use in corporate training programs. For more information, please write to the Director of Special Sales, Professional Publishing, McGraw-Hill, Two Penn Plaza, New York, NY 10121-2298. Or contact your local bookstore.

This book is printed on acid-free paper.

DEDICATION

Pat Tillman gave up a $3.6 million contract with the Arizona Cardinals to join the U.S. Army—and eventually the Rangers. In 2001 he turned down an offer of $9 million for five years from the Super Bowl champions, the St. Louis Rams, out of loyalty to the Cardinals.

He left the glory of professional sports for what he considered the good of the country and the world. He was killed in Afghanistan while on a Ranger patrol. He was one person who put his personal ethics and patriotism above the everyday selfishness that is so common in our world.

Tillman played linebacker at Arizona State University and was the Pacific 10 Conference's Defensive Player of the Year in 1997. He graduated summa cum laude in only three and a half years, earning a degree in marketing.

Tillman set a Cardinals record with 224 tackles in 2000 and warmed up for his last year's training camp by competing in a 70.2-mile triathlon in June. Tillman, who at 5'11" tall and 200 pounds was considered undersized for his position, nevertheless distinguished himself by his intelligence and appetite for rugged play.

"You don't find guys that have that combination of being as bright and as tough as him," said Phil Snow, who coached Tillman as Arizona State's defensive coordinator, in 2002. "This guy could go live in a foxhole for a year by himself with no food."

"It touches you pretty deep," Cardinals head coach Dave McGinnis stated at recent NFL meetings. "Pat Tillman is a guy that is full of fiber, full of fabric, everything that he does goes right to the core of what is good and sound in our country." John McCain, the senator from Arizona who was a prisoner of war for more than five years in Vietnam, lauded Tillman as "the quintessential definition of a patriot."

"He is a hero," said Michael Bidwill, vice president of the Cardinals. "He was a brave man. There are very few people who have the courage to do what he did, the courage to walk away from a professional sports career and make the ultimate sacrifice."

Denver quarterback Jake Plummer was a teammate of Tillman for seven years, three at Arizona State and four with the Cardinals. He said, "We lost a unique individual who touched the lives of many with his love for life, his toughness, his intellect. Pat Tillman lived life to the fullest and will be remembered forever in my heart and mind."

We and our players would do well to emulate the academic and athletic excellence of this young man—and even more important, his commitment to the higher ethical principles of pursuing the greater good for our world society.

A more complete man has probably never played our game, so we dedicate this book to Pat's memory and to the ideals it should inspire for today's generation and for the generations yet to come.

CONTENTS

Foreword by John Gruden, Head Coach, Tampa Bay Buccaneers **ix**

Foreword by Tony Dungy, Head Coach, Indianapolis Colts **xi**

Preface **xiii**

Key to Diagrams **xiv**

1 Coaching the Game of Football **1**

2 A Philosophy of Coaching and Playing **5**

3 Theories of Winning **11**

4 Theories of Developing a Running Attack **17**

5 Blocking for the Running Play **29**

6 Theories of Offensive Formations **39**

7 Passing Theory **49**

8 Attacking the Defense with the Forward Pass **59**

9 Theories of Defensive Play **69**

10 The Kicking Game and Special Teams **83**

11 Movement, Contact, Tackling, and Ball Stripping **93**

12 Offensive Line Fundamentals and Cadence **101**

13 Offensive Backfield Fundamentals **115**

14 Fundamentals of Passing and Catching **121**

15 Defensive Line Fundamentals **127**

16 Linebacker Fundamentals **139**

17 Defensive Secondary Fundamentals   **149**

18 Kicking Fundamentals   **161**

19 Scouting and the Scouting Report   **169**

20 Strategy: Deciding on the Game Plan   **179**

21 Strategy Planning Checklist and Game Plans   **189**

22 Tactics: The Adjustments During a Game   **197**

23 Coaching: It's More Than Xs and Os   **205**

Glossary   211

Index   219

FOREWORD by John Gruden

With over a hundred years of playing and coaching experience between them, Tom and Bob deliver the consummate book for football coaches. It is not a book on how to run the option play or how to develop a pass offense, although both of these topics are covered.

Rather it fills the gaps in many areas coaches may not understand or even think about.

Any competent coach, from the youth coach to the professional coach, must know what all the options are and why he chooses to do what he does. By looking at the history of our great game, we see that creative thinking in strategy and tactics is as old as the game itself. The illustrated old formations, used a hundred years ago, display imagination that rivals or surpasses some of the creativity we see today. Developing effective offensive, defensive, and kicking game strategies and tactics is one of the great fascinations and challenges for every coach. Knowing what has gone before, and seeing the evolution of football thinking, can help us to put our own theories in perspective. In football, as in life, if we don't know where we have been and understand all the options, we cannot intelligently choose how to go forward.

This book covers all aspects of coaching theory, and I believe that every coach can use it as a valuable learning resource. Young coaches can learn a tremendous amount about both the on-field and off-field responsibilities of coaching from this book. There is something important here for every coach and for anyone interested in better understanding the game.

JON GRUDEN,
Head Coach, Tampa Bay Buccaneers

FOREWORD by Tony Dungy

Tom Flores enjoyed a great career in the National Football League. He played for three different teams and later became the head coach for two different franchises. Along the way, he gained a great deal of knowledge about how to play the game of football. But it was more than his knowledge that made me appreciate Coach Flores. Whatever he did, he always did it with championship class and dignity. In *Coaching Football*, he presents a picture of how to teach young men about football and about life.

This is not just a book about strategy—what plays to run or what type of defense to employ; it is more about how the game is coached. It really talks about how to teach individuals to become not only better football players but better athletes and better young men. Coach Flores draws from all of his experience as a Super Bowl–winning player and coach. He gives you insight into how to develop a philosophy of coaching, how you're going to instruct players in-season and off-season, and how to get your players thinking like winners. His emphasis is not so much on *what* to teach, but *how* to teach. That's why this book is great reading for any coach. Whether you're at the Pop Warner level or coaching in the NFL, I'm sure you'll learn some valuable lessons that will make you more effective at doing what we are all trying to do—help our young men be the best that they can be.

TONY DUNGY
Head Coach, Indianapolis Colts

PREFACE

This book is designed to give you an overview of what must be considered in coaching. While it includes some specifics that should help you immensely, such as the strategy checklists or specifics on conditioning and fundamentals, space doesn't permit including all there is to know about football. We won't try to talk you into using the West Coast offense or the single wing. But we will attempt to get you to think through the whole coaching process—philosophy; theories of offense, defense, and kicking; some fundamentals; ideas on scouting and game planning; and so on. If you want to learn more on ways to block or offenses to run, you can buy books or tapes on the subject.

While we expect our reading audience to be coaches who are early in their careers (possibly high school or youth coaches) we address subjects that would be new to most pro and college coaches.

From youth football to the pro level, we coach an intensely interesting game. When we are developing blocking schemes, pass patterns, or blitz packages, we had better know something about those parts of the game; but there is much more. We must know how to motivate our players so that they will practice efficiently, learn the game, and play hard.

Young coaches often spend most of their time planning and teaching offense—even though most experienced coaches believe that defense wins championships. In spite of the importance of kicking, many coaches relegate only a few minutes of the Thursday practice to this essential part of the game. If the punt is the most important play in football, we should certainly spend more time on it than on the flea flicker! If you don't know it when you start coaching, it doesn't take too many seasons to realize that teaching techniques effectively is more important than having the league's thickest playbook. For championship contention, however, you'd better have a squad with an outstanding attitude. A few years ago at an American Football Coaches Convention, the first speaker at the junior college session talked about tackling; the second talked about the importance of attitude. The next lecture was a high school session; one coach talked about a trap play, but the next speaker talked only about attitude. The very next session was for Division 1, where the entire topic was attitude. Experienced coaches know that attitude is the heart of the game.

This book should have something for every coach from the peewee level to the pros. While we have included lots of "whats" and "hows" in many areas, we have emphasized the "whys."

So this book is not so much about plays—it's about evaluating and developing a comprehensive approach to theory and practice. Because of this focus, it is essential to look at the "whys": Why pass? Why double-team? Why use multiple formations?

Based on these we look at the "whats" and the "hows"—how to block effectively, how to develop an effective passing attack, how to develop the kicking game.

When coaches and players have thought out the "whys" and the "hows," we should all experience more success and learn more about winning in school and winning in life.

KEY TO DIAGRAMS

Drawings in this book use this traditional method of indicating how the play is to work:

◯ is an offensive player.

Ⓧ is the snapper. He will not always be in the center.

V indicates a defensive lineman.

B indicates a linebacker.

C indicates a cornerback or a defensive halfback in a 3-deep alignment.

S indicates the safetymen.

● indicates the ball carrier.

Ⓘ indicates a player who handles the ball, but does not complete the play as the ball carrier.
An example would be the player who starts a reverse play but hands the ball off to another player.

—— indicates the path of a player.

···· indicates the path of the ball—a pass or a lateral.

⌇⌇ indicates the path of the man in motion.

-|- indicates a fake handoff.

-||- indicates a handoff.

COACHING THE GAME OF FOOTBALL

"One of America's most important callings"

Hall of Famer Mike Singletary in his keynote address to the American Football Coaches Association in 2003 said, "If anyone would ask me what coaching really means, it's not really about winning. It's not really about Xs and Os. All those things go into it, but it's about influence." He then went on to say, "His coach would push them, would test them, would take them to the next level. But most importantly, love them."

"Football's been good to me. I've laughed and I've cried my heart out, just like, probably, many of you. But all in all, I wouldn't take anything for having the opportunity to do what I wanted to do most of my life, and that is to coach football"—so said the late Charlie McClendon, former executive director of the American Football Coaches Association and former head coach at Louisiana State University, on accepting the AFCA's highest award, the Amos Alonzo Stagg Award in 1992.

As a coach you have a deep responsibility to your players. It is your job to know the young people you are teaching, the game you are teaching, and how the game of football can bring your players to their highest potential as happy and contributing citizens, husbands, and fathers.

Those of us who have chosen to coach this great game follow in the footsteps of thousands of beloved coaches who have gone before us—from the gods of the game, Amos Alonzo Stagg, Knute Rockne, and Glenn "Pop" Warner, to the educational leaders of modern times, the Joe Paternos, Eddie Robinsons, and Grant Teaffs.

The fascination with the game continues for most of us. Amos Alonzo Stagg was still coaching after his 100th birthday. John Gagliardi of St. Johns University, at age seventy-seven, broke Eddie Robinson's all-time college win record in 2003 and then went on to win the Division III national championship, breaking Mt. Union's fifty-five game win streak in the finals. (His record at the end of the 2003 season was 414-114-11.) At age seventy-five, Joe Paterno is talking about another undefeated season this decade to match those he accomplished in each of the last four decades. Bobby Bowden, at age seventy-four, passed Paterno in 2003 and now holds the record for most wins by a Division 1A coach. Also in 2003, John McKissick of Summerville (South Carolina) High School increased his high school record to over five hundred wins. He is over one hundred wins ahead of his nearest rival. The beginning of the new century was a good one for old-timers!

We have a legacy to uphold. We must strive to defeat the often-believed idea that that we must win at all costs. Rather, we must always seek to win within the rules. Any victory gained by cheating is a personal loss to the players and coaches. In order to win fairly, we must understand as much of this complicated game as possible, understand our players, choose the possibilities of the game that will best fit our players, organize effectively so that we can make the most out of the limited time available, and then outthink our opposing coaches in the week before and during the game. This is the challenge of football—a challenge that no other game can match.

Approaching Coaching

As with any other worthwhile occupation, coaching football requires a thorough understanding of a body of knowledge. Strangely, a great many coaches don't understand the complete game. Because of this they limit themselves in the potential they can offer their players. Many coaches are knowledgeable only about the system they played. This limits their understanding of the possibilities of their own team, the advantages and the disadvantages of their opponents' approaches.

There is no one best way to coach. There is no one best offensive or defensive system. The pros use a system that allows them to attack the entire field. While most pro coaches want to emphasize the run, they have to pass.

The venerable and intelligent former coach of the Ohio State Buckeyes, Woody Hayes, once outlined the structure of how we should analyze the game of football. We will utilize this outline to look at the totality of the game. Coach Hayes said that our approach to football can be analyzed according to our philosophy, theory, strategy, and tactics.

Philosophy

Philosophy is "why" you play or coach the game. What is it that makes you play and coach? What outcomes result because of playing and coaching? Every player and every coach learns something every year from the game. Sometimes those lessons are negative. Hopefully the great majority of experiences will be positive. It is the coach's job to ensure that the experiences of his players are primarily positive ones. In the chapter on philosophy, some of the greats of the game will share with us what they have gained from this all-American game.

The Theory of the Game

The theory of the game is the overall approach you take to winning. On offense, do you try to get a first down on every series (as most teams do), or do you play a more conservative "field position" game while you attempt to reduce your mistakes and capitalize on those of your opponents? On defense, do you attack and gamble on creating losses, or do you merely attempt to limit your opponent's gains for three downs and then force a fourth down punt? How important is the kicking game in your plans? Is it a necessary evil while you wait to play offense or is it a key part of your approach to the game? These are very real concerns that many coaches do not consciously consider. Each has its advantages.

In this book, we attempt not to give you a playbook but rather to give you a number of options you might use in developing your own theories of offense, defense, and kicking. There isn't time to teach a complete power offense, an option offense, and a complete passing attack. So where are you going to put in your planning and practice time? If the punt is the most important play in football, how much planning and practice time are you going to devote to it?

If you think that the turnover ratio is critical to your success, how much practice time will you spend on ball security and stripping and intercepting techniques? Since time is your enemy, you must decide how to spend it effectively. We are just going to lay out the possibilities and the odds of winning using various approaches to the game.

Because the time available to teach your players is limited, you will not be able to teach them everything you know. You must develop priorities based on your theory—then use the time available to teach those parts of the game that you believe are most important.

Planning Strategy

Planning strategy is one of the most interesting parts of the game for most coaches. After scouting your opponent, you attempt to find how you can match your strengths against the weaknesses of your opponent—in personnel, formations, and situations.

Handling the Tactical Situations in the Game

Handling the tactical situations in the game is often the key to winning—especially in close games. Here is where knowledge and experience really count in coaching. How can you cope with your opponent's unexpected changes in attack and defense? How can you force your opponent to play your game? If an injury occurs to either team, how will that change your plans? Remember that every technical strength of a team will result in a technical weakness somewhere on the field. Can you find it and exploit it?

The Joy of Coaching

Yes, being a football coach takes a great deal of time. It requires constant studying to keep up. And it requires long hours with the players in conditioning programs, working on fundamentals, and meetings and functions with people outside of the team members. Few individuals ever make a significant amount of money in coaching—but that's not why we get into coaching. We coach because our lives are enriched by the people with whom we work and those whom we teach. We are rich because we are spending our time doing what we enjoy most. Aren't we lucky!

CHAPTER 2

A PHILOSOPHY OF COACHING AND PLAYING

"Why do we play and coach this very special game?"

The great composer Franz Liszt once said, "Every theater is a lunatic asylum and opera is the ward for the incurables." The same might very well be said about football coaches and players at the higher levels—for whatever reason, FOOTBALL IS FUN.

Every type of game excites its participants. Whether it is Monopoly, hide-and-seek, or football, people play for enjoyment. Those of us who have made lifelong commitments to the game of football obviously have some deep attachments to this very special game.

Players want to have fun. Will they have it only when playing a game? Will it occur in blocking drills, Oklahoma drills, playing keep-a-way with a football for conditioning, playing volleyball over the goalposts, running 7 on 7? In America, football is part of the total educational program. Therefore, we have a duty to help develop our players as total people.

Football tests a man's raw physical courage more than perhaps any other sport. Robert Lewis Stevenson once said, "Courage is the footstool of other virtues." In nearly all cultures, it is the badge of courage that separates the desirable young men from the rest of the pack. Whether it is the killing of a lion by a young African, the lonely battle against the elements of a young Native American during his initiation into the circle of braves, or the tackling of an opponent by a young football player— courage is exhibited. Every society recognizes that courage and applauds it.

What Is Your Philosophy of Life—and Your Philosophy of Coaching?

Why are you coaching? Is it for your ego or to develop young people to be the best they can be? At the Pop Warner and high school level, it is far more important to put the player's total development far ahead of your own interests. At the college level, the players are more developed, and winning becomes more important as a goal of the program. By the time you reach the pro level, it is all about winning—but even here helping the players to be the best they can be, to push them harder, becomes more important, if not vital.

The philosophy that we live by is a combination of psychological needs, such as the power drive, or love needs; it may be based on our religion, our upbringing, or the images presented by the media. But whatever elements make up our philosophy of life (such as the need to control and win, the drive for fame or fortune, the need to help our family grow and mature, or the necessity of following our religious beliefs), we should be aware of the forces that drive us. The Greek philosopher Plato popularized the idea that it was essential to know ourselves.

We should also understand our coaching philosophy. Certainly, no matter what level we are coaching we want to win. But at the youth level, the emphasis should be on making the young players the best people they can be. Even at the high school level, this is important—but the need to win games becomes much more important. This trend becomes even more important at the college level and all-important at the pro level. So readers of this book will primarily fall into the category of charac- ter- developing teachers rather than "win-at-all- cost" coaches.

Why I Played the Game

The reasons that men have played and the out- comes gained from playing are often different. It is not like building a house. When a person has the goal of building a house, he designs it and builds it. His goal is then attained. In football, a boy may begin to play because it is *the* prestige sport, or because his father wants him to play, or because it is the only thing to do after school. However, the out- comes may be a feeling of accomplishment, the development of a concept of self-worth, a college scholarship, or a lifetime job in playing or coaching.

Hall of Fame linebacker Sam Huff, of the Giants and Redskins, told us that he started playing just because it was expected. In the small coal-mining town in West Virginia where he grew up, boys were expected to go out for all three sports—football, bas- ketball, and baseball. "I was pretty good at football and baseball, but I never could dribble, shoot, or jump! And I liked the contact inherent to football. I liked the contact in baseball, too. I was a catcher."

The outcomes were different from what origi- nally attracted Sam to playing. He summarized his gratitude to the game by stating, "It taught me how to compete in life. It taught me patience. It taught me to give and take. But most of all it taught me to survive in a tough world." Sam's drive for success landed him the vice presidency of Marriott Hotels.

Otto Graham, the all-time Hall of Fame quarter- back, started playing for the same reason as most other boys—because it was fun. Otto had another motivation as well. His father had a great interest in music. Otto learned to play several instruments. While the violin and French horn did provide some

enjoyment, they did not offer the excitement of sports that so many young men crave. So basketball and football soon took up more of his time than did the strings and woodwinds. Otto's fascination with both playing and coaching has always been for the fun of the game, even at the professional level.

Otto went to Northwestern on a basketball scholarship. He didn't decide to play football until he was a sophomore. Of course, he had great suc- cess as a quarterback. Paul Brown, coaching Ohio State, was impressed. So when Paul approached Otto about signing with the new pro league (the All American Conference) he knew whom he was sign- ing. Otto signed for $7,500 a year and by the end of his career he was the highest-paid pro, making $25,000 a year.

The outcomes players have gained included devel- oping pride in themselves, learning patience, encoun- tering the "give-and-take" of the game, which teaches them about the real world, developing a sense of pur- pose in life, the place of discipline in accomplishing one's goals, developing leadership abilities, and for some, a lifelong profession in the game.

Detroit GM Matt Millan now has four Super Bowl rings—one with the 49ers, two with the Raiders, and one with the Redskins. He says that football helps you to learn a "zillion" things about yourself. One of the major lessons is to take care of the little things and the big things will take care of themselves.

He credits both his father and his high school coach, Andy Melosky, with developing his work ethic. His father would accept no marks in high school under 95 percent. His coach showed him the importance of working on the field.

Matt sets goals for himself daily. By working he was able to achieve them. Work will help everyone to get better. While you may not achieve your goals, you will come closer to them if you work hard. The poor player, with work, will get better. It became clear to Matt that the expectations in life are greater than their realizations: "Nothing is as good as you expect." You must come to terms with that concept so that you don't give up when life isn't perfect. Just work harder at the game, at your studies, in your business, in your marriage. Move up—don't give up!

In football, as in life, you must keep to the fundamentals. Even in the Super Bowl, when you are not playing your best, you must go back to fundamentals. Look first at your stance. Check your read progression to make certain that you are not overlooking an important key. The same is true in life. Check your fundamentals. When things are not going well in your personal or business life, check your fundamentals. Are you doing what you should be doing?

The Fascination of Coaching

Perhaps John Robinson said it best when, after leaving the head coaching position at USC for a three-month stint as a university vice president, he took the job of head coach of the Rams. "The thing that shocked me the most was that outside of the sports world, there isn't the passion for what you do."

John Madden got into coaching prematurely. An injury while working out with the Eagles gave him an opportunity to watch films with Norm Van Brocklin. The technical aspects of the game began to make an impact. He had a meteoric rise from junior college to college to pro coach. I think that a good part of his drive to succeed as the Raider head coach was to show Al Davis that he had made the right decision in giving John the job. He worked endlessly to develop the best team in pro football. He won the first Raider Super Bowl.

One of the things that excites coaches is the challenge of molding a team from a group of individuals. Former San Francisco 49er coach Bill Walsh had a reputation of being an innovative "Xs and Os" coach. Like many coaches, he had a penchant for drawing plays on tablecloths, napkins, and scraps of paper. He admitted, "Our fans liked our technical football, but I was really more concerned with two other things— the chemistry of the team and the proper evaluation

and selection of talent. Nothing on a pro football team is more important than the talent."

The Joy of Coaching

For many high school, college, and Pop Warner coaches, there is a keen desire and ability to help the youngsters of America. As Otto Graham said, "The high school coaches are the unsung heroes of America because so many of our youths will listen only to their coaches." Certainly knowing that they can be an important instrument in directing the lives of our youth is enough to make many coaches feel that they are living worthwhile lives.

There is certainly a feeling of power that a coach derives when he develops a new concept of offense or defense or when he develops a strategy that helps beat a favored opponent. There is a feeling of satisfaction when he makes personnel evaluations that turn out to help the team. There is the joy when he can help a player or the player's family. And there is the feeling of accomplishment when his team has won a game—especially a big game.

The Place of Football in American Society

Former football player General Douglas MacArthur said, "Football is the closest thing to war, that's why it would always be played at West Point." Football allows for a great deal more strategy than other games because after each play the teams can regroup and, based on the situation, can plan how to attack and how to defend the enemy.

Many former players testify that football has given them the means to be mentally tough. Successful programs emphasize the setting of both individual and team goals. Successful programs also give young men the hope and the heart to accomplish their goals in life. In an effective football program, young people can experience the success that flowers from the combination of lofty goals and hard work. And many will carry that lesson into their business, political, and family lives.

All Pro linebacker Jack "Hacksaw" Reynolds recently said, "The players that I used to play with were a lot tougher mentally. The softer our country gets, the softer our players get." Hacksaw's observation has been echoed by many coaches. The goal of so many people to "have pleasure now" sets up a psychological roadblock to a fundamental necessity of society—to defer immediate pleasure for a greater good in the future.

Former Dallas Cowboys coach Tom Landry concurred. He noted, "I came out of the Great Depression and was in a war, and I think that affected how we looked at things. You could treat us almost any way you wanted. Coaches could've kicked us and it wouldn't have affected us. When I first started coaching, there was no excuse for a player not playing the best he could. I've had to learn to motivate people to become that way."

We all know of some of the mentally tough people who have been around football since Pudge Hefflefinger played at Yale in the 1800s. They make up a smaller percentage of the players today than they once did. So it becomes the job of a coach to make young men desire to succeed. For a football team, or a society, to flourish there must be a commonality of purpose and a flaming desire to accomplish exalted goals.

Joe Gibbs, when he took over the Redskins in 2004, said he looked first for attitude, then intelligence, then ability.

Having a positive attitude helps winners develop the habit of doing the things that losers don't like to do. The young people of our nation must learn this lesson if our country is to continue to lead the world. There was drudgery in building the pyramids. Michelangelo spent many uncomfortable years lying on his back on a scaffold while painting the Sistine Chapel ceiling. There were cold unhappy days spent by the Army of the Revolution at Valley Forge. There have been many thousands of miserable seasick people landing at Ellis Island, anticipating their arrival into this country. Nearly everything valuable has occurred because of discipline—often in spite of great pain or adversity.

Vince Lombardi felt very strongly that "the quality of a man's life is directly proportional to a man's commitment to excellence." Every human being who wants to reach his fullest potential needs high goals and a strong work ethic. The game of football has given millions of American men the opportunity to pursue, in game conditions, the achievement of their goal of success; coaches universally have required a strong dedication to the work ethic.

Football has certainly played an important part in the lives of hundreds of our national legislators and executives. Dwight Eisenhower, John Kennedy, Richard Nixon, Gerald Ford, and Ronald Reagan all were involved in college football, and former congressman Jack Kemp was an All Pro.

What It Takes to Be a Successful Coach

We each bring different traits to our coaching. No coach is complete; in fact, it would be impossible to be complete. You can't be perfect for each relationship you are in—with each boy or with each coach. One boy may need a more directive approach, one may respond better to your verbal encouragement and criticism, another may sulk when criticized. You can't be Knute Rockne, Jon Gruden, Woody Hayes, Tony Dungy, Ken Hatfield, and Grant Teaff all rolled into one. You can't be the ultimate organizer, motivator, fount of football knowledge, and father equally to every boy and in every program.

Florida coach Urban Meyer, while remaining true to himself, incorporated ideas into his coaching style absorbed from several coaches with whom he has worked. From Earl Bruce, he learned to make certain he was doing things the right way.

From Lou Holtz, he learned motivation techniques. Bob Davies' approach to handling pressure influenced him. Sonny Lubick was just a great guy, a persona that made players run through walls because they liked him so much. So while you must "be yourself," you have learned both good and bad methods of coaching as you have evolved.

Be honest about who you are and what you want out of your players—and how you are going to go about developing and continuing your program. No coach can do everything he wants to do with his program; there just isn't enough time to do it all. We must trim our programs to allot time to what is important to us. Is it increasing takeaways or reducing penalties? Is it motivating players in the classroom? Is it developing a passing attack or an extensive kicking game? This is where your personal philosophy, your knowledge of the total game, and your goals for your team become the guideposts for developing your program and organizing your practices.

At the American Football Association meetings, it is revealing to hear how often the top coaches express their philosophies of life in terms of religion being primary, then family, and finally football.

There is no question that successful coaches are winners—but that winning doesn't always show on the scoreboard. Dr. Gloria Balague, one of the world's top sports psychologists, lists these essentials of coaching:

- The coaching process must emphasize the development of character.
- The coach must be competent in the necessary knowledge for the appropriate level for the sport.
- The coach must be committed to helping the players learn.
- The coach must really care for the players.
- The coach must build confidence in the players.
- The coach must be an effective communicator, knowing when to say nothing and when to praise, and how to criticize.

- The coach must be consistent in attitude and discipline.

The lower the age level of your players, the more you should involve the parents. They should know the direction you want to take in developing their children. Sometimes you have to reduce, in their minds, the importance of the scoreboard. The "win-at-all-costs" attitude at the pro level, and to a large degree at the college level, often works its way down to the high school and youth league levels. There is no question that some parents will want to overinvolve themselves in your program. They can't all understand that their son is not the next Payton Manning—in spite of his two left feet and his lack of leadership potential.

The values that can be taught through football include not only setting goals for the season and working hard to achieve them but also avoiding cheating, practicing good sportsmanship, and achieving improved academic progress. But you well know that you must live the values you are trying to teach. We all learn better by watching than by hearing.

Keep paramount in your mind that it is all about the players—as long as they are not getting paid to play. When they are professionals, we expect success. But even then the coach is responsible for helping players to be successful. The motivation to succeed and to win actually increases as a player moves up the talent scale. The coach at the pro level is at least as concerned with motivation and fundamentals as is the high school or youth coach.

What is it that you want to teach—blocking and tackling, life values, a passing attack, developing a work ethic, goal setting and the motivation of working toward goals in football and in life, playing pass defense, making every player feel important? We don't have time to teach everything well, so we must be clear on what is most important to us in coaching. Success is why we coach. But how do we measure our success, in championships or in the positive development of our players toward success in life? While you may do one or the other, these goals are not mutually exclusive. But whatever your goals, you must plan for both the content of your lessons and the methods of teaching that content—it doesn't just happen.

So coaching is a mix of many things that each coach mixes in his own way. No two coaches or programs are identical. You will put your own stamp on your program. What will that stamp bring to your athletes? Bobby Bowden said that he sees the essentials of coaching as honesty, loyalty, and compassion. The essentials for players are to be unselfish, to be a team player, and to love their teammates. The team, not the individual, must be primary in football.

The goals of winning through hard work and overcoming adversity are essential in a democratic capitalistic society. Football, properly taught, is a perfect vehicle to develop the feelings of cooperation and competition, of aggression and compassion, and of the joys of winning and the sorrows of losing. Football teaches how to be a successful person in our society better than any other subject in the school curriculum.

Football is the great American game—not because of its popularity in stadiums and on television but because of what it does for the youth of our country. Can football help to keep America tough with its eyes on the future? We think it can—and does.

CHAPTER 5

THEORIES OF WINNING

"There's more than one way to skin a cat."

Intelligent football coaches (just as generals and business administrators) must have an overall theory of how they expect to win. Since practice time is limited, coaches must determine their general approach to the game so that the alignments, plays, and skills required can be designed and practiced.

Some emphasize their defensive talents, some count on their knowledge of the kicking game, but most rely on their offensive ideas to produce their victories. Some believe that the best defense is a good offense. Others think that the best offense is a good defense. Advocates of both positions have won national and professional championships.

Field Position Theory

The field position theory of winning is probably as old as the game. Whether it was Knute Rockne or Darrell Royal—most of the legendary coaches of college football have been field position advocates.

Those who emphasize position football generally want to keep their opponents bottled up in their own territory. It is their belief that it is extremely difficult to march a team 70 or 80 yards for a touchdown. The odds are that somewhere during that march there will be a penalty, a fumble, an incomplete pass, or an interception that will stall or stop the drive. Field position advocates place their hopes in the old adage that "to err is human," and hope that their opponents are particularly "human" on game day.

By emphasizing defense and kicking, they hope to be able to slow down their opponents and to force the miscue that will result in a stalled drive or a turnover. These coaches will generally put their best players on the defensive team.

They will also spend a great deal of time perfecting the kicking game, especially punting. The 2003 Ohio State team is a case in point. Jim Tressel's team played strong field position football. It won three games without scoring an offensive touchdown by keeping the opponents backed up with interceptions, fumbles, and blocked kicks—which often become defensive touchdowns.

Likelihood of Scoring a Touchdown

Naturally the closer to the goal that the possession starts, the greater the odds of scoring. Therefore, most teams are not going to score on every possession. The opportunities for a long drive are often frustrated by an offensive penalty, a turnover, a big defensive play such as a successful blitz, or not converting on a third down. This means that a punt, or, if the team is close enough, a field goal must be attempted.

Jimmy Johnson's statistics for the pros, over the years, have shown that the following percentages work either for or against a team's ability to score from each zone on the field:

- From the goal line to the −25, the average team scores 7 percent to 12 percent of the time.
- From the −25 to the 50, the average team scores 25 percent to 30 percent of the time.
- From the 50 to the +25, the average teams scores 45 percent to 60 percent of the time.
- From the +25 to the goal line, the average is 80 percent.

Frank Beamer of Virginia Tech finds the college probabilities lower. Inside your own 20 he sees a 3 percent chance of scoring a touchdown. From the −20 to −40, about a 12 percent chance, at the 50 the chances are about 20 percent, at the +40 it raises to 33 percent, at the +20 it is now 50 percent, and if you get the ball at the opponent's 10-yard line, your chances are about 50 percent.

George O'Leary (former Georgia Tech head coach and Vikings' defensive coordinator, now head coach at the University of Central Florida) has developed a scoring percentage chart based on analyzing 10,000 plays. His scoring percentages (touchdown or field goal) are very similar.

How these three coaches break down the probability of scoring from various field positions is shown below.

Whether we want to admit it or not, football is a game of field position. The nearer you are to your goal line when you gain possession of the ball, the greater your chances of scoring.

Many coaches believe that it isn't so often that one team "wins" the game but rather that the other team "loses" it. This is particularly true in close games. So the field position advocates try to "not lose" the game. With the ball inside their own 10-yard line, they will probably punt it on first down. Inside their 20, they will probably punt on second down. And inside their 35, punt on third down. Of course, since they spend so much time on the kicking game, they may well surprise their opponents by a fake punt on first, second, or third down. If the opponent sends back one or two safetymen to field the punt, they are weakened against the run and the pass—so an occasional fake might get good yardage.

The quick kick is another important element in the field position general's arsenal. Since the idea is to keep the opponent deep in his own territory, and since a well-executed quick kick can gain 60 or more yards (compared to the 35 yards expected on a punt), the often-orphaned quick kick is a favored son to a dedicated field position coach.

The field position coach will generally divide the field into specific areas. As has been noted, inside his 35-yard line is going to be an early kicking down. From the 35 to the 50 is an area in which "safe" plays are called. Once past midfield, he will probably open

Probability of Scoring from Various Field Positions

Johnson

0 to −25	−25 to 50	50 to +25	+25 to goal
7 to 12 percent	25 to 30 percent	45 to 60 percent	80 percent

Beamer

Goal to −20	−20 to −40	50	+40	+20	+10 to goal
3 percent	12 percent	20 percent	33 percent	50 percent	50 percent

O'Leary

−10	−40	at 50 yard line
2.5 percent	11 percent	25 percent

up and may throw some passes. Then inside his opponent's 35-yard line, he will generally assume that he is in "four down territory" so he only has to make 2½ yards per play in order to score. So he may revert to a more conservative running game.

Knute Rockne divided the field into five 20-yard areas. From his own goal to the 20, he would kick on first down. From his 20 to his 40, he wouldn't pass and would punt on second or third down. Between the 40s, he might pass and would punt only on fourth down. From the offensive 40 to the 20, he would use some trick plays and would use a field goal if his offense was stopped. From the 20 to the goal, he would use the plays most likely to score.

Darrell Royal, the former Texas coach, thought in terms of three zones. From his goal to the 35, he wanted to get the ball across the 50 in any way possible—safe runs, passes, and if necessary, the punt. Between the 35s, he called "the alumni zone" where it was the duty of the coach to entertain the fans. From the offensive 35 on in, it was four down territory and he had to score.

Most field position coaches used colors to denote the area of the field in which they have the ball. It might be red, for danger, near the goal line you are protecting. Or it might be yellow for caution. Orange might be used in the middle of the field; then green, for "Go," or red for blood as you near your goal line. It is this "red zone" concept as you near your goal line that has now become the standard lingo. So even teams that do not label other areas of the field now nearly universally use the term *red zone* as they near their goal line.

"Play it safe and avoid mistakes" is the maxim that guides the thinking of the field position type of coach. His defensive ideas are geared to slowing the opponent. His offensive ideas tend to be conservative. He is likely to use an offensive attack based on power, with double-team blocking, putting two of his players against one member of the opposition. He is football's answer to Aesop's tortoise—who beat the swifter hare in their classic race.

One aspect of field position football when playing in the rain or on a soggy field may be to kick the ball on an early down, even on first down; wait for your opponent to fumble or have a punt blocked; then power the ball in for the touchdown.

Of course if you can't play good defense, this strategy won't work. But it can be very effective. The pros, with their usually high-scoring offenses, fields under tarps or under domes, and fresh balls on every play, wouldn't use this approach. In fact, the pro approach is usually that it is to the offense's advantage to play on a wet field because the pass defenders have a better chance to be defeated on a wet field.

At the pro level, wind is more often a factor in field position football. It is common in Chicago to take the wind rather than the ball if the wind blows more than twenty miles an hour. The idea is that the team will have better field position in the first or third quarters because the wind will be a factor in the kicking game and in the passing game. In a recent playoff game in Philadelphia, there was a serious debate over whether to take the ball or the wind in the third quarter.

Since a game of college football generally involves over 130 plays with twenty-two players in on each play, there are ample opportunities for errors. The old coaching adage that "football is a game of inches" indicates the small margin of error that can be the difference between winning and losing—and the field position coaches don't want to lose.

Ball Control Theory

The ball control coaches are more interested in offense—a safe offense. They hope to make 3½ yards on each of three running downs or 5 yards on two of their three passing downs so that they can get the first down. Naturally they want to avoid any mistakes, such as penalties (which would force them out of their short yardage theory) or turnovers (which would take away the ball).

Their emphasis is on safe running and safe passing plays. Most college and professional teams today are ball control teams. Whether it is done with the run or the West Coast style of passing attack, the objective is to make first downs.

The Big Play Approach

While all teams have their safe runs and passes, some seldom stray from their ball control theory. However, some coaches believe that better chances of winning lie in striking for the touchdown on one play. The Raiders have had the reputation of being such a team. Whether it is the long bomb, the deep reverse, the trick play, or the middle distance pass that "might break"—getting an immediate touchdown is always on the mind of the "big play" oriented coach.

While some coaches contemplate the "big play" with more prayer than preparation, the true "big play" advocates plan for the event. Each long-scoring play has been practiced and evaluated hundreds of times before it is used in a game.

The advantages of "big play" thinking go beyond the chance of the quick score. The defensive coordinators and their teams know that the "big play" team may "go for it all" on any play. They therefore must always defend against that long quick score. In so doing, they are often not quite ready for the basic ball control game. Their defensive backs may not support on the run quite as quickly because of their fear of the "bomb." Their defensive linemen or backers may not pursue quite as recklessly because of their fear of the reverse. If they rush the passer overaggressively they may open up the draw or the screen pass. So the threat of the "big play" makes the ball control game more effective.

Combinations of Theories

Most coaches will adopt more than one approach during the season. Perhaps the opponent is very

strong, so a "big play" approach is viewed as the only way to win. The coach may use a fake punt or put in trick plays, figuring it is his only hope.

Even the most "die-hard" field position coaches will go for the big play sometimes; it helps to keep the defense honest. And the "big play" people will use lots of ball control plays.

Successful coaches look at the probabilities of success for a certain type of play. For example, a field position coach might throw long from his own end zone—about once every ten years. He knows that the opposing coach is aware of his conservative bent, so once in a while he may throw long, knowing that the opposition expects him to stick to a safe running play.

Winning with the Run or the Pass

In analyzing the possibilities of these theories of winning it should be noted that the rule changes regarding the use of the hands in blocking give the offense a greater advantage than it used to have over the defense. It also gives the pass protectors much greater ability to protect the passer than they had when their hands had to remain close to the chest. Both the running game and the passing game are enhanced by the current use of the hands in blocking.

Both running attacks and passing attacks can be conservative or daring. Dive or power plays are "safe"—especially if the runner carries the ball with both hands so he won't fumble. Safe passing attacks will probably opt for lots of short passes to the backs—away from the major pass defenders. On the other hand, running option football (such as the veer and wishbone) increases the team's chances of fumbles while increasing the chances for long gainers. Remember the Oklahoma wishbone teams of a few years ago? It seems that every play was either a long touchdown run or a fumble. "Big play" passing teams don't worry about the interception as much, because when a long pass is intercepted it is about the same as having punted the ball. Of course "big play" coaches prefer the long completion to the long interception, given the choice.

Running advocates say that there are three things that can happen when you pass, and two of them are bad—the incomplete pass and the interception. So to avoid the incomplete pass or the interception, they stick to the run. Passing enthusiasts, on the other hand, believe that a good passing attack can be put together with less talented players than can a good running attack. Consequently, many coaches pass because of weakness, rather than strength.

A major fascination with the pass is that it is so much fun to design. Coaches are notorious for drawing plays on everything from tablecloths to the palms of their hands. On paper, there are no incomplete passes. So on the drawing board (or napkin), every coach can theorize his way to the Super Bowl.

Not only do coaches like to plan a passing attack, the players (at least the passers and receivers) like to practice it. It is a rare event when boys will go down to the park to block each other, but they will leave at the drop of a hat "to throw the ball around."

Then there is the weather factor. If your team plays in Nome, Alaska, or in Seattle, you must be concerned with the cold or the rain. Both can affect your passing attack more than your running attack. If you are guaranteed of playing every game on a clear and windless 70-degree day, your chances of success for your passing attack are greatly increased.

We see so many teams passing that many people believe that passing is the best way to win. While most coaches express their hope for a "balanced" attack—gaining nearly equal amounts of yardage from the run and the pass—in practice the running game has a lot going for it.

In the college game, the ten top running teams in the country generally average 80 percent wins, but the ten top passing teams generally average only 50 percent wins. At the pro level, teams that run forty times in a game will win 90 percent of the time.

Another pro statistic is that when the passer has a 300-yard game, his team wins 50 percent of the time. When a running back has a 100-yard day, the team will win 80 percent of the time. How many times does a team lose when one of its backs runs for over a hundred yards? Not often!

So the intelligent coach, from the youth or the high school level to the professional game, must do some hard thinking before he decides on the general theory of his approach to winning. He must consider the type of players with whom he will work (their toughness and their skills), the weather, and his own competencies and beliefs. At the college level, the coach can recruit for many of his needs so he may not be as influenced by player inadequacies. And at the professional level, the coach is nearly precluded from choosing a pure "field position" approach because the fans come to see the team score. For the pro coach, punting on first down would probably extend his tenure about as much as playing Russian roulette with all six cylinders loaded.

The coach's decision on how his team can best win is essential in determining his theories of offense, defense, and kicking. It will also play an essential part in the development of his week-to-week strategy for upcoming opponents and in the types of decisions he will make during each game. When a coach decides to punt on fourth and one on his opponent's 45, that decision was probably made months, or even years before, as part of his overall theory of winning. The boos from the stands will not persuade him to do otherwise.

Football is war with rules. How do you, as a coach, expect to win? You must have a grand plan. If you have great players, you may go for the ball control and the "big play" approaches to the game. With limited talent, you may opt for the more conservative "field position" approach. Neither is universally right or wrong; each has its place. Which is the best theory for you to use? Remember that you are the general, so it is your decision.

CHAPTER 4

THEORIES OF DEVELOPING A RUNNING ATTACK

"Should I trick 'em or run over 'em?"

Theories of running attacks can be categorized as power, quickness, and finesse. All coaches will use at least two of these theories, but in most offenses one will be emphasized.

If you plan to emphasize the pass, you will probably end up with a QB and two, one, or even no running backs. This will certainly affect your versatility in the running game. And remember that even at the pro level when a team has a 300-yard passer in a game, it has only a 50 percent chance of winning that game.

You may decide on a running attack based on your material or on your own preferences. You can adjust yourself to your material or your material to yourself.

The "power game" is predicated on the idea of having more men than your opponents at the point of attack. Most power teams will use double-team blocks by the linemen and/or blocking backs to accomplish this (see Figures 4.1 and 4.2).

The "quickness game" advocates will attempt to get the ball carrier to the line of scrimmage before the defense has a chance to react and pursue. The halfback dive play, the fullback buck, and the quar-

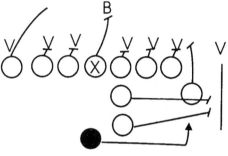

Figure 4.2 A Tennessee wing power play with two double-team blocks

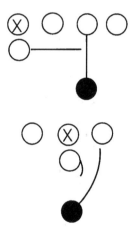

Figure 4.3 Split-T dive and fullback buck

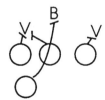

Figure 4.1 A double-team block with an isolated linebacker blocked by a fullback

terback sneak are examples of quickness plays (see Figure 4.3).

The "finesse game" utilizes deception or "reads" to fool the defense. Traps, counters, and reverses, as well as the various option series, fall into this category (see Figures 4.4 through 4.6).

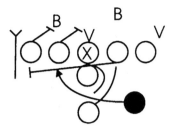

Figure 4.4 Crossbuck trap

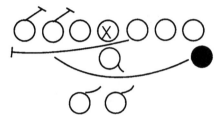

Figure 4.5 Wingback reverse

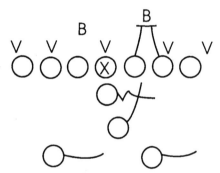

Figure 4.6 Wishbone triple option

Now for a bit more detail on these three approaches to the running attack.

The Power Game

Probably the most powerful was the Tennessee single wing attack. The basic series was an off tackle play in which the strong end and wingback double-teamed the defensive tackle, and the blocking back and fullback tandem blocked the defensive end (who was set up by the tailback faking to go wide, then cutting back behind the tandem block). Both guards would pull through the hole to block.

In the good old days, plays were called attacking the defensive positions. The defensive tackles always played in the area of the offensive ends. Today the plays are nearly always called over an offensive lineman because there are so many different types of defenses. So the off tackle play usually involves the end blocking with his tackle or a wingback. The man they block may be a defensive end, a linebacker, and sometimes the defensive tackle.

Today "off tackle" seldom means "off" the defensive tackle. Coaches just refused to change their old terminology as the defensive alignments and offensive numbering systems changed. It's like people calling all refrigerators "Frigidaires" or "iceboxes." (The old ways die hard, don't they?)

If the defensive tackle played wider than normal or fought hard outside to stop the double team, the blocking would change and the hole would be moved in one man—with the tackle being blocked out rather than double-teamed in.

In the single wing, if the defensive end crashed or played close to the tackle, he would be blocked in by the fullback and the tailback would run wide. The favorite inside power play was the fullback buck with a wedge block, in which the linemen formed a shoulder-to-shoulder wedge and pushed aside anyone in their path (see Figure 4.7).

With all of its power, the Tennessee wing had the disadvantages of hitting the hole slowly, having the center have to make a snap backward before blocking (much tougher than being a T formation center; also, many centers kept their heads down to

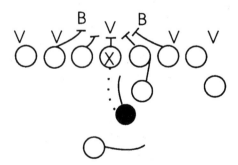

Figure 4.7 Wedge on the offensive center

make certain that they didn't make a bad snap), and of having to have a durable and outstanding triple threat back at tailback. The 1950 UCLA team lost its four top tailbacks for the duration of the season, before the first game. By the end of the season, its starting tailback was the former eighth string tailback. But the former eighth string tailback, sophomore Ted Narleski, made the All Pac Ten team. He was equivalent to a combination pro quarterback and an I formation tailback. For those that could survive the punishment, playing single wing tailback was the ultimate football position.

The Maryland I formation, developed by Tom Nugent, was also a powerful attack. In the Maryland attack, there were four backs lined up behind the center. Don Coryell, former San Diego Charger coach, when coaching Whittier College used a similar attack. During his last years with the Chargers, he brought back some of his old Whittier plays to reinforce the Charger running game (see Figure 4.8).

Here is a sample of the power that could be generated by such an attack. Note the similarities with the single wing power (see Figures 4.8 and 4.9).

While at USC in the 1960s, John McKay combined a power attack with the pro-style wide receivers in his "I" formation. This gained him a passing advantage but lost some of the running attack power. Here are two samples of power plays from the USC I, the off tackle play and an inside isolation play where the linebacker is not blocked by the linemen but is isolated, then blocked by the

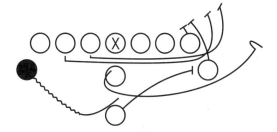

Figure 4.9 Off tackle from power double wing

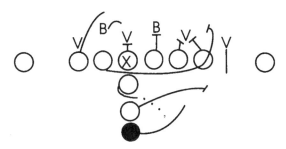

Figure 4.10 Pro-I off tackle

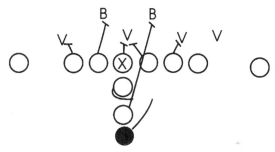

Figure 4.11 Pro-I isolation play

fullback—with the tailback having the option of running to either side of the fullback's block.

McKay's I attack is commonly used today at all levels of play (see Figures 4.10 and 4.11).

The disadvantages of the I formation are that it can't get outside quickly and it doesn't have the capability of crossing the backs in faking actions, so it is easier for the linebackers to key.

The power I is seldom used as the primary attack, but it is often used by I pro attacks in short yardage situations. Here the flanker is brought in to the halfback spot. From here, he and the fullback can lead the tailback to his side of the line, or the fullback and tailback can lead the halfback to the other side of the line (see Figures 4.12 and 4.13).

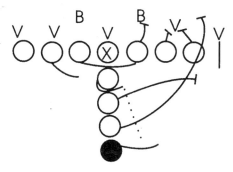

Figure 4.8 Maryland I off tackle

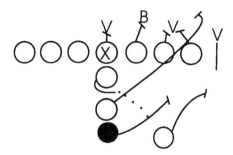

Figure 4.12 Power I—halfback lead

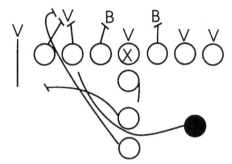

Figure 4.13 Power I—tailback lead

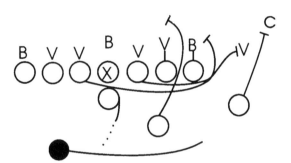

Figure 4.14 Lombardi's Green Bay sweep

The off tackle power game from the T formation was probably best emphasized by Vince Lombardi's attack at Green Bay. The Green Bay "sweep" could be cut "off tackle" or continued as a wide sweep—depending on whether the outside linebacker was blocked out or in (see Figure 4.14).

It is easy to see how the T formation types of teams have taken the blocking patterns from the single wing power play. But each time that a back is flanked as a wide receiver, a potential blocker is lost. If the quarterback is not called on as a blocker, because the coach is afraid that his signal caller will get hurt, another blocker is lost.

The Quickness Game

The quickness game is indigenous to the T formation. Because the center hands the ball to the quarterback, he can hand off to any of his other backs without them having to wait for the ball to get to them, as in the single wing.

With a quickness attack, there will be no special power blocking scheme. Most of the blocks will be one on one. And those blocks don't have to be sustained long because the back will be at the hole in about a half a second.

If the play is designed to hit between the guards, the fullback will probably carry it. If it is to go just inside or outside of the tackle, the halfback will usually carry it. This halfback dive was the basic play of the split-T attack.

From the I formation, it is the fullback who is the quick hitter. He can go to the same side as the tailback or to the opposite side, in a counteraction (see Figure 4.15).

Getting wide quickly is done with the quick pitch, a play designed by Hamp Pool, the former L.A. Rams coach. If the end plays close to the tackle, he can usually be flanked by the quick pitch.

(Note: if there is a fullback, he will usually run toward the defensive end to threaten him with a block, making it easier for the ball carrier to outflank him.) For maximum effectiveness, the halfback should line up at least as wide as the offensive tackle (see Figure 4.16).

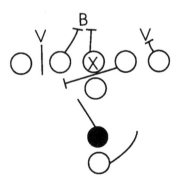

Figure 4.15 I fullback counter trap

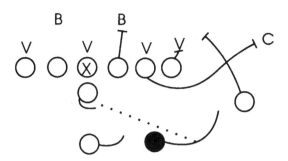

Figure 4.16 Quick pitch

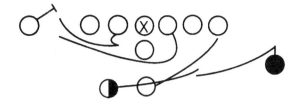

Figure 4.17 Reverse to wide receiver from a pro-set T

The Finesse Game

Possibly the most finesse-oriented offense was the old Michigan unbalanced line buck-lateral series. The ball was snapped to the fullback, who dove into the line. The blocking back might lead him or turn and have the ball faked to him or given to him. If it was given to him, he might run into a different hole, drop back to pass, hand to the wingback on a reverse, or pitch to the tailback—who might run wide or pass.

Dave Nelson and Forest Evashevski, who had played the buck-lateral system in Michigan, wanted to keep the elements of that series with the advantages of the T formation. They developed the often-used wing T. Most teams that use a wing T utilize the power, crossbuck, and reverses of the single wing but generally do not emphasize the potential of the halfback pass, although they often add the option element to the attack.

All attacks will have some elements of the finesse game. There will always be at least one play that ends up opposite of the way that it starts. This is to make the linebackers more cautious in their pursuit of the ball carrier. By keeping them aware of the countering action, they will be a bit less effective in stopping the team's primary power or quickness plays.

If the attack has a wingback, he will be the primary person used in the countering actions. When the wingback, end, or a wide receiver becomes the ball carrier, it is called a *reverse*. Figure 4.17 is an example of a reverse.

Figures 4.18 through 4.20 are some examples of countering actions (using the "set" backs rather than wingback, ends, or wide receivers).

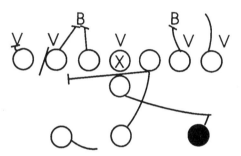

Figure 4.18 Crossbuck

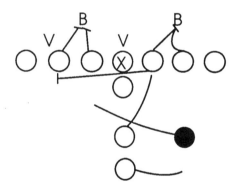

Figure 4.19 Crossbuck from power I

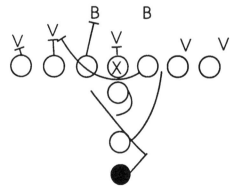

Figure 4.20 Tailback counter from pro-I formation (used if defense is keying the fullback)

Another part of the finesse game involves what has come to be known as "option" football. An option attack is an effective way to slow teams that blitz. It also forces teams to play assignment defense. In this type of attack, the quarterback must determine whether to give or keep the ball, depending on the action of a defensive player. On wide plays from the split-T attack, the quarterback would fake to the diving halfback, fake to the fullback (who was running off tackle), then when he came to the defensive end he had to decide whether to keep the ball himself and cut upfield or pitch to the trailing halfback. The man who is being optioned (in this case, the defensive end) is not blocked.

The quarterback had to determine whether the end was going to take him (if so, he would pitch) or take the trailing halfback (if so, he would keep it and run, perhaps pitching to the halfback farther up the field). Coaches would give the quarterback a "key" to help him with his determination.

Different coaches use different "keys" to help their quarterbacks. Here are some examples. Perhaps if the quarterback could see the front numbers of the defensive end (indicating that he was facing the QB and was probably going to tackle him), he would pitch. Or perhaps the key would be that if the end was closer than $1\frac{1}{2}$ yards from the tackle, he would pitch. Or it might be that if the end was on the line of scrimmage, he would pitch; if the end had penetrated into the backfield, he would keep it. If you are going to run an option attack, you must tell the QB exactly who is his key. He can't option off everyone who shows in an area!

The double options (two possible ball carriers, the QB and the pitch man) can be run after an inside fake or without an inside fake. The split-T option should freeze the defensive tackle and the inside backer (see Figures 4.21 and 4.22).

In either of these plays, the fullback can be used as a lead blocker for the halfback or can run the slant at the defensive end, then block in on a linebacker or lead the halfback downfield.

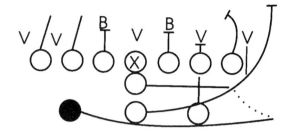

**Figure 4.21 Split-T option
(end playing tight, QB options to pitch)**

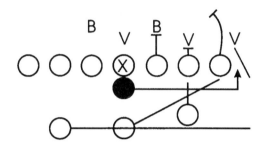

**Figure 4.22 Split-T option
(end playing loose, QB options to keep and run)**

The freeze option has an inside fake up the middle, then the double option wide. It should freeze the inside backers, allowing the outside blockers to wall off the inside pursuit.

The "speed" option does not rely on an inside dive fake. This play is generally run from a two-back set. What it loses in the inside fake it gains with the additional blocker.

TCU has used an option from its one-back set in which the QB reverse pivots, the running back fakes in that direction, then runs the option to the opposite side. The five technique defensive tackle is the man they are optioning.

The ultimate in "option" football is the triple option. The wishbone and the veer are the major triple option attacks, although some teams run a triple option from an I formation. The invention of the triple option is credited to former Georgia Tech athletic director Homer Rice when he was coaching in high school in the 1950s. He used it with the inside belly series. Bud Moore at Texas A&M used it from the I formation in the 1960s and Darrell Royal at Texas used it from the wishbone formation a bit later.

In a triple option, both the defensive end and the tackle are left unblocked. Because of this there are extra offensive linemen who can double-team the opposing defenders, especially the linebackers. This gives this type of "finesse" attack some of the elements of a "power" attack.

In the wishbone (named for the shape of the alignment of the backs), the quarterback reaches back to the fullback and puts the ball in his belly as he looks and "reads" the defensive tackle. If the tackle has an outside responsibility, the ball is given to the fullback. If the tackle comes in to stop the fullback, the quarterback takes the ball back, while the fullback blocks the tackle. The quarterback then moves quickly down the line to option the defensive end. Here he "reads" the defensive end, just as he did in the split-T option (see Figures 4.23 and 4.24).

The triple option has the elements of finesse, power (because of the double team), and quickness. As such it is very difficult to stop. The problems are that with the quarterback having to make the two

options in less than a half a second, there is ample opportunity for mistakes—the fullback may think he is keeping the ball, while the QB is trying to pull it away; the pitch may go astray; or the quarterback may make the wrong read. Also, because the true wishbone has three set backs, there is not the pro type of threat of the pass, with two wide receivers.

Bill Yeoman, when coach at the University of Houston, attempted to rectify the passing weakness of the wishbone by substituting a wide receiver for the fullback and splitting one of his ends. This formation is called the "veer" or the "Houston veer."

In the veer, the first option is to the diving halfback, rather than to the plunging fullback. The second option is to the "off side" halfback. In the wishbone, both halfbacks ran wide, so that if the ball was pitched, the ball carrier had a lead blocker. In the veer, the halfback must go it alone, hoping that his fleetness of foot and his keenly intelligent fakes will help him elude that killer cornerback (see Figures 4.25a and 4.25b).

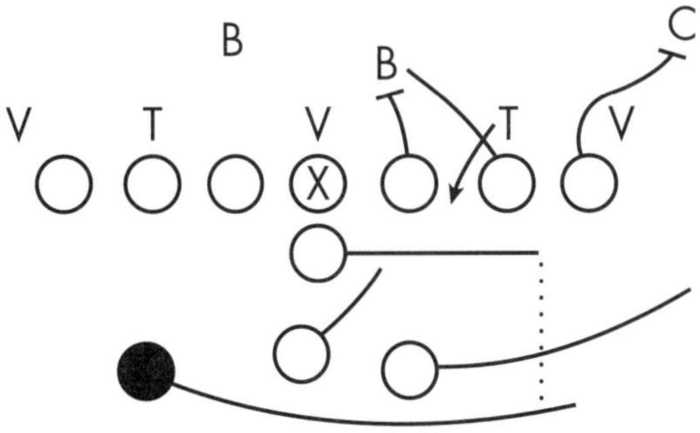

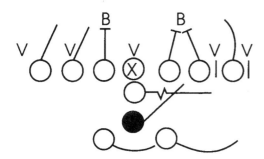

Figure 4.23 Wishbone triple option (defensive tackle has responsibility for the fullback)

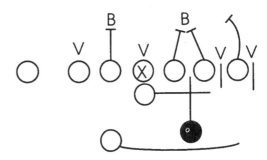

Figure 4.25a Veer option (give to halfback)

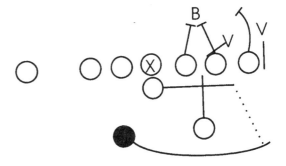

Figure 4.24 Wishbone triple option (defensive tackle has outside responsibility)

Figure 4.25b Veer option on the end

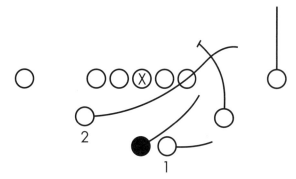

Figure 4.26 Florida-type double option

Utah's and Florida's highly effective offenses feature the quarterback running from the spread, then having the option to pitch to a trailing back or forward to another eligible receiver who is being accompanied by a pulling lineman. Most teams that use a spread or shotgun offense will use an option with the quarterback heading toward the defensive end, then having the option of pitching to the other back. But Urban Meyer's ingenious concept really puts the pressure on the defense (see Figure 4.26).

Still another type of finesse play starts with the ball carrier 6 to 8 yards deep, then running behind zone blocking, picking his hole which is often on the back side of the formation. This requires great vision by the ball carrier. This deep set one- or two-back formation has become a staple lately for teams with great running backs.

Developing the Primary Running Threat

Every play, with the exception of the quarterback sneak, is part of a series. The play series will be based on a power theory, a quickness theory, a finesse theory, or some combination of the three. In selecting a play series, the coach must be guided by his overall theory of what he expects to do from that series. If he wants maximum power or finesse, having three backs in the backfield will probably be more effective. Does he want to pass? If so, he will probably want three or more immediate receivers next to the line of scrimmage. And he will probably

want his set backs wide so that they can get into the pass pattern quickly.

He may want his backfield action such that it will yield a good faking action should he decide to pass. The split-T series would be a terrible series from which to pass because the wide line splits make it difficult to hold out the pass rushers, and the only immediate receivers are the ends. But there are other series that will offer a good deal of faking and pass protection.

In theory, in the T formation, any back can hit any hole. However in practice the fullback is the tough hard running and hard blocking type of player while the halfbacks are speedier and perhaps more elusive. Some coaches want a total power game and go with all backs being fullback types. Others go with all backs being racehorse types. Once in a while the coach is lucky enough to get a back who can do it all. Such a back makes the coach a genius.

Plays Starting with the Fullback Threat

Many coaches will set up their basic attack with the fullback. He may buck at the guard and set up a cross-buck or a belly series. (see Figures 4.27 and 4.28).

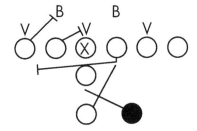

Figure 4.27 Crossbuck (straight blocking)

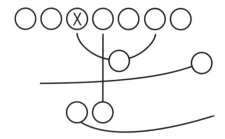

Figure 4.28 Buck lateral series

In the crossbuck series, the fullback goes toward one of the guards, then the halfback on that side comes back either behind the QB or between the QB and the center. This is often done with the guard trap blocking

Either crossbuck can be done with straight-ahead blocking or with a guard trapping while the fullback blocks the guard's man.

The inside belly series is another type of buck. The QB reaches back and puts the ball in the belly of the fullback. If the fullback play has been called, the QB gives him the ball, then fakes to the opposite halfback. If the halfback's play has been called, the ball is slipped away from the fullback at the last second and given to the halfback.

The fullback buck is also the beginning of the I formation isolation series, but the fullback is generally the lead blocker rather than the primary ball carrier. But in the fullback counter he is the ball carrier (see Figures 4.29 and 4.30).

And, of course, when there is only one running back in the backfield, as in the "A" formation popu-

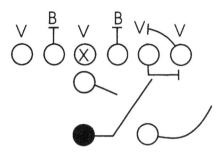

Figure 4.31 Fly series (quick pitch slant)

larized by the Washington Redskins Coach Joe Gibbs, that lone runner had better be an animal.

The slant play has the fullback going toward his tackle or end. This action is generally used as part of an outside play—the fullback either gets the ball as the primary runner or he fakes and blocks while the halfback or quarterback goes wide (see Figure 4.31).

- As part of the split-T series, the fullback might get a cross block between the end and tackle or a double-team by the end and tackle and an outside block by the diving halfback.
- As part of the quick pitch (or fly) series, the quarterback fakes the pitch to the flying halfback, but gives to the fullback.
- A third series that incorporates the fullback starts wide and is called the "outside belly." In this, the QB moves wider and puts the ball in the fullback's belly ("rides" him). If the fullback's play is called, the QB gives it to him. If the wide play is called, he pulls the ball from the fullback, then options the defensive end.

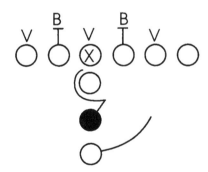

Figure 4.29 Fullback counter from the I (QB reverse pivots)

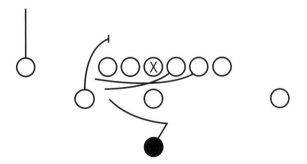

Figure 4.30 Counter trey

Plays Starting with the Halfback Threat

The quick-hitting halfback play is the dive. If the halfback is set behind the tackle, he will generally attack just inside or outside the tackle, often having the option, depending on how his tackle has blocked the opposing lineman. If he is set behind the guard, as in the veer, he will be able to attack from inside the guard to outside the tackle (the outside veer series; see Figures 4.32 and 4.33).

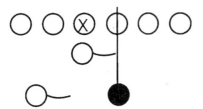

Figure 4.32 Inside veer at guard

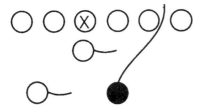

Figure 4.33 Outside veer at tackle

Plays with the Tailback Threat

When the coach calls the halfback a "tailback," look out! It means that he is the primary ball carrier. Whether it is the single wing, the double wing, the I, or the one-back ("ace") set—there's a stud back there ready to score. Whether it is Emmit Smith, Marcus Allen, or Marshall Faulk in an I, or Bruce Smith, Tom Harmon, or Paul Cameron in the single wing, you know that you have a ball carrier back there who is either very fast, very powerful, or very tricky—usually all three.

So while some coaches believe that their offense is better served when they let their two or three running backs carry the ball in equal amounts—a theory that balances the attack—other coaches want their best man to carry the ball 80 or 90 percent of the time.

In 1984 Auburn ran a wishbone with all the backs getting a chance to run the ball. One of those backs was Bo Jackson. When the 1985 season opened, Auburn had changed its basic formation to the I and old Bo, as the tailback, got to run the ball far more often than he had the year before.

As was earlier noted, the seldom-used Tennessee single wing is the most powerful offense. Here are the two ways that the tailback attacked the off tackle hole with power.

When running to the wingback side, he started as the ball was snapped. When going to the weak side, he would stand up and fake the pass while the fullback and blocking back ran in front of him; then he would start his run.

The Basic Running Series of Football

The type of running attack that a coach chooses will influence the type of formation he will use. (Formations will be discussed in Chapter 6.) But the theory of the play (power, quickness, or finesse) and the primary running threat (fullback, halfback, or tailback) can usually be incorporated into a different formation than that in which it was originally used.

So the off tackle power play or the run-pass option of the single-wing series have been adapted to the T formation. Certainly the spread offense or shotgun adjustment that most T teams use is really an offshoot of single- or double-wing football. Similarly, teams that still use the single-wing attack will often split wide receivers—an idea borrowed from the T-formation teams.

The commonly used spread attack with the QB deep and four or five receivers, while having the potential to have a single-wing type of attack, generally uses typical T-formation plays such as the handoff to the other back, the draw, or the option. When John McKay was at USC, winning his four national championships with Heisman runners Mike Garrett, O. J. Simpson, and Marcus Allen, he ran single-wing power out of the T formation. He pulled both the off guard and tackle and led with a fullback.

Coaches borrow from each other continually. They borrow, invent, and adjust in order to make their offenses as effective as they can possibly be. Here are some of the most influential running series in football.

The Traditional "Tight T" or "Full House"

This formation made quicker plays more possible than did the single wing. There is also a better possibility for faking and for quicker countering than allowed by the offenses that featured the direct snap, such as the single wing. The quick dives and bucks along with the threat of the immediate quick pass made this formation almost universal by the early 1950s.

The Inside Belly Series

This was made famous by Eddie LeBaron, a diminutive quarterback for College of the Pacific in the 1940s. His uncanny faking ability caused many long runs to be called back because the referee blew the whistle when the fullback was tackled—but the halfback was carrying the ball goalward. Eddie started for the Washington Redskins for a number of years. Bobby Dodd, the legendary Georgia Tech coach, perfected the series.

In the inside belly series, the quarterback calls for either the fullback or the halfback to get the ball. It is not an option. The quarterback puts the ball into the belly of the fullback as he attacks the area of the offensive guard. The quarterback "rides" the fullback as he goes into the line. If the fullback is to be the ball carrier, the quarterback leaves the ball with him. If the halfback is to carry it, the quarterback rides the fullback as long as possible then pulls the ball out and hands it to the halfback.

The Outside Belly Series

This series starts with the fullback attacking the tackle-end area. The quarterback rides the fullback and gives him the ball if that is the play called. If the halfback's number has been called, the QB takes the ball away from the fullback, then either pitches directly to the halfback or runs an option at the end with a possible quarterback keep or a pitch to the halfback. The coach will decide if he wants to use an option as part of the play.

The Split-T Dive-Option Series

This series was developed by Don Faurot, coach of the University of Missouri. It was popularized by Jim Tatum, at Oklahoma and Maryland, and reached its pinnacle under Bud Wilkinson at Oklahoma. This attack was a combination of quickness and finesse, which threatened every offensive hole. By splitting the linemen up to 8 feet, large holes were developed in the defensive front. Also, the large splits put the defenders on the side away from the play (the "off" side) a great distance from the attack point. Nearly all teams in that era (the 1940s and 1950s) used eight-man defensive fronts that made it easier to split them. (Ironically, it was Bud Wilkinson who developed the 5-2 Oklahoma defense that greatly reduced the effectiveness of the attack. That same 5-2 defense is the most universally used defensive alignment in football and is the father of the 3-4 defense, which is so commonly used today.)

The split-T attack is based almost entirely on quickness, with only the FB counter as a finesse variation. The quarterback sneak was also an important part of the attack. The guard could split from 1 foot to 6 feet, the tackles 2 to 8 feet, and the ends 3 to 8 feet. The split depended on how far the defensive linemen would split with the offensive line. When a defensive lineman would play "head up" on any split, some coaches would say "take them to the sidelines with your split."

Another advantage of the split-T quickness attack was that the fakes were done at the line of scrimmage. This meant that each defender had to commit to the play in his area immediately so was not able to pursue the play as quickly as he might be able to do when the fakes were deeper in the backfield.

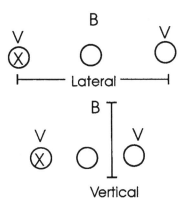

Figure 4.34 Creating lateral and vertical holes

The split-T series was based on the principle of creating lateral holes along the line of scrimmage by the split of the linemen, with vertical holes resulting at every spot where there was a linebacker. Since the holes were already present when the teams lined up, all that the offensive lineman had to do was to keep his defender in the same spot; he didn't have to move him away from the hole as was necessary in the single wing (see Figure 4.34).

The Wing T

This series, developed by Dave Nelson at Delaware and made famous by Forest Evashevski at Iowa, attempted to use much of the power and the wide reverse counter play of the single wing with the speed of the T or split T.

The Pro-I Formation

This creation of John McKay (USC) incorporated much of the power of the single wing, with some of the quickness of the T and the passing potential of the professional wide formation. While the fullback buck and the outside belly series were integral parts of the attack, he added the isolation play for power

and a new idea of "option running" for his talented tailbacks. If the linemen just stayed with the defenders, the tailback could pick his holes. He might run to where the play was designed to go, or he might run wider or cut back.

You can see that coaches have a great many options from which to choose in developing a running attack. They can't have it all. Each coach must choose whether to emphasize a power, quickness, or finesse attack. He must then decide whether he is going to feature one primary ball carrier or spread the ball-carrying responsibilities around and balance his attack. He must decide whether to fit the players to his system (making small changes each year to accommodate the abilities of his players) or to fit a system to his players (possibly making great changes every year or so). In doing this he might emphasize a tough fullback one year and a fast halfback the next.

The number of possible running plays are countless. The problem is that there isn't enough time to teach all possible plays to each team. Some coaches have tried to mix formations using a "multiple offense." Biggie Munn did it at Michigan State. He used the T, wing T, single and double wing—fourteen different backfield sets in all. Today it is common to use combinations of single back, I, offset I, and various combinations of receivers with trips or doubles (possibly double tight, double flanker or double slot, or a combination of flanker to one side and slot to another).

The general theory of most successful coaches is the "KISS" approach. (KISS is an acronym meaning "Keep It Simple, Stupid.") It is generally felt that a team is better served by doing fewer things well than many things poorly. Consequently, most teams will have three or fewer basic running series. And many very successful teams, particularly at the high school level, use only one series.

CHAPTER

5

BLOCKING FOR THE RUNNING PLAY

"The work in the trenches"

It's a lot easier to draw up a backfield series than it is to make it work on the field. What makes it work is the blocking pattern and the skills of the blockers.

In coaching circles, it is often argued as to which is the most important segment of a football team. Some coaches hold that it is the defensive cornerbacks, but most maintain that it is the offensive line. The media hype the so-called skilled positions, but you better believe that the offensive line is all-important in making any offense effective!

You may have heard about the time that Knute Rockne's famous backfield, called the "Four Horsemen," got a bit cocky because of all the publicity they had received. So in one game Rockne took out the "Seven Mules" (the nickname for the first-string Notre Dame line). To the surprise of the Horsemen, they were totally ineffective. Only when the Mules were inserted in the game did the backs start to run with abandon.

It is no small wonder that great backs appreciate their offensive lines. Expensive gifts and sumptuous dinners are rewards that these appreciative backs sometimes give to the often-unheralded linemen who make them look so good.

In designing your offense, it is essential that you think long and hard about the types of blocks you will use and how you should teach them. This is where the offensive game is played. Your Os have to know how to effectively block the opposition's Xs or your offense won't be worth a nickel. Offensive blocking schemes and techniques do not just hap-

pen. Further, your blocking scheme and techniques must coordinate with your overall theory of offense. If your tailback is back 8 yards and is going to run to daylight, your blocking techniques will likely emphasize zone blocking, with the linemen playing higher and more balanced in blocks that can be maintained for a few seconds. If your offense is based on quick-hitting power, you will undoubtedly use quick shoulder blocks and double teams. Blocking is not a "one-size-fits-all," but rather a tailor-made, custom-fit idea. The blocking techniques, schemes, and lessons must be appropriate for the offense.

Techniques of Blocking

Blocking techniques vary. For example, a one-on-one block might be executed by stepping into the opponent, getting under his shoulder pads, getting the blocker's head on the same side of the defender as the hole where the back will run, and lifting the defender while driving him backward. It might also be performed as a scramble block, in which the blocker stays low (possibly on all fours) and drives at the defender with little or no lift. It might also be carried out by working the defender upward but not particularly trying to drive him anywhere—just maintaining contact.

Each type of block has its place, depending on the type of attack and the size and skill of the blocker. (For complete coverage of offensive line play, see Nelson and O'Connor's *Playing the Offensive Line: A*

Comprehensive Guide for Coaches and Players, McGraw-Hill, 2005.)

When you are teaching blocking, there are several things you must consider before you step onto the practice field:

1. *What stance do you want?* If your team only blocks straight ahead or at a slight angle right or left, you might use a bunched four point. If you have linemen who pull both ways, the feet may well be parallel. Some teams whose linemen pull only across the center will have the inside feet of all linemen back, so the right-side linemen will have their left feet back and the left hands down, while the left side linemen will have their right feet back and their right hands down. The pros, because of their pass protection responsibilities, will often have the outside hands down and the outside feet back. Most coaches teach knees in front of ankles, neck bulled, back arched, butt down, eyes on the belly of the defender.

The stance you teach should allow the player to do whatever is required of him in a game: drive forward, drop in pass protection, pull right or left, reach block, goal line block, and so on. So one stance may not fit all. There will be variations in stances unless all of your players are the exact same size. For example, taller players may need a wider stagger or a wider base; as a coach you must be able to adjust the requirements of an effective stance to the body type and ability of the player.

Quick-hitting teams, such as those that employ the wing T and veer attacks, are more likely to use number or rule blocking. Deep set I backs or single back offenses often use zone blocking (described in Chapter 12).

2. *What is the aiming point of the block?* Near number, far number, sternum, inside thigh, near arm pit, and so on.

3. *What surface will you hit with?* Near shoulder, hands, forearm, shoulder and forearm.

4. *What footwork do you want to teach?* This essential fundamental is often not taught effectively. The feet should slide across the grass in short, choppy steps. The first step should position the body; normally it will be a 3- to 6-inch step. Then contact should be made on the second step (the power step).

5. *What is the proper body position?* Teach the proper body position—knees bent, back flat or arched, angle of the back to the ground for the type of block you want: low for goal line or scramble, high for zone block, higher for pass protection.

6. *What should the hands do?* For many years, coaches were teaching to keep the hands back when zone blocking, almost like they were going to draw a gun, then shoot the hands to the target. The pros have now recognized that there isn't enough time to move the hands from the hips to the opponent's chest; consequently, knowledgeable coaches are teaching to keep the hands higher so that they can punch quicker. The hands should punch through, not to, the defender's chest.

7. *How important is the hip roll or explosion in the block?* Do you merely want a stalemate or are you trying to drive the opponent off the line?

Individual Blocking Assignments

Individual blocking assignments can also take several approaches.

- The straight one-on-one drive block has the lineman taking the man nearest him away from the hole.
- A reach block has the lineman blocking one on one on the next man out.
- A down block has the lineman blocking the next man down with the near shoulder.
- A reverse shoulder block has the lineman blocking the next man on the line with the blocker's shoulder that was farthest from the defender being the point of contact. This type of block gives the offensive man an angle on the defender so he should be in a more advantageous position to move the defender.

- A cross block has the two adjacent linemen blocking the defenders aligned near the other. If the two defenders are both on the line of scrimmage, the outside offensive lineman blocks first and the inside lineman moves slightly behind to block his man. This block is often used when a linebacker is on the inside man. The outside lineman moves first and blocks the linebacker while the inside offensive lineman moves behind and blocks the "down" lineman.

- A fold block is like a cross block but the lineman blocking the "down" lineman goes first while the blocker who is assigned to block the backer goes behind his teammate, and then blocks the backer (see Figure 5.1).

- A scoop block is another combination used on a down lineman and a backer. In this block, the man on the down defensive lineman hits him while the man to his inside moves to help him. Once the inside man has made contact, the outside man releases and blocks the backer. If a backer is "reading" the block of the man on him and sees him blocking, the backer will probably "fill" into that area rather than pursue the play. This makes it easier for the outside blocker to seal him away from the play (see Figure 5.2).

- A trap block has a blocker, usually one who was lined up inside, run outside and block a defender—who has probably penetrated into the backfield (see Figure 5.3).

- A lead block has a player running through the hole, ready to block the most dangerous defender (see Figure 5.4).

- A double-team block puts two offensive players, usually two linemen, against one defender.

- A wedge block has three or more players blocking an area—getting under the defenders and moving them backward. In a wedge block, the offensive linemen are not assigned specific players to block.

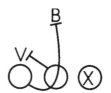

Figure 5.1 Fold block

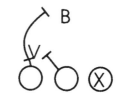

Figure 5.2 Scoop block

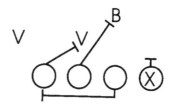

Figure 5.3 Trap block

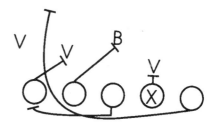

Figure 5.4 Trap and lead block

- An inside zone block is a combination of a double team and a scoop. One type of zone rule is for the man on the defensive lineman and the first lineman inside to double-team the down defender, having all four hands on him. But all four eyes will be on the backer. If the backer blitzes or scrapes, the lineman near where the backer is moving will come off the double team and block the backer.

Another type of block is for the offensive ¹ man covered to be helped by the man outs⸏ him blocking down.

• An outside zone block has the lead man moving to the linebacker, possibly ripping the down defender with his inside arm. He walls off the backer from the wide play. The inside offensive lineman, the trail man, takes his bucket step and reads the defenders. If the backer comes through his gap he takes him; if not, he blocks the down lineman by getting square or outside and walling him off from the wide play. If the defensive lineman's move is outside, the lead blocker will stay with him while the trail blocker will take the backer, either attacking straight or pulling around the lead blocker to wall him off.

• In the outside zone or "stretch" blocking, the linemen still step out first, but there's no worry about a double team.

Zone teams use other blocking schemes as well. They may trap inside or outside, run "isos," or rule-block on some plays.

Zone blocking works best against defenses that are set in one position rather than those that may stem (shift to a new defense before the snap) or those that "rover" or "prowl"—those in which the linemen and backers are continually shifting. This is because the zone-blocking linemen must be aware of which down defender is down so that they can know which two blockers will begin to double-team the down lineman. The rovering of the backers is not really a problem for the zone blockers.

A short yardage play in the middle will often use a wedge block. In making the wedge, the apex man stands up his defender. His teammates in the wedge block into his hips to assist him in driving the defender off the line. It is important that the lineman being blocked is not allowed to fall down or the wedge will be defeated. Wedges may include from three to five offensive linemen and possibly a wingback or inside slot. While the block is designed for short yardage plays, it is often an 8- to 10-yard gainer and may break for bigger yardage if the ball carrier is taught to break out at the right time.

Designing the Blocking Schemes

Blocking schemes should be simple, yet still present the defense with problems. If you are coaching a small squad and there is a likelihood the linemen will have to play more than one position because of possible injuries, the simplest rule is best. If you are coaching at the pro level and have more than forty hours a week to practice and adequate reserves, your blocking scheme and rules can become much more complicated. At the high school level, you probably will be able to have a base blocking rule, possibly a zone concept, an inside trap rule, possibly a wedge block, and an outside power sweep block. Remember, your primary concern is what the players can execute perfectly.

Every running and passing play has blocking rules for every lineman and usually for some of the backs. The coach who develops the rules for each play must take into consideration the multitude of possibilities in defensive alignments. Some common defensive alignments are shown in Figures 5.5 through 5.14.

Sometimes linebackers are stacked behind a lineman (as in Figure 5.3, page 31). Other times they are stacked in a gap. A "gap stack" presents some real problems in blocking, especially with a one-on-one blocking scheme—where one offensive player must block one defensive player without the help of a teammate in a double-team block).

Many defenses put linemen or linebackers in the gaps, or put them on the inside or outside shoulder of an offensive lineman, giving the defender the gap responsibility. The gap placement or gap responsibility is needed to reduce the splits of the offensive linemen.

Blocking Rules

Base blocking rules (meaning the "basic" rules) are an essential part of planning your blocking scheme. Some teams use their "base" rules on all plays. Others

- Playside end: block safety in four deep, corner back in three deep
- Offside guard: block first man to your side of the center (whether he is on or off the line of scrimmage)
- Offside tackle: seal first man outside guard or block the second man on your side of the center (seal means get in front of him so that he has to go behind you—before you make your block)

Calling the Defensive Front to Aid in Knowing What Rule to Follow

Many coaches find it helpful to the blocking scheme for the center to call out the type of defense he sees:

- *Clear:* no lineman or backer over the center
- *Odd:* man-on or shading the center
- *Stack:* odd defense with a man behind the nose tackle
- *Solid:* linemen on the center and guards
- *Even:* no man on center but linemen on the guards
- *Double:* stacks on both guards

Calling the Blocks on the Line of Scrimmage

Call blocking is often used between two linemen to determine whether they will block the men on them, crossblock, scoop, fold, and so on, and who will go first when exchanging assignments. Teams that use this technique generally have all the linemen say something, such as "you," "me," "go," or other code words. When the linemen are allowed to call how they will block a given play, they use code words or letters. Usually, every man on the line will call out a word, but the only one that counts is the key man on that particular play. The key man may be the man on the inside or the outside of the hole.

Some teams label each block with a letter. Following is a traditional use of letters for calling the blocking (see Figures 5.23 through 5.28).

The trap block was first called the "mousetrap." In the old days when all linemen charged hard into

Figure 5.23 A—Basic rule: block near man

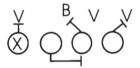

Figure 5.24 B—Cross block, outside man goes first

Figure 5.25 B—Fold block, inside man blocks a linebacker

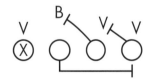

Figure 5.26 C—Onside guard traps

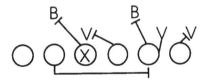

Figure 5.27 D—Trap block with linemen blocking down

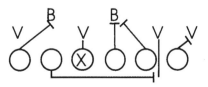

Figure 5.28 D—Trap block with double-team call

the backfield, one man would often be unblocked and coaxed into a "mousetrap" where the pulling guard could easily block him. Modern defensive techniques have made this a more difficult block to execute; however, it is still used often.

Some teams have a code word when they want to exchange blocking assignments; only the two men at the hole will be involved. Perhaps the inside man will say, "me," meaning that he will go first. Or he may say, "you," meaning that his partner will block first while the man calling the block will go behind. If the key man doesn't want to exchange assignments, he might say, "go," meaning to go ahead with the basic rule for that play. (Remember that all the linemen are saying "me," "you," or "go," so the defensive linemen don't know which lineman is calling the "live" word.)

One-on-one blocking at the hole between the guard and tackle versus an Oklahoma 5-2 can be done four ways if only the guard and tackle are involved. The guard is calling the block in Figures 5.29 through 5.31.

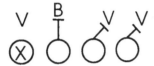

Figure 5.29 "Go" call

Figure 5.30 "Me" call

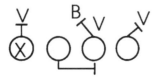

Figure 5.31 "You" call

Instead of a "me" or "you" call, the coach might decide to use a more variable code. An example might be for the inside man to call any city—meaning that he will go first. So whether he says *Dallas*, *Baltimore*, or *Paris*, it all means the same thing. Similarly, if he wants the outside man to go first, he might call any color. So whenever a coach refers to a cross-block with the inside man going first (whether in a practice, chalktalk, playbook, or game), he calls it a "city" block. Whenever he refers to a crossblock with the outside man going first, he calls it a "color" block.

Still another type of call block has one man call the block for the playside of the line. For example, if he calls a "teen" number (11 thru 19), it means that everyone blocks one on one. If he calls a 20 number, it indicates a 2 on 1 (double-team) block, and if it's a 30 number, it indicates a double team with the man outside the double team sealing down. Then a second number could be added to determine if there was a pull and, if so, who would pull. So if the last number is a 2, it means the guard pulls, a 3 means the tackle pulls, a 4 means the end pulls, and a 5 means the guard pulls with the tackle sealing through. So a 32 call would be a double-team block with the outside man sealing and the offside guard pulling (see Figures 5.32 and 5.33).

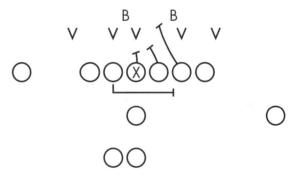

Figure 5.32 A 32 call versus an Okie defense when the play was called over the center with the center and guard double-teaming, the tackle sealing down, and the off guard pulling to trap trapping

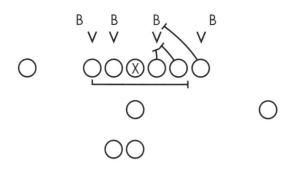

5.33 A 33 call versus a 4-4 with the play called over the guard, and the off tackle trapping

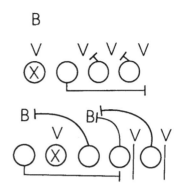

5.34 Examples of trap plays with pulling guards

Making Adjustments to Unexpected Defenses

When the defense aligns in a manner that was not expected by the offense, the QB or the linemen must make adjustments in order to avoid a bad play. The quarterback can change the play at the line of scrimmage. Often these plays are called *automatics*. This adjustment is more often used by teams that use very simple blocking rules.

For teams that allow the linemen to adjust their blocking on every play, "call" blocking may give the advantage back to the offense. Linemen usually like to have the option of calling their blocks; after all, they know better than anyone else what is working well in the game. Additionally, the offensive linemen are often very intelligent—the intelligence tests given by professional teams indicate that the offensive linemen are generally the smartest people on the team.

Today's blocking schemes have become more and more complicated. No longer are the guards the only linemen who pull and trap. No longer are traps only from the inside of the formation to the outside (Figure 5.34).

While the guard is still the primary pulling and "trapping" lineman on most teams and the inside-out trap is the most common type of trap, today the

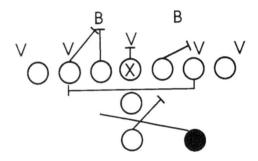

Figure 5.35 Tackle trapping on crossbuck

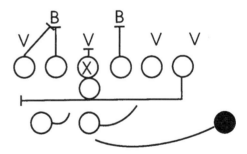

Figure 5.36 End trapping on reverse

center, tackles, ends, wingbacks, or the man in motion can all pull and perhaps trap (Figures 5.35 and 5.36).

Downfield Blocking

It isn't enough to block defenders near the point of attack. Nearly every play in modern football is designed to score a touchdown. This requires that some linemen be released downfield in front of the ball carrier. If the play is in the center of the line, both ends will usually be released. It is possible that one or both tackles will also release downfield.

Blocking Schemes

Normally a coach has several blocking schemes in his arsenal. For example, a fullback slant against a 3-4 or Okie 5-2 might be blocked with straight base blocking, with a crossblock, with a near or far guard trapping, or with the near halfback blocking out or

logging. In preparing for a game, however, it is preferable to reduce the number of blocks so that execution during the game is better.

In fact, one of the coach's major jobs is to determine which blocking schemes will probably work best against the next opponent's most likely defenses. Since teams don't have fifty hours a day to practice, coaches are greatly limited in their ability to meet every possibility that the next opponent might use. That's why every play doesn't work on the field like it does in the playbooks. This is also why we must have a "base blocking" rule to use so that any unusual defensive alignments won't confuse the offense and create a big play for the defense.

CHAPTER 6

THEORIES OF OFFENSIVE FORMATIONS

"How can you gain an offensive advantage through formations, shifting, and motion?"

Obviously, a coach chooses a formation that will best allow him to attack most effectively according to his theory of attack. Today's pro teams nearly always use a formation that allows at least three immediate pass receivers into the defensive secondary. Often they set up to allow four or even five men to attack the opponent's pass defense. College or high school wishbone offenses may keep both ends tight and all three backs in the backfield in order to make their running games more effective.

Nearly everyone is familiar with the variations of the T formation seen in most present-day football games. Let's go back a few years and look at some of the formations that have been used—and are still being used by a number of high school and college coaches. Most of these were employed in the 1920s and 1930s. But note how modern formations have evolved from ideas in existence over fifty years ago (see Figures 6.1 through 6.11).

There were more variations of formation then than now! Does that mean that we are all copycats now—or have we reached the "ultimate" in offensive alignment? Probably neither, because the offense must align itself to attack the defense. As the defense adjusts to strength, so must the offense change its strength.

When the "nickel" defense (using five rather than four defensive backs) came into play to stop the pass on an obvious passing down, many offensive teams adjusted by using a running formation and a running play. And when the defense substitutes an

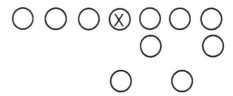

Figure 6.1 Rockne's Notre Dame box

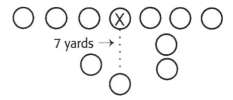

Figure 6.2 Harvard's short punt

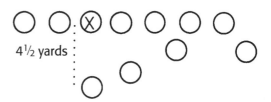

Figure 6.3 Pop Warner's single wing

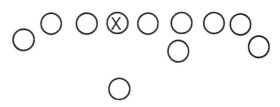

Figure 6.4 Pop Warner's double wing

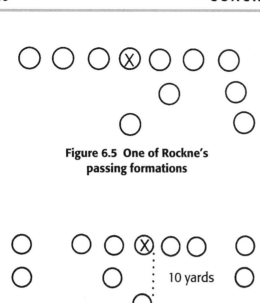

Figure 6.5 One of Rockne's passing formations

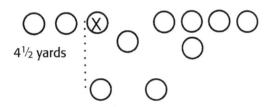

Figure 6.6 Minnesota's spread

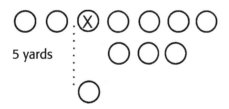

Figure 6.7 Louisiana State's formation

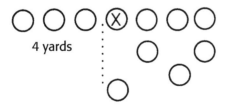

Figure 6.8 Yale's formation

Figure 6.9 Penn State's formation

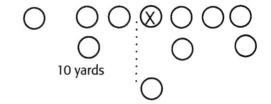

Figure 6.10 Idaho's formation

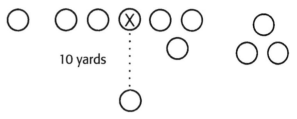

Figure 6.11 Princeton's formation

additional lineman to stop the run in a short yardage situation, many teams exploit the pass.

Selecting the Offensive Formation

Before starting an offensive play, the coach or signal caller must decide which offensive formation to use. He may choose a formation because it is especially advantageous for that play (such as a split-back pro formation for a pass), or he may choose a formation just to see how the defense adjusts so that any weakness can be exploited on an ensuing play.

The T Formation and Variations

The tight formation (T, wing T, double-wing T) has the advantages of running power, good faking, and quick counters, but lacks the quick wide pass threat. Teams with good passers and receivers will want to spread the defense so that it has more area to defend. With the defense spread, there are more possible openings between the defenders for the receivers to exploit (see Figures 6.12 through 6.15).

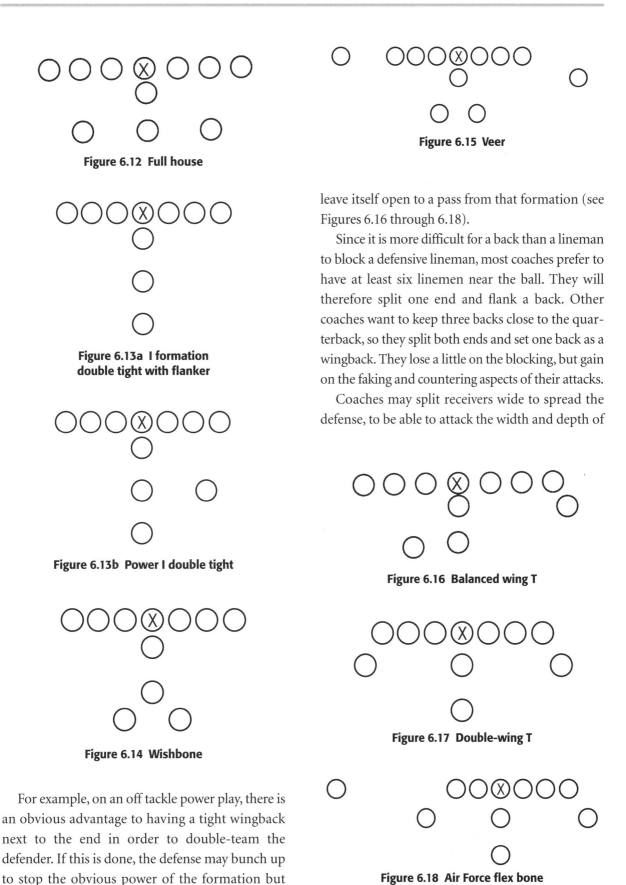

Figure 6.12 Full house

Figure 6.15 Veer

**Figure 6.13a I formation
double tight with flanker**

Figure 6.13b Power I double tight

leave itself open to a pass from that formation (see Figures 6.16 through 6.18).

Since it is more difficult for a back than a lineman to block a defensive lineman, most coaches prefer to have at least six linemen near the ball. They will therefore split one end and flank a back. Other coaches want to keep three backs close to the quarterback, so they split both ends and set one back as a wingback. They lose a little on the blocking, but gain on the faking and countering aspects of their attacks.

Coaches may split receivers wide to spread the defense, to be able to attack the width and depth of

Figure 6.16 Balanced wing T

Figure 6.14 Wishbone

Figure 6.17 Double-wing T

For example, on an off tackle power play, there is an obvious advantage to having a tight wingback next to the end in order to double-team the defender. If this is done, the defense may bunch up to stop the obvious power of the formation but

Figure 6.18 Air Force flex bone

the field better, or to hide weak players because they can't match up 11 on 11 and they want to run the ball; by flanking two weak players they can run 9 on 9. Here are some examples of wide formations. Coaches set flankers not only to open up the pass, but also to spread the defense. If you can get the opponents to put a cornerback and a linebacker far to one side of the field to stop one of your receivers, it is going to be difficult for those defenders to stop a run up the middle or a play to the opposite side of the field. There are some examples of two, three, and four wideout sets (and Ace back sets) in Figures 6.19 through 6.24.

A major reason for using varying sets and motions is to be able to get a mismatch. Offensive football is about gaining mismatches—getting a faster player on a slower player, a taller player on a shorter player, a fresh player on a tired player or an injured player, or more men to one side of the ball.

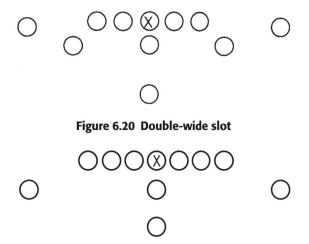

Figure 6.19 Two split ends and a wingback

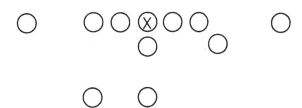

Figure 6.20 Double-wide slot

Figure 6.21 Double tight and double flanker

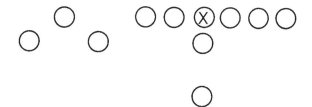

Figure 6.22 Tight end right, trips left

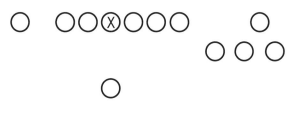

Figure 6.23 Wide slot left, bunch right

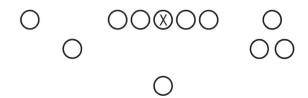

Figure 6.24 Split left, quads right

Choosing the right formation is the best way to accomplish this.

Placement of the Linemen

The rules say that the offensive team must have at least seven men on the line of scrimmage and that the end men on the line are eligible for passes. Today, most teams use balanced lines, with a guard, tackle, and end on each side of the center. When a team occasionally goes unbalanced, it often catches the defense off guard (see Figures 6.25 through 6.28).

The coach also must determine what he wants from his linemen. Typically, the guards will be more agile, but some want the guards bigger for power blocking and will pull the tackles more often. If you are going to dropback pass with a right-handed passer, you'd better have an outstanding pass blocker at your left tackle.

The spacing of the linemen is another factor for a coach to consider. If the linemen are close to each other (a tight line), they can pass-protect, double-team block, and crossblock more effectively. Also, it is more difficult for the defenders to penetrate the offensive line of scrimmage (LOS). The backs can also get around the end faster on sweep plays. On the other hand, the defenders are all closer to the point of attack.

If the offensive linemen are split wider, they spread the defense better and create either holes or blocking angles. If the defensive lineman moves out with the offensive man, a hole is created. If the defender splits only partway, perhaps playing on the inside shoulder of the offensive man, a blocking angle is created. Most offensive linemen are taught to be creative in their splits—often splitting wider on the side away from the play, to put the defender farther from the hole.

In the early days of football, line splits were only a few inches. The split-T spacing of up to 8 feet between linemen reached the opposite extreme. Today, most teams split 1 to 2 feet between the tackles, with the tight ends splitting 2 to 4 feet (see Figures 6.29a and 6.29b).

Another factor in determining the placement of the linemen is their strength and abilities. In a basic T formation, the linemen have the same assignments on either side of the center. But in some attacks, such as the single wing, power I, and some pro attacks, the assignments may be quite varied from one side to the other.

On one team, the strong side of the line may emphasize double-team blocks while the "weak" or "quick" side of the line specializes in pulling, one-on-one blocks, crossblocking, downfield blocking, or other such skills.

When the two sides of the line have different types of blocking responsibilities, they will "flip-flop."

Figure 6.25 Balanced line

Figure 6.26 Unbalanced line right

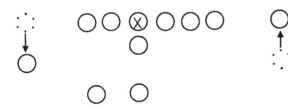

**Figure 6.27 Shift to unbalanced line
from pro set**

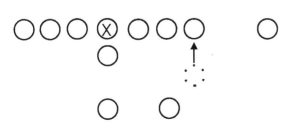

**Figure 6.28 Shift to eight-man line
(slotback moves up so he can block better)**

6.29a Creating a hole with line splits

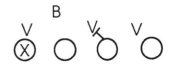

6.29b Creating blocking angles

A flip-flopping team will always have its "strong-side" linemen on the side of their basic power plays and their "quick-side" linemen on the side to which they will counter or run quick plays. Teams that flop their line will do so by crossing their linemen as they break the huddle or by serpentining them. (The strong end or wingback leads the team in a motion that looks like a serpent's path.)

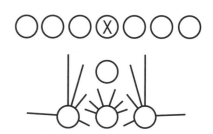

Figure 6.30 Possible paths of set back in a full house T

Setting the Backs in a Formation

It is obvious that if all three backs are set in the normal T formation, there will be a great threat to the defense in quickness and countering. Each back removed from the three-back formation reduces the running attack while adding to the passing threat. When a coach decides to remove a fullback, he gives up the buck, the fullback trap, the fullback counter, and the fullback slant. When he removes a halfback, he gives up the dive threat and the quick pitch to that side, and the halfback traps and counters to the other side. The defense knows this and can afford to reduce its defense in the areas where it is not threatened (see Figure 6.30).

Once the coach decides where he wants to set the backs, he may have to adjust their position somewhat by what he wants the back to do. For example, a very fast back in a wing-T formation might beat the quarterback to the hole, so he might have to be set a foot or two deeper than normal. In most offensive running attacks, the timing of the backs is very important, so backfield coaches often use "cheats" to make the timing better.

Examples of "cheating" the backs are setting a halfback wider or deeper when the quick pitch is used to his side, moving a halfback up or in for certain trap plays or for pass blocking, or moving the fullback up when he is faking and blocking.

The way the backs set their feet and place their hands is also a factor in their effectiveness as blockers or runners. In a "two-point" stance, the back will not have a hand on the ground. This allows him to

see the defense better and to get wide fast, but he can't go forward as fast, so he may have to line up closer to the line of scrimmage. One of the problems with the two-point stance is that the back often is eager to go and is in motion early, causing an unnecessary penalty.

If the back is expected to go forward, right, and left, his toes should be parallel to the LOS. If he is expected to go only forward or to his right, his right foot can be back. (It is slower to go to his left from this stance.) If he is going to go laterally much of the time, he won't want much weight on his hands, but if he is going forward, he might well take a sprinter's stance.

In the mid-1950s, Coach John Johnson of Red Sanders's staff at UCLA noticed that John Brodie, the Stanford quarterback, kept his feet parallel when he was going to pivot to hand off for a running play, but when he was going to pass, he had one foot back so that he could drop back faster. Each time that the defense saw his feet staggered, they yelled "Omaha" to attack him with an eight-man rush. The Bruins' attack was at least as effective as that of the Allies at Omaha Beach in World War II. Stanford, which had beaten UCLA the year before, 21-18 went down to a devastating defeat, 72-0. The primary reason was the tipoff on the placement of the quarterback's feet.

When a coach is running an I pro attack, he may put his tailback from $4\frac{1}{2}$ to as far as 7 or 8 yards back. If he wants the back to hit a certain hole, he will have him closer. But if he wants him to pick his hole, depending on how the defense adjusts to the play, the back will be deeper. The USC attack under John McKay and John Robinson used this deep set, which allows the skilled back to improvise. It took a very intelligent coach to let a Mike Garrett, O. J. Simpson, or Marcus Allen run where he saw an opening. Many coaches have now adopted this theory.

Shifting the Offense

Knute Rockne is given credit for developing the backfield shift. After lining up in a T formation, the backs would shift right or left into their Notre Dame box formation. The ball would be snapped as they were finishing the shift. This put a great strain on the defense to adjust to the power in time for the play. (The rule now is that after a shift, a player has to remain motionless for a full second—so that the defense can adjust to the new formation (see Figures 6.31a, b, and c).

Bob Zuppke, at Illinois, used a line shift to help spring Red Grange to his legendary running exploits. The guards were set behind the line and gaps were left on each side of the center. Then they shifted into the right or left gap to give an unbalanced line for the "galloping ghost" to run behind (see Figures 6.32 through 6.35).

Today, many teams use backfield shifts to upset the defensive strategy (see Figures 6.36a and 6.36b).

Perhaps no modern team has exploited the shift as much as the Dallas Cowboys did under Tom Landry. They would line up in one set, and then everybody would move. The linemen adjusted their splits, and the backs would move to another position. They knew where they were going, but the

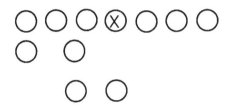

Figure 6.31a Rockne's box left

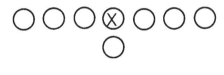

Figure 6.31b Rockne's T formation

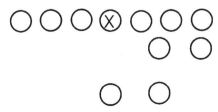

Figure 6.31c Rockne's box right

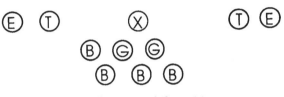

6.32 Illinois preshift position

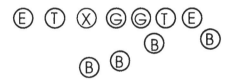

6.33 Shift to unbalanced line—single wing

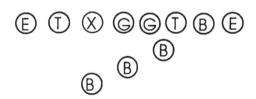

Figure 6.34 Shift to an eight-man unbalanced line

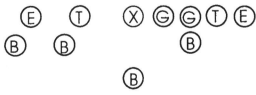

Figure 6.35 Shift to an unbalanced line, backs opposite

defense didn't. They might shift to an I, split backs, pro set, one back, or any other set they could devise. The defense, of course, had to be ready for a play from the original set, then adjust to whatever plays might be run from the final set.

As defenses became more specialized with a strong safety, strong cornerback, strong and weak linebackers, and perhaps strong and weak defensive linemen—all with special responsibilities—it was inevitable that someone would shift to upset such defenses. Since the defenders declared the offense "strong" to the side of the tight end, many teams declared the tight end to one side, let the defense set, then moved the tight end to the other end of the line. This movement of one offensive man could force the defense to move at least two defenders—and probably six or more men (see Figures 6.37 and 6.38).

This shift might force the movement of the strong and free safeties, the strong and weak side inside and outside backers, a "rover back" (if one is used), and perhaps the cornerbacks. That's a lot of defensive confusion for the shift of one lineman. If you are double tight and have the offensive backs left, the defense should adjust to your strong side. A simple shift of the offensive backs to the right may require a similar defensive adjustment. If the

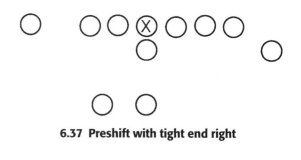

6.37 Preshift with tight end right

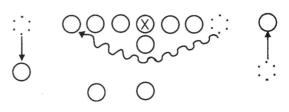

6.38 Shift to tight end left

offense snaps the ball shortly after the one second required for a shift, the defense may be caught shifting and may not be ready for the offensive play.

The Use of Motion

American football teams are allowed to have a back in motion going parallel to the line of scrimmage or moving backward. (Canadian rules permit several backs to move sideways or forward at the same time—a factor that is directly responsible for the high suicide rate among Canadian defensive coordinators . . . just kidding!)

Motion can be used to change formation by changing the strength of the formation (changing from a flanker to a slot or a slot to a flanker formation). See Figures 6.39 and 6.40.

Motion can be used to stretch the formation from a tight to a wide set, or to reduce the formation from a flanker set to a tight set (see Figures 6.41 and 6.42).

When teams don't adjust to the motion, they make themselves vulnerable to the offense changing the formation strength and then attacking to strength. It is amazing how often teams will disregard the change in formation strength. Some teams

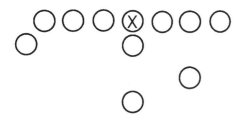

6.36a Wing T left . . .

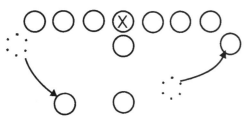

6.36b . . . shifting to wing T right

adjust to any motion, even when it doesn't unbalance the formation (see Figures 6.43 and 6.44).

Sometimes "short motion" is used. This is almost like a shift. The types of motion that a wingback could use: (1) short motion to the halfback position, (2) short motion to a power I formation, (3) motion to the slot area, (4) motion to the flanker area.

While a back in short motion cannot run a dive play, he can run a trap or counter to the other side and can certainly run a sweep. This type of motion is used extensively by wing-T teams. If the defense adjusts quickly to the short motion, the motioning back can reroute to another responsibility (Air Force does this).

Motion can also be used to bring a slotback or flanker into a position where he can execute an outside-in trap block. This is often a great surprise to the lineman being trapped, and often a greater surprise to the flanker who learns that he can block as well as catch passes.

Another major use of motion is to determine whether the defense is playing a man-to-man or a zone defense on that play. This makes it easier for the quarterback and the receivers to determine which patterns will work best on that play. If a zone shows (the motion back is not followed by a defender), perhaps a deep curl would be run. If

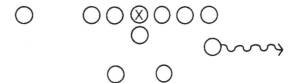

Figure 6.41 Stretching the formation from a wing to a flanker

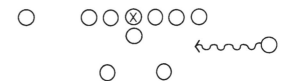

Figure 6.42 Reducing the formation from a flanker to a wing

man-to-man shows (a defender follows the motion man), perhaps a crossing pattern or a comeback would work best (see Figures 6.45 and 6.46).

Modern-day teams are usually multiple-formation teams which employ a good deal of motion. A good part of the "chess match" element of the game involves setting one's formations and evaluating the opponent's adjustments to them. Finding and

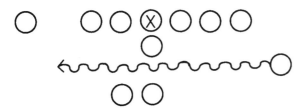

Figure 6.39 Flanker set motioned to slot set

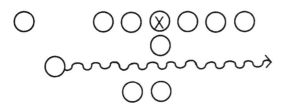

Figure 6.40 Slot set motioned to flanker

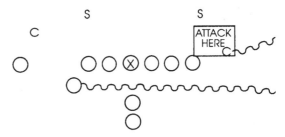

Figure 6.43 A balanced defense that doesn't change in formation strength (attack toward the motion)

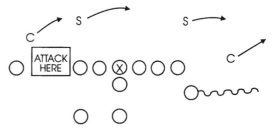

Figure 6.44 A defense adjusting to motion, which doesn't change the formation strength (attack away from motion)

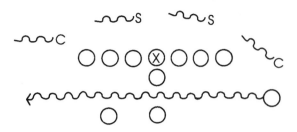

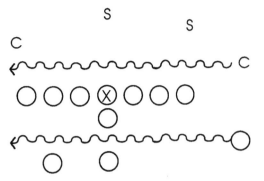

Figure 6.45 Crossing motion—defense shows it is in a zone

Figure 6.46 Crossing motion—defense is in man to man

exploiting the weaknesses in a defensive team's adjustments to formations can often be the key to winning the offensive battle.

Coaches must be aware of the importance of choosing formations. Some coaches use only a few plays but many formations. By noting how the defense adjusts, the coach can get a good idea as to where the defensive weaknesses will be with each offensive set.

He can then set his formation and call a play that will attack the vulnerable area of the defense. Other coaches will use few formations, believing that they

would rather know where the defense will be, then plan their attack.

Today the multiple formation idea has more adherents. However, in order to use formations most effectively, the coach must have a great deal of help in spotting the defensive adjustments. Scouting reports will give some indication of where defenders will generally be aligned, but during the game the coach must know exactly who is where on game day. He must then be able to attack the defense appropriately.

The Spread

The spread formation is a variation of the shotgun. It is like the single wing with the QB as runner and passer. It is becoming a more common offense in high school football. It uses four or five immediate receivers in slot, flanker, trips, and quads sets. The pros are still not likely to expose the QBs to running. The same is often true in college. It is often done with no huddle: the formation is signaled in and the QB checks the number of men in the box to determine whether it will be a run or a pass.

If you are in the middle of the field and are in a balanced formation (such as a wide double slot) you might expect a corner and an outside backer with your wideouts. This gives you five in the box, and a run is a good possibility because you have five linemen and two backs and outnumber them. (The "box" is an area approximately 5 yards deep and a yard or two outside the offensive ends.) The formations should get the linebackers out of the box.

PASSING THEORY

"Choose the approaches that fit your offensive potentials."

The forward pass is the heart of the pro attack and the delight of the fans. This present-day phenomenon was once a lowly orphan in the game. It wasn't even legal until thirty-six years after the game was invented. Some pressure on the rules committee by John Heisman (the man after whom the Heisman Trophy is named) resulted in Walter Camp, the head of the football rules committee, legalizing the forward pass in 1906. A few years later, Camp tried to have it again ruled illegal because he wanted to increase the running game's effectiveness.

In the classic football movie *Knute Rockne, All American*, starring Pat O'Brien and former president Ronald Reagan, Knute was shown practicing the pass during the summer at Cedar Point, Ohio. Then several months later, he sprang the surprise of all time on the heavily favored Army team, as little Notre Dame from the West defeated the Cadets in their 1913 game.

Well, it really did happen that way, but the forward pass had been used by teams in the Midwest since St. Louis completed the first pass against Carroll College in early September 1906. Still, the big roughhouse teams of the East weren't ready for the "sissy" pass so it remained for the teams from the Midwest and the South to develop it.

In those days the ball was still somewhat like a blimp—like a rugby ball—so it was very difficult to throw. So the first passes were more like basketball chest passes or were thrown underhand, end over end. However, it didn't take players long to learn how to throw the overhand spiral. In fact, Bradbury

Robinson of St. Louis University was credited with several 50-yard pass completions in 1906.

While Eddie Cochems is generally credited with the earliest development of many aspects of the passing game, Pop Warner at Carlisle, Amos Alonzo Stagg of Chicago, and Jesse Harper, Rockne's coach at Notre Dame, are all considered among the pioneers in the development of the forward pass.

The rules relating to the pass have changed a bit over the years. At first the passer had to throw from a spot at least 5 yards deep and 5 yards to the side of where the ball was snapped, and an incomplete pass cost the throwing team a 15-yard penalty. In 1910 it was made illegal to pass more than 20 yards downfield—because the pass was taking away from the "real" game of football. This rule lasted only two years. Also in 1910, the passer was no longer required to pass from 5 yards wide of the center, but he still had to be 5 yards deep when he threw.

By 1931 the shape of the ball was changed to make it easier to throw. And by 1934 the rule requiring a 5-yard penalty for the second incomplete pass in a series was eliminated. By 1945 it was legal to pass from anywhere behind the line of scrimmage.

The last major change was to allow any back less than a yard behind the line (such as the T-formation quarterback) to be an eligible receiver. This rule was passed in 1963.

The passing game is an essential part of any offensive plan of attack. While the running game allows a team to attack the width of the field, the passing game allows the offensive team to attack both the width and the depth of field.

A great passing attack starts with the offensive line. The receivers must have the time to run the proper depth. A potentially great passer isn't going to be worth much without receivers who can get open and catch and a line that can give him the needed time. Of course, you can sprint a passer away from a weak offensive line or you can pitch to the running backs and let them throw.

For a few teams the pass is primary. Brigham Young University under LaVell Edwards achieved a great deal of fame, and a national title, with this theory. The San Diego Chargers under Don Coryell and the "West Coast" offense of Bill Walsh's 49ers certainly brought the pass into more prominence than it had previously enjoyed.

Even before the West Coast offense achieved notoriety, the "run-and-shoot" offense developed by Glenn "Tiger" Ellison and popularized by Mouse Davis when at Portland State centered the offense around the pass.

Teams using the forward pass want to "stretch" the defense vertically and horizontally. They want to be able to hit "out" patterns right on the sidelines (a horizontal stretch) and they want to be able to throw the 50-yard pass deep (a vertical stretch). Once they have established that they can do both of these, the defensive team must be prepared to defend the entire field.

The Action of the Passer

The most common type of pass is the "dropback" pass. The quarterback either backpedals or turns and runs to a set depth before setting up to pass. Dropback passes are designed for the quarterback to drop one, three, five, seven, and sometimes nine steps. His depth depends on the depth that the receiver is to run in his route. When Miami upset the Bears in 1985, they did it primarily with one-step and three-step drop patterns. Dan Marino was

able to get his passes away before the vaunted Bear rushers could get to him.

The passer who turns and runs to his passing spot can get back quicker. On the other hand, the passer who backpedals is better able to see what the defense is doing and "read the defense" more effectively. While many coaches employ only one or the other type of drop, many pro teams use both. For teams that use both types of drop, the "presnap read" (how the defense is aligned) may be the key to which type of drop the quarterback may use.

Most teams also use play-action passes. This action usually holds the linebackers and opens up the underneath zones effectively. If the line blocks aggressively, as they would on a running play, the defensive backs may also be fooled. This aggressive blocking may not give the quarterback effective protection. But if the line does its normal pass-protection blocking (standing up and retreating), it will generally not fool the defensive backs.

In a rollout action, the quarterback runs deep behind the protection of his backs. He may pass from 10 to 20 yards wider than he lined up. This rolling action puts a great deal of pressure on the defensive player who is assigned to cover the short, wide area and to support on a wide running play. If the defender drops to protect for the pass, the quarterback may be able to run; if the defender comes up to support the run, the pass is open (see Figure 7.1).

In the partial rollout, the movement of the quarterback past the offensive tackle often signals the defense to change their assignments, with a wide pass defender moving up to support the possible

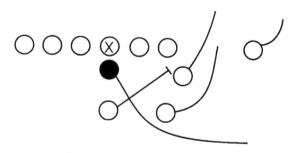

Figure 7.1 Rollout

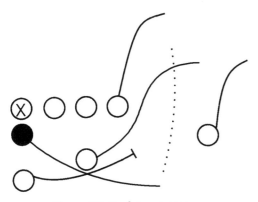

Figure 7.2 Sprint out pass

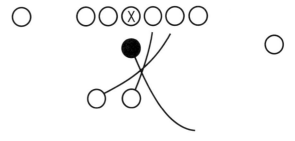

Figure 7.4 Waggle

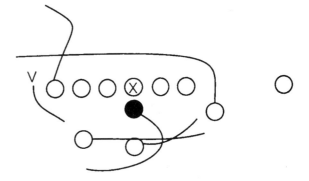

Figure 7.5 Boot with flood pattern

run. This may open up another man in the pass pattern. As the defenders rotate their pass coverage and change their zone responsibilities, the throwback pass may open up.

The sprint out pass is similar to the roll, but it is faster and more shallow, so it puts more pressure on the defensive cornerback to make up his mind quickly as to whether to play the run or the pass. The sprint out is similar to the option play discussed in Chapter 4. But while in the option play the QB can run or pitch back, in the sprint out he can run or pitch forward (see Figure 7.2).

The moving pocket ("rove," "dash," or controlled scramble) is a more recent development. What looks like a dropback pass becomes more like a rollout (see Figure 7.3).

The waggle is a type of short rollout with the quarterback moving behind the running backs on a running fake. A few coaches call it a waggle if the QB drops slightly away from the flow of the backs, but not as wide as a bootleg (see Figure 7.4).

The bootleg is like a rollout, but it is away from the flow of the backs. The QB will fake to a back

and keep the ball, going the opposite direction. He may or may not have a pulling lineman to block for him. This play is highly effective on the goal line or in short yardage situations in which everybody but the quarterback has a man assigned to guard him (see Figure 7.5).

Play-action passes are especially important to teams that rely on the run. Some teams have the linemen perform the normal "retreat" pass protection; others block aggressively as if the play is a run. Aggressive blocking is more likely to fool the defensive backs who are often keying the linemen—but the passer will probably not be protected as long.

Protecting the Passer

There is no question that you can't have a good passing attack unless the passer can release his pass. The more time he has, the more effective he will probably be. Consequently, the blocking schemes

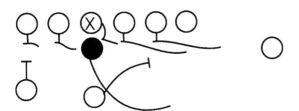

Figure 7.3 Moving pocket

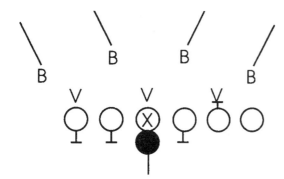

Figure 7.6 All backers drop to their zones

that an offensive line must learn in a sophisticated passing attack are quite complicated.

As an example, let's take a simple "man" blocking scheme. The player is responsible for the defensive man who lines up on him. Here is how it would look in an Oklahoma 5-2 or the pro 3-4, with the linebackers reacting back as the passer "shows" the pass by dropping back (see Figure 7.6).

"Big on big" is another type of commonly used man scheme. If there is a four- or five-man defensive line, the center, guards, and tackles will be responsible for those linemen. If there is a free blocker, he can help the linemen or look for blitzers. The center takes the "0" man, the guard the "1" man, and the tackle the "2" man. In a pro 4-3, it is quite simple; the guards and tackles take the men on them and the center drops back to help where needed—assuming that his linebacker doesn't rush. Against the old Oklahoma 5-2, the guards would block the defensive tackles and the offensive tackles would block the defensive ends. The backs in this scheme are responsible for the linebackers should they rush the passer.

Generally the backs are assigned to block if they see the linebackers rushing, but they may be allowed to swing to the outside if the linebackers drop back.

Another type of blocking scheme is "slide" protection. If an offensive lineman is having trouble blocking his man, he might get help by sliding another man over to help him. When the protection is "slide left," the right guard checks to make certain that his linebacker is not rushing, if not he is

free to slide to his left and help the center on the nose guard/nose tackle. In slide protection, the offensive linemen move a man to the right or left—usually toward the strong side or toward a very effective pass rusher.

Here is what is more likely to happen in a pass rush when the defense decides it really wants to "sack" the passer. (Defenses and the theories of stunting will be more thoroughly discussed in the chapters on defense.

Meanwhile, just sit back and be as confused as offensive coordinators are when their pass protection breaks down and their quarterbacks wonder why they aren't playing pro golf instead of pro football!) When the quarterback lines up in a shotgun formation, he is better able to read the stunts and blitzes and has more time to unload the ball. It looks relatively simple on paper, but on the field it is complicated (see Figures 7.7 through 7.12).

In order to take away the advantage of the defenders switching positions in a stunt or a twist, a zone blocking scheme may be used. In a "zone" scheme, the blocker sets up and waits to see who comes into his area. It might be the man who lined up on him, but it might well be somebody else. You always hope that your quarterback can see this all happening and dump off the ball to a tight end or a back.

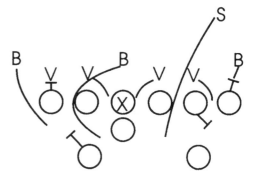

Figure 7.7 Backer and safety blitz

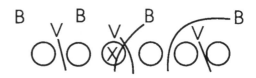

Figure 7.8 A stunt from a 3-4

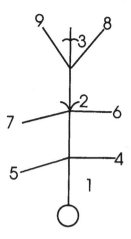

Figure 7.21a Sample of a passing tree—left-side patterns (odd numbers)

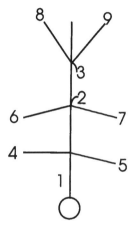

Figure 7.21b Sample of a passing tree—right-side patterns (even numbers)

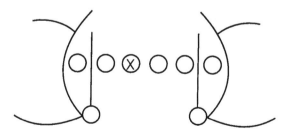

Figure 7.22 Some backfield patterns

receiver. The other receivers might run "complementary" patterns.

For example, if the coach called a "Y-9" or a "Y-corner," the tight end would run a corner pattern and the other two receivers should know which complementary patterns to run. Perhaps the nearest

other receiver knows that he should run an intermediate-level pattern in the same line of sight as the Y receiver, and the other receiver might have been coached to run a short pattern in the line-of-sight area. This would create a vertical stretch on the defense. If they were in a typical zone, the Y end should have the deep zone person near him. The second receiver would probably be in the deep curl or out area, 15 to 20 yards deep and behind the flat zone cover man. The other receiver would be between the line of scrimmage and 5 to 7 yards downfield, in front of the flat cover man (see Figure 7.23).

Often the coach wants to totally control the pattern and take the guesswork out of the players' minds, so he might call 483—meaning the X runs a 4, the Y runs a 9, and the Z runs a 3. This would give the same effect as the pattern explained in the above paragraph, but would be more explicit. The quarterback may not be as aware of his primary receiver when the coach calls a 483, however, so he has to look for the open receiver. (When the quarterback called "Y-8," he had a pretty good idea of who the coach thought would be open.)

A horizontal stretch could be accomplished with four receivers hooking at 8 to 10 yards or curling at 15 to 18 yards and working between the underneath cover men. It could also be done with one or two receivers going deep, then three others running hooks, ins, outs, circles, and so on to one side of the field. The stretch doesn't have to be all the way across the field but can stretch just half of the field.

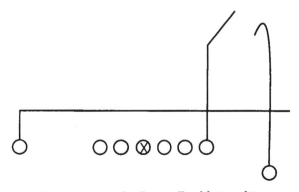

Figure 7.23 Y-9 (or "corner") with X and Z running complementary patterns

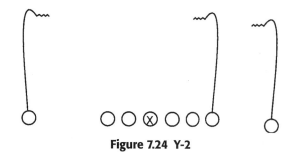

Figure 7.24 Y-2

There just must be more receivers in the under zones than there are defenders.

A simple type of complementary pattern would be all receivers running hooks—two patterns, or curls—three patterns (see Figure 7.24).

Obviously some patterns work better against certain defenses. A fast halfback has the advantage over a slower linebacker if the coverage is man to man. Deep curl patterns (at 18 to 23 yards) work against most zone coverages. And sending three players deep against a two deep zone may work. But since coverages are generally disguised, the offensive team is never quite sure what defense will develop as the quarterback drops to pass.

Team patterns are often called to put some special pressure on the defense. In a "flood" pattern, the offense tries to flood one area with more receivers than can be covered by the defense (see Figure 7.25).

Getting the Receiver Open

Many coaches attempt to get their best receiver against the poorest defender on the defense. This is a "mismatch"—they put their best or fastest "wide outs" against the poorest or slowest cornerbacks and their fastest running back against the slowest linebacker. This certainly gives the offense a "leg up" on getting a man open. Every game plan should have a few ways to make big plays for each receiver through alignment, motion, or deception.

If the receiver is being bumped by a defender, he must first get free of him. He may use a head fake, fake a block on the defender, then get into his pat-

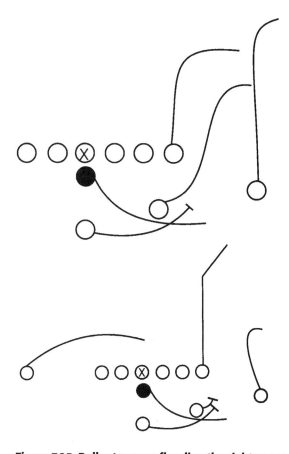

Figure 7.25 Rollout passes flooding the right zones

tern, spin away from the defender, or use his arms to knock the arms of the defender away.

Once he is free of the defender's bumping, he may attack a defensive back. Some coaches teach the receiver to run a straight line to the place where he will make his cut; others approach the defender in a weave.

Some coaches teach a hard 90-degree angle cut. A receiver who wants to cut right will plant his left foot and drive hard to the right. Sometimes, especially on deeper routes, the receiver makes a double cut. Some coaches prefer a rounded cut. The rounded cut gets the player wider faster, but doesn't fool the defender as much. However, if the receiver can get close to the defender and make the defender turn and run with him, then make his cut when the defender has his legs crossed or his shoulders turned, he can increase

Figure 7.26a Square cut

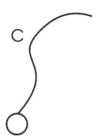

Figure 7.26b Weave and rounded cut

the distance between himself and the defender (see Figures 7.26a and 7.26b).

Making good cuts and making the cut at the proper time are particularly important with man-to-man coverage. If a team is playing a zone defense, the defenders should be paying more attention to being in the proper place on the field in relation to the ball than to the cut of the receivers. So receivers are often less concerned about faking a defender than they are about getting to an open area between the zones.

Some coaches don't worry so much about making a perfect cut but tell the receiver the area in which he should be. The passing tree can be used to call this area. The receiver is then taught to recognize man or zone cover as he comes off the line. (The defender generally watches the receiver in man and the QB in zone, or he will obviously be near his man in man and dropping to an area in zone.) The receiver, if he finds man cover, will (1) make a double cut; (2) approach or bump the defender, then break away; or (3) run deeper, then hook back. If it is a pure zone, he merely finds the open area—over or under the cover man or between the cover people.

This chapter has covered the basics in setting up a passing attack, but if this were all that there was to a modern pass offense it would be relatively simple. The real work in today's air attacks is developing techniques that allow the quarterbacks and the receivers to "read" the defense as the play unfolds. That is the mission of our next chapter.

CHAPTER

8

ATTACKING THE DEFENSE WITH THE FORWARD PASS

"Hit 'em where they ain't."

The forward pass is an integral part of many offenses. Usually the more skilled the players, the more likely it is to be successful. On paper, the passing coach can always beat the defense; however, doing it on the field takes a great deal of planning and practicing. Since most skilled players like to pass and catch, practice is more likely to be fun for them.

If you are going to pass, the most important factor is to have a great pass-blocking offensive line. If the QB is worried about being sacked or doesn't have time to read the defense, there is a reduced chance of a completion. Also, the receiver must have the time to run the proper depth. Second in importance is whether the receivers can get open and whether they can catch. The passer is the third consideration. Of course, you need all three to have a chance of being successful.

There Is More Than One Way to Design a Passing Attack

Some teams, stimulated by the success of Bill Walsh when he guided the 49ers to successive Super Bowl wins, opted for the shorter passing attack—the West Coast offense. The receivers must run disciplined routes and the quarterback makes his reads in a definite progression. The quarterbacks are more likely to use three- and five-step drops. The short pass receiver is expected to run for good yardage after the completion.

The West Coast offense is actually an evolution of thinking from Sid Gilman (Hall of Fame coach), Don Coryell, Ernie Zampese (former Ram offensive coordinator), and Bill Walsh. But a number of coaches have utilized the concept of short passes to replace some of the running attack. So the West Coast offense is really a theory in which short passes have become more important than they had been in the past.

Another concept that was pioneered in high school but has been used by the pros is the run-and-shoot approach. In this approach, the receivers are given more leeway in which way they will get clear. The quarterback must see what is happening and make the delivery to the open receiver.

Still another approach is the use of timed patterns, with different patterns becoming open at various times and the quarterback's reads progressing from early- to late-breaking patterns. (Timing patterns were the secret of the success of LaVell Edwards's BYU teams.)

In any of the approaches to passing theory, a coach may design patterns versus a two-deep and three-deep zone and against man-to-man and blitz packages. The pass patterns may be called depending on how an opponent is normally playing against you in the game—this is simpler for the QB. Or, patterns may be adjusted during a play to take advantage of how the defenders are actually playing on that play. This requires an advanced ability to read the defense.

Attacking the Defense

There are several theories of reading the defense. One is to read the progression from receiver to receiver; for example, curl to flat to safety valve or corner to curl to flat. Another method is to look at the flat defender to see if he is covering the curl or the flat, then throw the open pattern.

There are a number of different ways a defense can cover a pass on any given play; therefore, the quarterbacks and receivers must learn to "read" the defenses. This is the most technical area of modern-day football.

The first question to be answered by the quarterback and receivers is whether the coverage is a regular "man for man" (with the defensive backs 5 to 10 yards off the line), a press or a bump-and-run man for man, or a zone defense. If it is "man for man" (M4M), the best patterns are crossing patterns, comebacks (sidelines, hooks, curls), fakes—especially double fakes (Z out or in, hook and go, out and up)—or patterns in which the receiver can get the defender to turn and run one way and then just as the defender crosses his legs, the receiver cuts behind him. This makes it very difficult for the defender to recover in time to stop the pass. Versus bump and run, the receiver may lean into the defender, then make a break; he may run some sort of a comeback pattern; or he may simply try to outrun him.

In the following paragraphs, we will illustrate some successful pass patterns that are being used across the country. In designing your own attack, you will want to decide on which concepts, not which patterns, you will use—then design the patterns. Will you have vertical and/or horizontal stretches, high-low patterns on an underneath cover man, timed patterns, read high to low or low to high, do mostly drop back or play action, utilize a number of formations and motions, run a West Coast or a run-and-shoot attack? You can't do everything, so what is it you intend to feature? In the following paragraphs, we will look at how some of these possibilities can be developed.

Attacking Man-to-Man Coverage

When it is quite certain that there will be a man-to-man defense, crossing receivers is often effective in screening out the defenders. One such type of pattern is a "pick" play similar to those common in basketball. Just as in basketball, moving picks are illegal. However, if a potential receiver hooks and stops and somehow gets in the way of a defender covering another player, it is legal. Crossing patterns can accomplish the same thing when the receivers cross near each other. Such plays are often used on the goal line where man-to-man coverage is common (see Figures 8.1, 8.2a, and 8.2b)

An interesting pattern that Kentucky uses is to release the tight end (Y) across the field at a 6-yard depth. The X comes under him. (If it is man to man, you have a pick action and the receivers just keep running to clear themselves. Z runs a quick postup and corner ending somewhere between 13 and 23 yards. F (fullback) runs a swing—so you

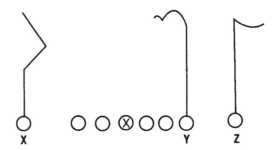

Figure 8.1 Patterns effective against a man defense (L to R): X running a "Z-out" pattern, Y hooking, and Z sideline

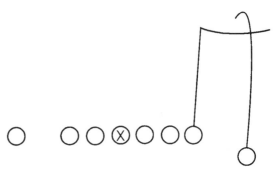

Figure 8.2a Z hook, Y out—a pick play

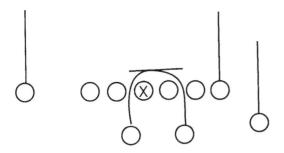

Figure 8.2b Backs crossing—a pick play

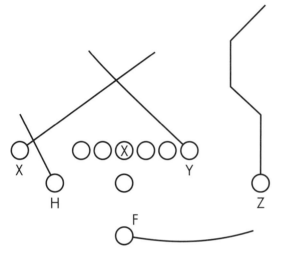

Figure 8.3 Kentucky crossing pattern

have a high-low over and under the flat defender in a zone. H (halfback) runs a shoot route to about a 3-yard depth. This route handles man-to-man cover with the X and Y patterns, zone cover with the Z and F pattern, and has H as a safety valve. F and H check the near backer before releasing—blocking him if he comes (see Figure 8.3).

The running backs must get width to force the backers wider so that X and Y can more easily find a window. The QB's read is deep to short.

Attacking Zone Coverage

When the defense uses a lot of zone coverages, as most teams do, patterns can be called in the huddle and the "read" is relatively simple.

Quite often the coach will design patterns that stretch the defense either horizontally (across the field) or vertically (up the field).

An example of a horizontal stretch is to have all the receivers doing hooks (going 10 to 12 yards, then coming back 8 or 9) with each receiver trying to get between and "under" the defenders in the short zones. The quarterback merely looks for the open defender. He can usually see who will be open if he watches the retreat of the linebackers into their zones.

A vertical stretch has two or three receivers at different depths up the field. One might run a very long pattern, another breaking at about 18 yards (between the deep and the underneath covers), and another staying close to the line of scrimmage. The passer looks at the defenders on that side of the field and determines which receiver will be the deepest open target.

Here is a vertical stretch pattern using two receivers in a pattern that reads only one defender. This pattern is often called an "orbit" because the two receivers are in a partial orbit around the defender. The defender being "read" is the man responsible for the flat area. If he chooses to cover the deeper receiver, the QB will throw to the shallow man; if he covers the shallow man, the pass will be thrown to the man running the deep curl (see Figures 8.4a and 8.4b).

This same principle can be used on any short zone defender with a man curling deep and another up to a 5-yard depth.

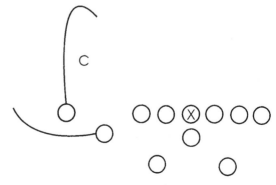

Figure 8.4a Orbit pattern with split end and slotback

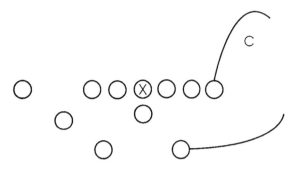

Figure 8.4b Orbit pattern with tight end and running back

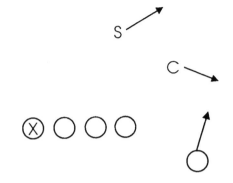

Figure 8.5a "Cloud cover" to two-receiver side

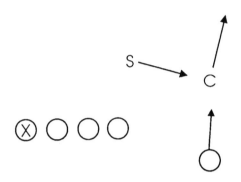

Figure 8.5b "Sky cover" to two-receiver side

Threatening a deeper vertical stretch is the traditional Raiders approach. The deep pattern is constantly run, even though it is only planned to be thrown a half dozen times a game. More of the patterns will break at 18 to 20, under the deep routes. Texas Tech has done a good job with the vertical game. An example of a vertical stretch pattern has four receivers releasing. If they read man cover, they may try to outrun their defender or hook. If they read zone, they settle in an open area 10 to 15 yards deep. Starting with four verticals, depending on the cover, they can continue, hook, or settle into an open area.

Another type of pattern against a zone is a flood pattern in which two or three receivers are sent into one or two zones. The passer is expected to determine who is the open receiver, then fire the ball to him.

Most teams play four defensive backs but need to cover only three deep zones. One of the defenders can be freed to cover a flat zone to the strong side. (The strong side can be the side to which the QB rolls, the wide side of the field, or the side of the two receivers.) If the cornerback is assigned to cover the flat, it is often called "cloud" coverage. If the safety is assigned the flat for that play, it is often called "sky" coverage (see Figures 8.5a and 8.5b).

Here is a common "read" used against teams that use cloud and sky covers. (Only one defender is read and there is only one receiver who is the major concern of the passer.) It is called a "post-read" pattern. The wide receiver starts to run a post pattern,

and both he and the quarterback watch the safety. If the safety starts wider and deep, the receiver changes his pattern to a corner and is ahead of the safety. If the safety starts wide but does not get depth, it means that he will be covering the flat, so the cornerback will have the deep third of the field. In this case the receiver breaks inside the cornerback and runs a post pattern. The passer must get the ball to him quickly so that the other safety, who is now moving to the deep middle zone, cannot react to the ball.

If it turns out that the defense is in man-to-man coverage, the receiver breaks back toward the passer after he has run about 15 yards downfield (see Figures 8.6 and 8.7).

Still another type of read occurs when an offensive receiver is assigned to watch a linebacker to see if he will blitz the passer. If he sees the backer stunting, it means that the backer's zone has been vacated. If he sees the backer stunt, the receiver yells

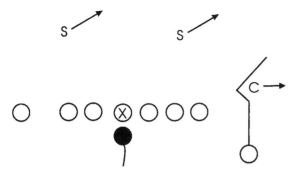

Figure 8.6 Post-read, safety has deep outside zone (cloud)

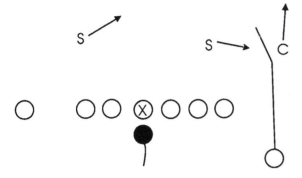

Figure 8.7 Post-read, safety covers flat (sky)

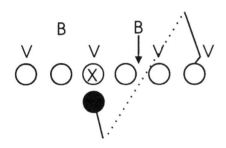

Figure 8.8 Tight end as hot receiver

"hot" and runs to the vacated area. The QB passes immediately—no matter what pattern had been called in the huddle. Some teams will make the strong linebacker the first read so they don't have to yell "hot"—they just read it (see Figure 8.8).

More complicated reads can involve looking at two or three defenders to determine the coverage. Usually there is an "alignment" key and a "movement" key.

Simple Read Concepts

Here are the rules and keys (greatly simplified) and how they would be applied to this pass.

Flanker (Z) looks at the near cornerback and safety. If the corner is 5 to 10 yards deep, it could be a man to man or a zone. If the safety is closer to the line of scrimmage than the corner, it is probably a zone. In any case, run a 10-yard out pattern (the basic pattern just shown). But if the cornerback is up close, he will probably try to press cover or bump and run (a tight man to man) or bump and play the short flat zone. In either case, run a fade pattern (angling for a spot 18 yards deep and 4 yards from the sideline).

Split end (X) is similar to the flanker, but he must also look at the near linebacker for additional keys. The weak safety may also give him a key. His primary responsibilities are the same (run a 10-yard out or a fade pattern if defenders are up close), but he may also get to the 10-yard out area (2 yards from the sideline) by splitting wider, then hooking out at the 10-yard area.

The tight end (Y) looks first at the strong safety to attempt to determine whether he is in a zone or man coverage. On the snap of the ball, he concentrates on the nearest linebacker. He tries to run an 8-yard hook over the middle, but if the linebacker won't let him inside, he breaks to the outside. If the defense is blitzing, he can break wherever there is an opening. If he gets man coverage from the free safety, he works upfield, then comes back for the ball.

Running backs check to see if they are needed in pass protection, then release to an area 4 yards deep and between the offensive tackle and the wide receiver. Against an excellent pass rusher, the back may be assigned to block the rusher before releasing. This is a good way to hide his intent before releasing on short check-off routes.

The quarterback looks at the secondary first. He will have called for the flanker side or the split end side to be the primary target area. He will concentrate on that side first in his read. If the safeties are closer than normal (inverted), there is probably strong run support or man-for-man coverage. He should throw the out pattern to the wide receiver. If it is covered, he should look at the halfback and tight end to see who is open. If the alignment shows that the wideouts are tightly covered, he should look at the defensive end or outside linebacker to the primary side to see if he has dropped off in pass coverage. If he hasn't, one of the backs or the tight end should be open.

Remember that this is just one of many patterns, each with its own set of reads—and each read is more complicated than just described because the keys must consider three- and four-deep alignments, regular formations and inverted formations, tight and normal zones, and man-to-man defenses, as well as situations in which the blitz occurs.

Here is an "all-curl" pattern that many teams use as a horizontal stretch. On the two-receiver side, it is probable that only one of the receivers will be double covered. Once the QB sees who the linebacker is covering, he can be reasonably certain that the other receiver can break free (see Figure 8.9).

Any team that uses a sophisticated passing attack should have adjustments that will be made as the receivers see the short zones open. The deep routes do not need adjustment because they are still threats and will stretch the defense vertically. Inside routes may gear down in the short zones so that they are under the coverage. Outside routes may not need adjustment unless the corner forces the run and opens up the zone. Then shallower routes or even fade patterns may open.

Run and Shoot

Run and shoot is a theory developed by "Tiger" Ellison, a former high school head coach and assistant to Woody Hayes at Ohio State. It was refined and popularized by Mouse Davis when he was head coach at Portland State and later with the Denver Gold of the now-defunct USFL. He also is responsible for its use in the NFL, where he became an offensive coordinator. Originally it offered five series, each with its own reads. It had reads in its running attack and reads in its passing plays.

Here is the tight double-slot formation with the left half in motion. This is called the "Gangster pass right" series. When this play was called in the huddle, no one on the offense knew which of the options would develop.

Option 1. If the man covering the left end was 3 or more yards inside the end, the QB could throw the "automatic" pass. The X end would run an "arrow" pattern (see Figure 8.10).

Option 2. Where would the fourth defensive man from the center play after the left half went in motion? Was he close to the slotback (blitz position), head up on the split end (hardnose position), or halfway between and dropped off a bit (walkaway position)? If the number 4 defender was in a "blitz" position, the right end would run a "look in" pattern. The QB would run down the line and throw on his third step (see Figure 8.11).

Versus the "walkaway" number 4 man, the right end would start downfield, make a 30-degree break, and curl. The slot would hook near the inside line-

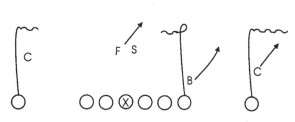

Figure 8.9 Raider all-curl pattern

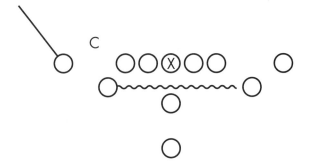

Figure 8.10 Automatic pass to X end

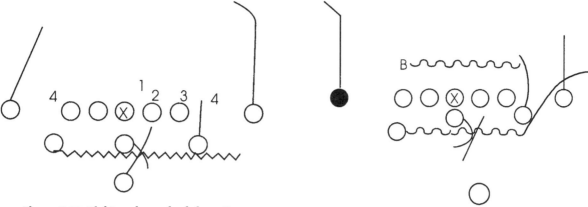

Figure 8.11 Right end runs look-in pattern

Figure 8.13 Throwback

backer so that he could "cherry pick" him, and the motion man would swing wide. The rule is "He left-I right; he right-I left; he up-I back; he back-I up." In other words, if the walkaway number 4 man came up or went wide, the pass would be thrown to the end running a curl; if the walkaway man dropped off or came to the middle, the QB would hit the halfback in motion (see Figure 8.12).

The right halfback might also be the pass receiver. His rule is that if the near linebacker red-dogged, he would release upfield as a "hot" receiver and catch the ball over his inside shoulder. If the backer followed the motion man, the right slotback would release and catch the ball over his outside shoulder. If he played in his normal position, the slot would "pick" him by running a hook pattern between the linebacker and the curling end.

Should the defender come across with the motion man, it is most likely a man-to-man defense, so the quarterback has the ball snapped earlier than normal.

The motioning back then cuts upfield and "picks" the man covering the right wingback. They cross. Whoever is free gets the pass (see Figure 8.13).

Attacking Man-to-Man Defenders

The simplest strategy is to just outrun the defender who is playing man to man. But there are two possible problems: If you are playing against a top pro team and you are being bumped near the line of scrimmage, then you are going to have to outrun the cornerbacks who run 4.4 for the forty. In high school and college, the defender can continue to bump the receiver until the ball is in the air, so it is easier for the pros to work against bump coverage than it is for high school and college players.

If you are playing a team that plays a looser man-to-man, the defender has a head start of 3 to 10 yards on you. Consequently, most man-to-man routes require that the receiver use techniques to break away from the defender. The simplest such moves are the hooks and the outs.

In order to free himself, the receiver may lean into the defender to get him off balance, then make his break. If the defender stays close to the receiver, a double-breaking route such as a "hook and go," an "out and up," or an "in and out" (Z out) can be called—if the QB has time for these slower patterns.

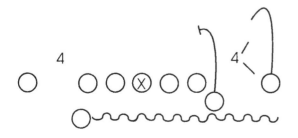

**Figure 8.12 Right end runs curl,
halfback goes in motion**

Another common route against bump and run cover is the "fade" route. In this route, the receiver runs to the corner of the end zone, "fading" away from the passer. The ball must be thrown over the defender while the receiver uses his body to keep the receiver away from the spot where the ball will be caught. A short pass is an easy interception, so the passer must hit it exactly—or overthrow it.

A pick play, where one man screens another's defender, is a common pattern, especially on the goal line, where most teams play "man" coverage (see Figures 8.14, 8.15a, and 8.15b).

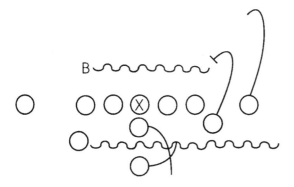

Figure 8.14 Picking M4M defender

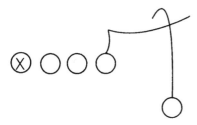

Figure 8.15a Hook and out pick

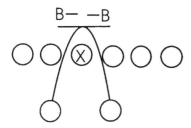

Figure 8.15b Crossing backs pick

Counters for the Passing Attack

Just as running teams must have counters, so must passing teams. Teams that drop their linebackers quickly to stop the pass may be countered with the fullback or quarterback draw. Against teams that rush a good many players, screen passes may work. While the receivers run deep and the quarterback drops nine or more steps, the linemen set up a screen for the receiver (see Figures 8.16 through 8.18).

The shovel pass was developed by Jack Curtice and popularized when Lee Grosscup played for him at Utah. In the Curtice shovel pass, one side of the line drops back in a retreating pass protection; the other side blocks aggressively as if for a run. The

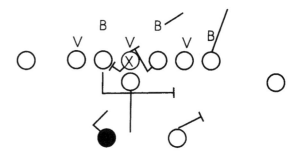

Figure 8.16 Fullback draw with a trap

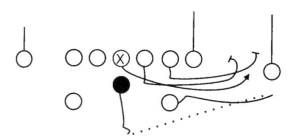

Figure 8.17 Halfback screen right

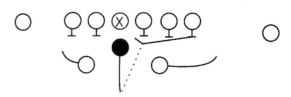

Figure 8.18 Tight end middle screen

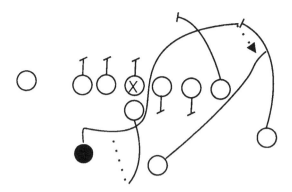

Figure 8.19 Jack Curtice's shovel pass

receiver runs to the gap created by the different blocking schemes and takes a short pass, often underhanded or a basketball chest pass; he then runs into the secondary where he "options" the first man who tries to tackle him. The player to whom he laterals often scores (see Figure 8.19).

The shovel pass has come back in style, especially with the shotgun spread attacks, but coaches seldom use the lateral to the passer, which Curtice used so successfully.

Quarterbacks generally want to throw long, so except for those patterns that you want to go long, get your quarterback used to hitting the first receiver open.

Attacking the Blitz

Your passing attack design must take into consideration the alignment of the backs (two, three, or four deep); the number of zones usually covered; the types of zone, man, and combination defenses they use—and when they use what.

But you must also consider how you will pick up blitzes and whether you will be facing a man blitz, zone blitz, or both. If you are going to have a sophisticated passing attack, you must then have some sort of reads that can take care of every situation. Blitz pickup and patterns against the blitzes require some special consideration.

When the defense blitzes and plays man to man or zone behind it, you must be prepared to recognize it quickly and adjust your pattern. Your scouting reports should indicate whether your opponent is most likely to use a man or a zone blitz, and if a zone, whether it is a three or four under zone. Also under what situations is the opponent most likely to blitz—when behind, outside of red zone, third down?

If you can get a presnap read, it will help, but effective blitzing teams aren't going to tip off their intentions often. That means you must always be prepared to block or to attack the open zone or the weak man-to-man cover person. Use the running backs against M4M cover because you usually get a speed mismatch on a backer. Versus a zone, you get the easy underneath completion with the possibility of a big gainer on the run.

Just one player asleep at the switch can cause a disaster.

When an offensive team has developed a high level of confidence in its ability to pick up and exploit the blitz, it often plays with a confident attitude. Only practice time will develop that kind of confidence in the team. The coach should spot the opponent's blitz situations and alignments through video study, then communicate to the offense how to handle the blitzers, and most important, practice against them.

This blitz analysis might indicate that the opponent blitzes more than the other teams played thus far. They are likely to do it on their side of the 50. Their backers usually sneak up a bit, and their cover people come up from 8 yards to about 6 yards. Now the quarterback has a good picture of what to expect, and when. The tight end or slotback may look for the same things as the quarterback and be alert to make the hot call when the near backer goes. What may have been a sack can turn into a 10-yard completion because the offense was prepared and practiced against the blitz.

The offense's preparation should include presnap blitz looks, but it should still be prepared for the well-disguised blitz after the snap. Decide on a key for the running backs to use on whether to block or release. Decide whether to zone block or use a man protection, then determine who will block the most likely blitzers in a blitz situation. Also, decide whether to use hot calls, and if so, by which players.

The Goal-Line Passing Attack

Near the goal line the defensive team will usually play a man-to-man defense. Because of this, the pick plays such as crossing patterns to the tight ends or between a tight end and a flanker often work. Also, a delayed pattern may work. In a delayed pattern, a receiver first blocks (making the defender think that the play will be a run) and then releases after the defender has committed to the run (see Figures 8.20 and 8.21). Play-action passes often work near the goal line because the defenders are so ready to stop the run

Another pattern that often works is the bootleg run or pass. Defenses usually don't assign a man to watch the quarterback so he is often free. Some teams will use him as a pass receiver on occasion for that reason. He may pitch out to a running back who stops and throws to the opposite side of the field to the uncovered quarterback.

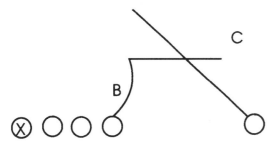

Figure 8.20 Pick pattern vs. goal-line defense

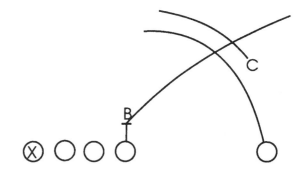

Figure 8.21 Delay pattern vs. goal-line defense

Planning for the Scramble

Nearly every game will find the quarterback scrambling at some point; the receivers must be aware of what to do in this case. Some coaches say to come back toward the quarterback in the direction of the scramble. Others send the farthest receiver from the scramble running a post, for the possible touchdown. Other receivers may then work outside of the QB to the scramble side, working at different depths. The widest receiver to the scramble side may be drilled to come to the sideline at first-down distance and sit there. The passer's reads now become short to long.

Passing Is More Than Throwing and Catching

Don Shula, former Miami Dolphins head coach, has described "passing" as a mental achievement, while "throwing" is strictly physical. He said that his quarterback, Dan Marino, read the defense and made up his mind as to where he would throw faster than anyone who has ever played the game. He not only recognized where to throw but how to throw—hard or soft, high and outside, or low and inside.

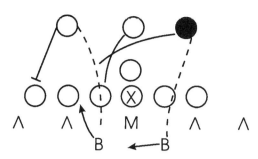

Figure 9.29 Straight read through guard; inside belly series; crossbuck with guard pulling

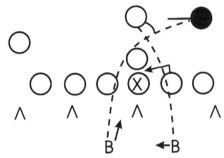

Figure 9.30 Cross read—guard to far back

Stemming

Changing the alignment of the defensive linemen and/or backers before the snap is called "stemming." Ray Graves, when he was the defensive coordinator at Georgia Tech, is credited with originating this move.

He called it "jitterbugging." Originally, the movement was from one standard defense to another, such as an Okie to an Eagle.

As it has developed, the movement shifts defensive gap responsibilities. By stemming, you force the offense into either short or long counts and you confuse the offensive linemen.

If the offense opts for short counts, you merely move a bit earlier. If they go on long counts, you can change twice. The verbal signal for the change must not be similar to the offensive snap count. "Change" or "move" are words that may be used to signal the shift.

Linemen can also move on their own along the line as they change positions. This is generally called "prowling" or "rovering." Here the lineman knows where he will end up, but he moves along the line, getting closer to his responsibility as the snap becomes more likely.

Rovering or prowling, the defensive linemen and backers can confuse blocking assignments. Whether the blocking is zone or rule, the movement of the defenders confuses the offensive linemen. However, the defensive linemen may have problems if they are playing a typical gap control pursuing defense. They have a greater advantage if they make a slant charge through the offensive line. This makes them more vulnerable to the trap, however. But a plus is that they get a head start on a pass rush. If they are taught to charge low, they add still another problem for the higher-blocking zone linemen; the lower charge greatly reduces the opportunity of the blocker to grab cloth and hold.

Stunting

Line stunts include slants and loops. Twists or cross charges are also in the category of line stunts. Traditionally, a stunt means to include one or more backers coming. Some coaches now call this a blitz.

Blitzing

Blitzing is sending a backer or defensive back across the LOS at the snap of the ball to get a sack or to tackle the runner behind the line. It can be done with a man-to-man defense or a zone defense behind it.

Since one or more pass defenders are involved in the blitz, there will be one or more holes in the zones. Some teams drop off a lineman to pick up a zone or to cover an end or back man to man.

Theory of Techniques for Defensive Backs

The defensive back's technique depends on whether he is playing a man-to-man or a zone. Generally the back will take a few steps back as he reads his key. A defensive back may key the offside end or end and tackle. If both go downfield (in a college or high school game) it is a run or a pass behind the line. (In high school and college, linemen can go downfield on passes completed behind the line of scrimmage.) Of course, in a pro game the tackle going downfield can only indicate a run (see Figure 9.31).

The back might also key any uncovered linemen, such as the guards in an Okie alignment. But with so many teams pulling their uncovered linemen behind the line of scrimmage, they have taken away this key. Zone teams drop to their zones if a pass shows. They may also rotate their zones if the passer moves to a new position.

With teams passing more, especially in certain situations, defensive coaches have begun to put in more defensive backs than the standard four. The five back (nickel defense) and the six back (dime defense) have defensive backs coming in to substitute for linebackers on "passing downs." The advantage of such moves is that the backs have better speed and pass defense skills—and are less likely to be "burned" in one-on-one man-to-man coverage against running backs. The disadvantage is that they tend to be weaker against the run than the linebackers would have been.

Theory of Secondary Alignment

Coverage players must play pass first. If there is one free safety, he should be in the middle. If there are two deep safeties, they should be about 13 yards in from the sideline. This would be about 4 yards outside a high school hash mark.

It takes three men to cover the deep secondary zones; therefore, many teams use the three deep secondary, which has been around since the earliest days of the game. Others rotate or otherwise disguise their intentions as to what player will be in each zone.

With more teams using two wide receivers, it became impossible to rotate up to stop the run because this leaves the wide receiver unattended. Consequently, many teams started to "invert" their safeties. The safeties then become responsible for run support while the corners are primarily responsible for the pass (see Figure 9.32).

With the umbrella defense or the invert, when teams play a zone defense they generally play with three deep backs in the zones and an extra man in the flat.

Some college and high school coaches decided that they could teach better if they had the same three people in the deep zones all the time. However, they liked the seven-man front of the Okie defense. So with seven up front and three deep they had an extra man. He was called the "rover" or "monster."

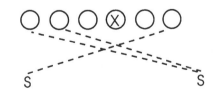

Figure 9.31. Keying the offside tackle and end

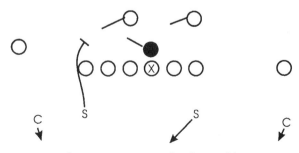

Figure 9.32. Inverted 4 deep with safeties supporting to the flow

The rover or monster could be put in the middle of the defense, but usually he went to the wide side of the field or to the strength of the offensive set. In determining the strength of the offense, his rules were to go to the side of a flanker or slotback or away from a split end. This rover back usually had responsibility for wide runs and for the wide flat pass zone.

In man-to-man defense, the defenders can play up close and "bump and run" with the receiver or they can play 5 to 10 yards off a receiver. While there is usually a "free" safety, he cannot cover the whole deep secondary, so the cornerbacks must do most of the job themselves.

If the receiver is faster than the defender, he can easily get open on a streak pattern. Teams running the bump and run have the theoretical advantage of being able to take away all of the patterns that the receiver might run. The major disadvantage is that the man covering a wide receiver can't be much help in stopping the running play.

So, as you can see, there are a lot of possibilities of alignment and of technique. The important point is really the effectiveness of the individuals playing defense. How well do they read their keys? How well do they escape ("shed") their blockers? How well do they pursue to the ball carrier? How well do they play pass defense?

Of extreme importance is the type of defense called to counter each offensive situation. Do players have the proper pass defense when the offense is most likely to pass? Have they properly selected a pursuing or a penetrating defense when they expect the offense to run?

Factors to Be Considered in Zone Coverage

If you are playing three deep, the free safety will be in the middle of the field; the middle of the outside zones is 9 yards from the sideline. If you are playing two deep, the middle of the zones is 14 yards from the sideline (4 yards outside the high school hash marks). The safeties should line up 10 to 14 yards deep, depending on their speed. In a zone defense, the QB's eyes and the ball take the defender to the reception point. In man defense, the receiver takes you to the ball.

For deep defensive backs, when a receiver is 10 yards deep when the ball is thrown, the interception point will be about 15 to 18 yards deeper downfield. For this reason, those with deep responsibility need not be close to the receiver for deep passes. They should be close to where the ball would be caught. On shorter patterns in the middle, the interception point is about 6 yards from where the receiver was when the pass was thrown. Field position, yard line, and hash mark can affect the type of coverage:

- closer to the offensive team's goal line restricts the vertical distance of the pattern
- closer to the defensive team's goal line reduces the chances of completing the long pass because of the time factor and chance of a safety if the passer is sacked.

Formation and backfield set tell how the perimeter of the defense is being manipulated. The wider the wideouts, the wider or deeper the defensive backs must set.

If the backs are set wide, there is a greater threat of a swing pass or another type of pass pattern to a back.

Flow of the backs can signal the most likely area that the offense can attack. They can all flow to one side, they can split, they can cross, the QB may boot away from flow.

The quarterback setup point should have a direct relation to the depth of the patterns:

- three-step drop. Expect a short pattern in the 5-yard area or a timed pattern.

- five-step drop (about a 7-yard set up). Expect intermediate routes in the 14- to 18-yard area or delayed patterns such as an end dragging or a back out of the backfield.
- seven-step drop (about a 9-yard setup). Expect deep vertical routes such as streak, post, or corner.

Knowing the depth of the QB's drop should give you an idea as to the depth of the pattern. Then watching the passer's eyes or chin should give you an idea as to the direction he will throw.

Taking Away Specific Areas

The most common type of zone coverage is the four-under three-deep responsibility. Against a team that throws short often the coach may want to play five-under and two-deep zones. Both may be open to intermediate-area passes of 14 to 18 yards. To take away this intermediate area, the coach may play five-under man with two-deep zones. This should take away all passes under 18 yards but could allow vulnerability to long passes, splitting the seams of the deep two safeties. With the undercoverage men watching men rather than the ball, this five-under man defense is vulnerable to the run.

The coach must recognize that there is a defense for whatever the offense wants to do, but every defense has its weaknesses. Because of this, the coach may want to change covers at certain times (but not be predictable in so doing). For example, if he plays a five-under man two-deep zone on every third-and-long situation, his team may be open to a quarterback draw or bootleg or even a sweep into an area being cleared by receivers.

You may find that a team screens a great deal to an outside receiver or running back. You can put a spy on the running back and play M4M on the wideout—even if you are otherwise in a zone.

The Blitz

Stunting linebackers in pass situations has been around forever. But blitzing corners, strong safeties, and even free safeties is a relative newcomer to the defensive arsenal. Defensive coordinators have had to look beyond what had been done to counteract the pass attack.

At the pro level, the blitz is one of the biggest troublemakers an offensive coordinator can encounter. Originally, the blitzes were packaged with man-to-man coverage. Knowing this, it became easy to attack, so the zone blitz was developed. Since the blitz is designed to get to the quarterback quickly by sending more people to an area than can be blocked, the passer and receivers must be able to recognize the blitz and the coverage instantly to be able to attack it.

Playing Man Coverage Behind the Blitz

Man coverage, possibly bump and run, should be considered when blitzing in a pass situation. The free safety may or may not be used. In any case, the defense has to cover five people. The defenders committed to cover the setbacks can go to them and occupy their block, or defenders can wait to see if they come out of the backfield, then play them man to man. With a five-man rush you can play man for man and still have a free safety. If you rush six, you won't have a free safety.

Playing Zone Behind the Blitz

With zone coverage, you will end up with a four-under two-deep zone, or even a three-under two-deep. You may even gamble with four-under zones and one deep or four or five under and no one deep. You might even slide the zones over to protect the most likely target area, and also drop off a lineman to cover a zone or to spy for a draw or screen. Playing a zone behind allows for much better run recognition and for the potential of having more people reacting to the ball and to the receiver.

Goal-Line Defense

Goal-line defense is an essential aspect of many games. Since most teams prefer to run in this area, because of the reduced passing area, teams must stop the run. In order to do this, they usually play man-to-man pass defense. The defenders on the wideouts will possibly be able to help on a wide run. The linebackers assigned to the running backs will be available whether their men are involved in a run or a pass.

Occasionally, some teams play a zone defense against a team that does a lot of drop-back passing near the goal line. Usually they will commit five men to the short zones.

Stopping the run is usually done by penetrating at least six defenders. Usually two will be in the center-guard (A) gaps, two in either the guard-tackle (B) gaps or tackle-end (C) gaps, and two attacking from outside the ends (see Figure 9.33).

Figure 9.33 6-5 goal line defense

Being Balanced

Every offense poses different problems to a defense. It stretches it horizontally, and possibly vertically, differently. Defensive coaches must understand the strengths and weaknesses of each offensive set. Then, as shifting and motions change the set, the defensive coach must have considered each possible problem and how it will be encountered. Many coaches start their adjustments with two markers. By drawing an imaginary line through the center, then counting the number of offensive players on each side of the line, they match those numbers with defenders. A second, often-used marker is the rule to have two and a half men outside the offensive tight end. This is adjusted for flanker, slot, or other wide formations, but it provides a rule of thumb regarding the force possibilities of the defense.

As a defensive coach, you therefore have a large number of factors to consider. Will you attack and contain or pursue?

Will you go with two or three deep? Do you have the speed to play the kind of defense you want? Can you adequately cover everything the offense can throw at you? And can you teach it all in the limited time available?

CHAPTER 10

THE KICKING GAME AND SPECIAL TEAMS

"It's a third of the game"

Today with the emphasis on "special teams," the kicking game has become more important in the eyes of the fans. Coaches, especially the "field position" coaches, have long known the importance of the "kicking game" and have emphasized it in practice and in their games. A great number of the most successful coaches place the kicking game second in importance only to defense (with the offensive game being third).

Many coaches believe that if a team makes two more mistakes than its opponents in the kicking game, it will almost undoubtedly lose that game. A blocked punt, a long kick return, a muffed catch, or a missed extra point can be disastrous to a team's chance of winning.

Many of the so-called breaks in a football game occur during the kicking phase of the game. They are not really breaks at all because the "lucky" team has practiced all season to make those breaks occur. This is not the part of the game to let the subs play. Frank Beamer of Virginia Tech is generally considered the major exponent of the kicking game. Understanding how important it is to start your possessions in a zone that gives you a better chance to score, he plays his best players on special teams.

The Kickoff

Most teams prefer to receive the kickoff if they win the coin flip. Strong defensive and kicking teams will often choose to kick the ball. Their hope is that they can hold their opponents inside the opponent's 30, make them punt, then take over somewhere around their own 40-yard line.

The basic kickoff play puts the kicker in the middle of the field with five tacklers on either side of him. Some teams will kick the ball from a hash mark, rather than the middle of the field, in order to reduce the opponent's options for a return. The thinking is that it will be more difficult for a team to return to the other side of the field. Every step that the ball carrier takes to the far sideline gives every member of the kicking team one more step into the receiver's territory.

So the chances of an effective return are reduced. If the receivers return to the side of the kick, the defenders each have less territory to defend.

Some coaches use two kickers, aligning one to kick deep to one side of the field with the other kicker ready to kick to the opposite field or to kick an onside kick.

In Figure 10.1, kicker "1" is used to kick deep to the right side of the field, and kicker "2" is used to kick shallower to the left or to kick the onside kicks.

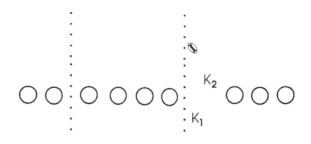

Figure 10.1 Two-kicker kickoff

With all the soccer-style kickers around today, there are many who can kick the ball into the end zone consistently. It doesn't take a genius to realize that this is the ultimate in kickoff strategy. The problem for the coach is when he doesn't have that great long-ball kicker. One solution is to "squib-kick" the ball.

To squib-kick the ball, the kicker will generally lay the ball on its side rather than tee it up. He will generally kick it off center so that it will take those uncontrolled bounces that only a football can take.

The onside kick is often used near the end of the game when the team that has just scored is still behind. However, it is also used by some daring and intelligent coaches when the return team peels back too quickly. Some coaches threaten the onside kick on every kickoff. They may start with all of their players close to the kicker. The kicker can kick straight ahead 10 to 15 yards and the kicking team will have eleven players near the ball. The players may then either align in their onside kick formation or take their normal kickoff positions. If the receiving team comes up close to stop the onside kick, the kicking team can kick to an area of the field left vacant by the receivers.

A few coaches use the onside kickoff at least 70 percent of the time. Their thinking is that they have between a 30 and 50 percent chance of recovering the ball. Even if they don't recover it, the opponents will have the ball only 10 to 20 yards closer to the goal than if they had made a normal return.

The onside kickoff alignment can be the same as the regular kickoff or, in obvious onside kick situations, more of the cover men can be placed near where the ball will be kicked. Usually the ball is set on one hash mark and kicked to the wide side of the field.

The assignments of the cover men include those who will block the receivers, those who will attempt to recover the ball after it has gone 10 yards, and a "fielder" who will be near the sidelines to stop the kicked ball from going out of bounds (see Figure 10.2).

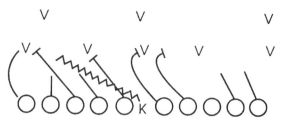

Figure 10.2 Onside kick coverage from normal alignment

Kickoff Coverage

Covering the kickoff is another important consideration. Every kick coverage will have two men responsible for the outside—these are the ends. There will also be one or two men who act as safeties.

The other seven or eight men will attack the ball carrier in one or two waves, keeping appropriate distances between themselves so that the ball carrier cannot easily go around them or run through a gap in the wave. Most teams have a couple of "mad dogs" who will sacrifice their bodies as they attempt to break the wedge of blockers who convoy the ball carrier until he finds a gap in the defense and runs for daylight.

It is essential that the defenders stay in their assigned lanes as they run down the field. If they all run directly to the ball, they will open a hole in the defense that the running back might exploit for a long run. The lanes are generally about 5 yards apart but will reduce to 3 or even 2 yards as they get close to the ball carrier.

Kickoff coverage has three areas of concern: the run and read area (from 40 to 40), the avoidance area (from 40 to 25—assuming a kick to the goal line), and the contact area. In the run and read area, the defenders must see where the ball is going and how the blockers are setting up; for example, wedge, man, or cross blocking. The avoidance zone is where you expect to encounter the blockers. Here you can dodge a blocker, running behind him, then getting back into your lane. The contact zone, about

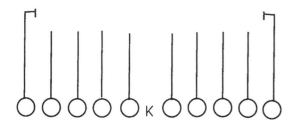

Figure 10.3 Straight kickoff coverage

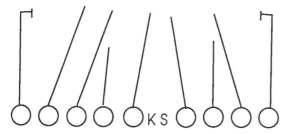

**Figure 10.4 Coverage with two waves
(mad dogs and safeties)**

The Kickoff Return

Generally the kickoff can be considered a success for the kickers if they hold the return team inside their own 25-yard line. It is a definite success for the returners if they get the ball to their own 35.

Kickoff return strategies involve a wedge block, cross blocking, double-teaming, trapping, or the setting up of a wall of blockers to one side of the field. These may be used in combination (see Figures 10.6 through 10.10).

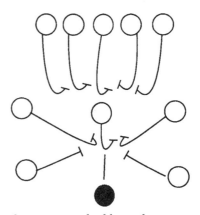

Figure 10.6 A double-wedge return

15 yards from the ball, has the cover people running through any blocks—extending the arms and hitting the blocker in the armpits while the fingers are up so that the blow is upward. The distance between the cover people is reduced to 3 yards, then 2, then contact (see Figures 10.3 and 10.4).

Because some teams designate which men to block on the return, many coaches cross their rushers as they run downfield. (Usually, the return team will number the men on the kicking team.) This is particularly true of the ends, because many teams use a trap on the end as part of their blocking scheme. So crossing the end and one or two other men can foul up the blocking assignments of the return team (see Figure 10.5).

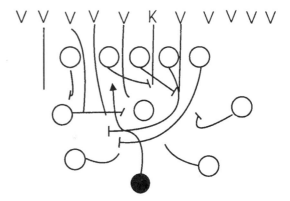

Figure 10.7 A cross-block return

Figure 10.5 Coverage with crossing rushers

When to make the block is a question that is seldom addressed. In a wedge, you set the wedge and make the blocks when the kicking team arrives. That's pretty easy, which is why the wedge is so often used. It became popular when low blocking

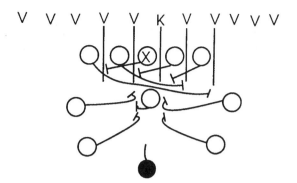

Figure 10.8 Cross block and wedge

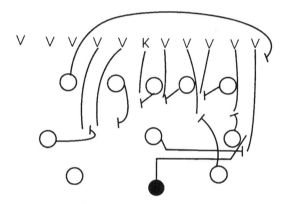

Figure 10.9 Trap on the end

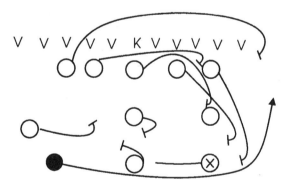

Figure 10.10 Reverse with a wall

on kickoffs was made illegal. It is relatively simple to teach and to time properly. Other blocks, like crossing blocks or straight-ahead blocks, are often done early. If properly done, they will delay the cover people a second or two.

The most difficult blocking technique—but the most effective when properly done—is to make the block 10 to 12 yards in front of the ball. This requires that the blocker find his man and drop about 30 yards

while still keeping his position on his target. By making the block 10 to 12 yards in front of the ball carrier, the block will be effective if held only for a second. This block is effective on trapping returns and middle returns. The block is made by jamming two hands into the chest of the cover man while keeping the body in a position to protect the runner.

The Punt

Most coaches believe that the punt is the most important play in football. How many plays average 35 to 40 yards? In designing the punt play, the coach must be concerned with the protection of the punter, the direction and height of the punt, and the coverage of the kick.

The best protection is very tight, which reduces the effective coverage; and the best coverage places the kicking team members far apart, which reduces the protection of the punter. So a happy medium must be achieved.

In high school and college, the kicking team members can release to cover the kick at any time. At the pro level, only the widest two players can release immediately. Commonly, in high school and college the blockers will block for two counts, then release with the personal protector(s) waiting for the "thud" of the kick before releasing. They then release to their landmarks (the spots on the field that will put them 5 yards apart and give them an imaginary vertical line to run on), then proceed to cover the punt.

The traditional "tight punt" formation gives good protection but is poor on coverage. It is often used today when a team is punting from its own end zone and must avoid a blocked kick. In this formation, the punter is generally 10 yards behind the center.

In the classic spread punt, the kicker lines up 13 to 15 yards behind the center. The halfbacks are in the center-guard gaps, and the fullback lines up 5 to 7 yards deep as a personal protector for the punter. This gives the effect of a 9-man line.

Another formation is the semispread or the "tackles back" formation. In this alignment, the team has the advantage of seven men releasing quickly to cover, yet having three big linemen as protectors for the punter. It can also be done with three backs in a line. This provides a more effective fake punt possibility (see Figures 10.11 through 10.14).

The pros use a formation with two wide gunners, two wings, and a personal protector. The linemen and wings start in a semicrouch with the outside foot back. On the snap they take two quick steps back (the forward foot moves first), then they set to pick up the blockers. By retreating first, then blocking, they are better able to pick up stunts by the defense. Of course it also reduces the punt coverage because the linemen have stepped back first. Many colleges and some high schools now use this type of punt protection. It makes more sense for the pros to use it because the linemen can't release until the punt—but at the lower levels a great deal of coverage depth is lost.

An effective punting team will generally take .6 or fewer seconds to get the snap to the punter, then 1.2 or fewer seconds for the punter to get the kick away. If the time from the snap to the kick is 1.8 or fewer seconds, it will probably not be blocked. If the time is 2.1 seconds or more, there is a good chance of a blocked punt.

Punt-protection blocking can be done by attacking the defenders at the line of scrimmage, then releasing after two seconds; controlling the LOS without retreating; or using the retreat blocking done by the pros.

Punt coverage usually starts with one or two men getting to the ball immediately. A second wave, generally the center, guards, and tackles, will be 5 or 10 yards behind the first men. They must stay in their proper coverage lanes-about 5 yards apart. Two people are designated to be "ends" or contain men, who can stop any wide plays or reverses. Then there is a safety man or two.

When practicing this, it is a good idea to blow the whistle after players have released downfield about

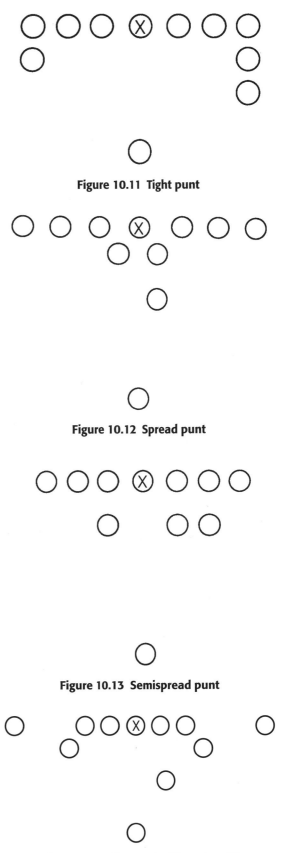

Figure 10.11 Tight punt

Figure 10.12 Spread punt

Figure 10.13 Semispread punt

Figure 10.14 Pro punt with ends split

20 yards to check their spacing and whether they have stayed in their lanes. As the players begin their coverage, they will probably encounter opponents who will attempt to slow them up or disrupt their lane responsibilities. You must therefore teach the cover men to avoid by faking or ripping up through the blocker's hands, then getting back in their lanes.

Direction, Distance, and Height of the Punt

Since the object of the punt is to gain as many yards as possible, it is generally not best to kick into the end zone. The pros now keep statistics on how effective their punters are in starting their opponents inside their 20-yard line. To kill the ball inside the 20, kickers either kick out of bounds or use a pooch punt, in which the ball is kicked to about the 10 while the covering team attempts to let the ball bounce toward the goal line but not cross it.

You can punt high and hope to cover without a return, or you can punt directionally (possibly punting lower to maximize the distance gained with the ball bouncing). Directional punting is developing more adherents; it is effective if your punter can be taught to kick wide enough to make the returner run about 15 yards to catch it. Catching while running sideways increases the chance of a fumble. Also, if the punt is to the short side of the field, it reduces the area that the punt team must cover. It may also disrupt the timing and the direction of the planned punt return.

Make your punt-coverage people aware of the rule on downing a punt. The punt is not dead until the referee blows his whistle. If a punt cover man touches the ball at the 25-yard line, then it rolls and another touches it at the 20, then the returner picks it up, runs it 10 yards, then fumbles, the rule is that the return team can take the ball at "any spot of touching;" so even though the returner lost the fumble, he still has the option of taking the ball at the 25-yard line first and 10.

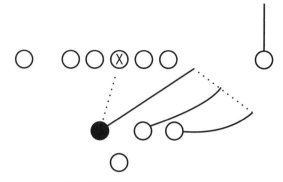

Figure 10.15 Fake punt from semispread

Fake Punts

Fake punts are particularly important if you are a field position coach and plan to punt on early downs occasionally. They may also be made as automatics in fourth-down situations—depending on defensive placement. When the gunners are not covered by defenders, the punter may be instructed to throw the quick pass to the uncovered gunner. Some very successful teams use this strategy.

If you have a personal protector or punter who can pass, there are other options (see Figure 10.15).

The Punt Return

The team defending a punt has the option of trying to block the punt or attempting to return it—or both. Since it is so difficult to block a punt and it is so easy to rough the punter and give the punting team 15 yards and a first down, most teams opt to return the punt. A team attempting to return the punt generally tries to hold up the tacklers on the punting team. With the pros able to release only the two widest men on the snap of the ball, most pro teams use two men to hold them up.

At the high school and college levels, all potential tacklers should be delayed. Your scouting report should tell you which players release the quickest and who are the best cover people. Obviously, they are your primary concerns in setting up your return.

If the kicker can kick the ball high and get a good "hang time," the tacklers have more chance to cover the punt. Since it takes about 2 seconds for a kicker to get off his punt and most good punters hang the ball up for about 4 seconds and kick about 35 to 40 yards, the punt-coverage team has about 6 seconds to cover 35 to 40 yards. And since most special teams players run a 40-yard dash in under 6 seconds, there will be no chance for a return unless the coverage people are held up for at least 2 seconds.

Once the punting team members escape the men delaying them, the receiving team members set up for their return. Most teams form a wall of players on one side of the field. They generally choose the wide side of the field or a return left—against a right-footed kicker. Generally the ball will drift to the right of a right-footed kicker and to the left of a left-footed kicker (see Figures 10.16 and 10.17).

If the punting-team coverage men take wide lanes, the return team may elect to return to the middle. An example of such a return is shown in Figure 10.18.

Another type of return starts up the middle; then one of the defenders is blocked out (trapped) and the play breaks outside.

The punt can be considered a success for the punting team if it nets 35 yards. It is a success for the returners if the punt nets less than 25 yards.

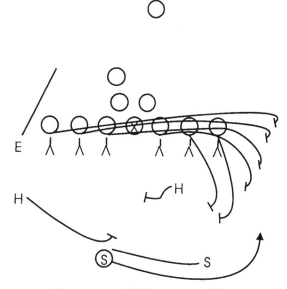

Figure 10.17 Sideline return with a reverse or fake reverse

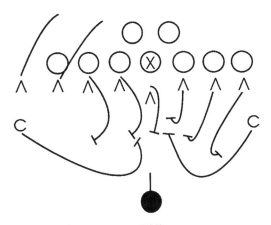

Figure 10.18 Middle return

Punt Blocking

Often the scouting report plays a large part in determining whether to attempt to block the punt. A center who makes slow passes or who is often inaccurate may issue an invitation to block his team's punt. A kicker who takes too long to get off a punt or who takes more than two steps before kicking is a prime target for a block. And, of course, there are tactical situations in which a block may be called, such as when behind late in the game or when the opponent is backed up close to its end zone. (Scouts

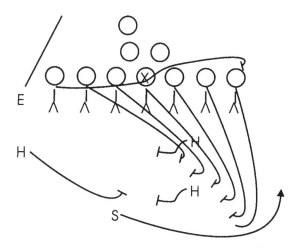

Figure 10.16 Sideline return with a single safety

time the punter in the pregame practice and in the game to determine whether he is a good candidate for a punt block.)

Since the ball is generally kicked from about 4½ yards in front of where the kicker started, punt blockers should aim for a spot 1½ yards ahead of the spot where the ball will leave the kicker's foot. This is about 8 or 10 yards behind the center if the punter is 13 to 15 yards deep. So the punt blockers have about 1.8 seconds to run 8 to 10 yards—depending on whether they are in the middle or the end of the defensive line. Aiming ahead of the kick spot should eliminate the chance of roughing the punter—the mortal sin of punt blocking.

Here is an example of a heavy rush in which there are six potential punt blockers against six offensive blockers (excluding the offensive center, who cannot be counted on to make the long snap, then block effectively). If any of the blockers choose the wrong man to block, a blocked punt may result. Many coaches always put a defender near the center to charge a gap. This may rattle him and increase the chances of his making a poor snap (see Figures 10.19 through 10.21).

Every team has at least one man rushing just in case there is a bad snap. And some teams try to block every punt. Here is an example of a punt block that tries to spring three people free with the

Figure 10.21 A 10-man rush

other eight in a return. If a punt is partially blocked and has not crossed the line of scrimmage, it can be advanced by either team. This is essential to tell your team (see Figures 10.22 and 10.23).

Get as close to the LOS as possible because every inch counts in blocking a kick. If close to the snapper, watch his fingers tighten on the ball just before he snaps it. Some snappers lift their hips just before snapping. Sprint from the stance, avoid the blocker (sliding the shoulders perpendicular to the ground may aid the sprint to the ball), sprint to the block point, and put your hands up at the last second. To

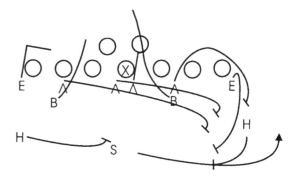

Figure 10.22 Double tandem rush and return

Figure 10.19 Heavy rush one side

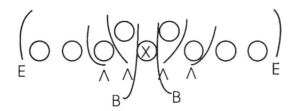

Figure 10.20 Middle rush

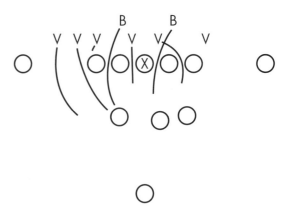

Figure 10.23 Versus 3 tackles back, 3 on 2 on wing

take the ball off the punter's foot, the hands should be waist high. If the ball has been kicked, the hands can be higher. The ball is kicked when it is about $1\frac{1}{2}$ to 2 feet above the ground. It leaves the punter's foot about $2\frac{1}{2}$ feet off the ground. It then goes about 1 foot forward for every $1\frac{1}{2}$ feet of height. It is imperative that the blocker keep his eyes open as he blocks the kick. After reaching the block point, the blocker slides to the side of the kicker to avoid any contact. Once the ball is blocked, the nearest person to it scoops it up to score while the others turn back to pick up any punt-team members who are in pursuit.

Here's a suggested drill: Either in a pitching cage or with a backstop in front of the kicker, have the punter kick softly (about a 20-yard punt) with partially deflated balls. The coach stands behind the punter and watches the approach of the blocker and whether he is looking at the ball and placing his hands correctly.

Most lower-level teams will block man. Here you can think of crossing your rushers. Or you can leave one or more blockers free and overload another blocker.

Against zone protection, you may be better off attacking straight ahead until you can escape inside and move to the block point.

Field Goals and Extra Points

There is no question that the abilities of modern kickers have increased the chances of success of a field goal or extra point. Experience shows that it is best to tee up the ball about 7 yards behind the center. (With tall or high-jumping defenders, 8 yards may be used.) The blockers then can block solid and force the defense around the kicking formation. If the kick is made within 1.2 to 1.4 seconds after the ball is snapped, it will probably be successful.

The normal field goal formation has the wing-backs outside the ends. Since teams will usually try to block field goals and extra points by charging inside and outside the wings, some teams move

their wings in behind the ends. When a wide wing has rushers inside and outside, he must hit the inside rusher with his inside arm, then the outside rusher with the outside arm. This is difficult to do effectively. By moving the wing behind the end, the two outside rushers are outside the wing and can be handled more effectively (see Figure 10.24).

Blocking must seal the inside. To do this, the guards can overlap their feet with the center. The tackles and ends are allowed to step behind the man inside after the ball has been snapped. After the inside movement, the linemen can take on the defenders with their hands and block aggressively. The simplest way to block effectively, which can be used at lower levels of play, is to have all the linemen thrust their heads inward to overlap the hips of the lineman inside. This gives an effective seal.

A newer field goal formation now sometimes seen is unbalanced to the left side but with the two wings to the right. This has obvious advantages for fake field goals and fumbled snaps ("fire" situations) because you have three immediate receivers, so the defense must have three pass defenders (see Figure 10.25).

On short field goals, the defending team has an opportunity to return the kick, so the kicking team must be alert to covering the ball after it is kicked.

Every team has at least one fake field goal as well as a special play that can be signaled if there is a foulup or "muff" on the snap or the hold. In this

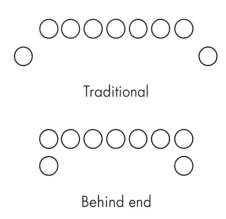

Figure 10.24 Normal and tight wing

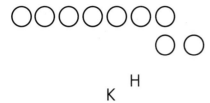

Figure 10.25 Two wings right

emergency play, the holder yells "go" or "fire" and the ends release for pass.

Defending the Field Goal

The defense must nearly always be ready for a fake field goal or extra point. Most teams try to block the field goal or extra point by either attempting to collapse the middle of the offensive line or by overloading at the end of the line. Teams with tall, high-jumping players are often successful in collapsing the middle of the line a bit, then sending the jumper up. The longer the field goal attempt, the lower the ball will generally be kicked. The scouting report is very useful in determining the most obvious weakness in the offensive blockers and how quickly the kick rises.

Making the Breaks

As you can see, there are many opportunities for a big play when a team kicks. A blocked punt is at least a 50-yard gain for the blocking team (35 yards that would have been gained on the punt and the 15 yards behind the line where the kick was blocked.)

A blocked field goal that is returned for a score by the defense is considered a 10- or 11-point play—the 3 points that the kicking team didn't score and the 6 to 8 that the kick blocking team did score. Such a play is a great momentum builder for the defenders.

CHAPTER

11

MOVEMENT, CONTACT, TACKLING, AND BALL STRIPPING

"Football is a game of movement and contact."

Your players must be able to move quickly in any direction. After moving they must be able to make contact effectively. Movement and contact are the most fundamental of the fundamentals of football. Your players are never too accomplished to not need to practice the fundamentals. Bill Walsh tells of working alone in the off-season with Joe Montana on QB mechanics when he was thirty-eight years old and already a pro MVP. He also tells of working with Jerry Rice, in his later years, in the off-season on pass patterns—without a passer. If two of the best players in history were still working on fundamentals during their final years of playing, perhaps your high school players should spend a bit of time perfecting the fundamental skills that they need in order to compete effectively.

Movement

A football player must be able to move—forward, backward, sideways, on all fours, and in many awkward positions. He must therefore be agile. He must be quick. At times he must be fast. (There is a real difference between quickness, which can be greatly improved through learning, and all-out speed, which is largely God given.) He must be able to move so that he will be ready to make contact. That movement must be trained by the coach.

Running forward is the basic form of movement. In the old days, coaches often told their players to

just "fall then put your feet in front of you." Today there is a great deal of information and research on how to increase a runner's effectiveness.

Speed is a combination of stride length and stride frequency. A 2-inch increase in stride length, assuming no reduction in stride frequency, drops 0.1 second from a 40-yard time. Stride length comes from increased flexibility in hip flexion and extension and from greater pushoff power. Doing the splits, with the right leg forward, then backward, increases hip flexibility. The mechanics of running require that the player does the following:

- Runs on his toes. The final power of the pushoff comes from the muscles that extend the ankle. By running on the toes, his landing is cushioned, thereby reducing the shock of his landing, and the eccentric contraction makes the muscle more ready to contract forcefully on the pushoff.
- Lifts his thigh to reach forward for the stride. This helps to lengthen the stride.
- Pushes back powerfully with his hip extensors—the gluteal muscles and hamstrings. He must think of "clawing the ground" with his foot as he pushes back.
- Keeps his torso and head slightly forward.
- Keeps the arms flexed at the elbows at approximately 90 degrees. The arms should move forward and back, not across the body.

A major weak link in sprinting ability is the slowness of the quadriceps (front of thigh) in pulling the thigh forward fast.

The power leg should be "popped backward" (extended quickly) in order to get maximum thrust. At the end of the pushing phase of the stride, the knee should "punch" forward, not upward.

The runner should stay low to get going but should straighten up in order to get speed. The eyes control the head and the head controls the rest of the body. Keep the eyes forward. This will bring up the head.

The back should be slightly arched and the butt should be under the torso. The palms of the hands should face inward. The thumb should lightly touch the forefinger. As the arms swing up and down, the hands should move from the chest to the hip pocket.

Speed comes from what happens in the downward and backward phases of the stride. While basic "all-out" speed is largely inherited, the strength and form necessary for developing one's maximum speed can be taught.

Running backward (backpedaling) is essential for defensive backs. In running backward, the muscles in the front of the thigh and leg supply the power. The upper body must lean slightly forward. The chin should be held down. The arms should be held similarly to the way they would be held if running forward. The runner must reach backward with the toe in order to extend the stride as far as possible.

Another type of backward running involves the legs running forward but the head and eyes facing backwards.

This is used by some zone defense teams. The movement for a "three-step and turn" drill would be this: start to the left with a left lead step (the line of the foot should be in the exact line of the run), the next step is a crossover step with the right leg, then another left leg step. As the left toe is planted, the toe pivots to the direction of the next direction of the run. The next step is a right step, then a left crossover, then a right step. The right toe then pivots and the left leg opens for the next step.

The pivot is essential to making this drill effective; it is a very long pivot. If the player is making 90-degree cuts, the pivot must be 270 degrees. If the player is going straight back, the pivot will have to be 360 degrees. The extensive pivot is necessary because the player continues to face the coach (or the passer in a game) as he runs backward (see Figure 11.1).

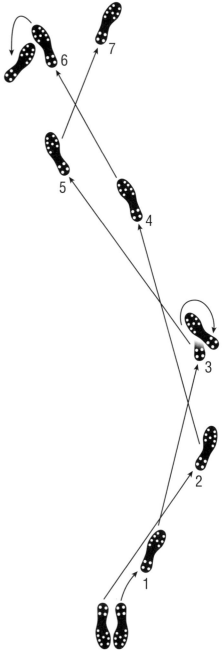

Figure 11.1 Proper foot action for three-step and turn drill

Moving sideways is another important football fundamental. Players must learn to move laterally while keeping their bodies squared to the line of scrimmage. The first type of sideways running teaches the player to move sideways facing the LOS but not crossing the feet. The player assumes a hitting position (knees bent, torso leaning forward, head up, feet 1½ to 2 feet apart). The player moves the feet as quickly as possible.

Developing Quick Feet

It is important to do movement drills such as jumping rope, ladder drills, dots, step over bags, and so on. So many players, especially linemen, don't have the quick feet necessary to play the game fast. You can make your own ladder; make it with adhesive tape on the floor or make it with thin rope. Make the squares 15 to 18 inches per side. The quick-feet drills you can do are endless: moving sideways, moving forward or back with feet skipping in and outside of the squares, and so on.

Training for speed is done with quality work. Long runs do not help in the development of speed. Long runs help to develop more of slow-twitch muscle fibers while speed work or heavy weightlifting helps to develop fast-twitch fibers. Football is not really an endurance activity—develop the fast-twitch muscles.

Plyometrics works on increasing the number of muscle fibers contracting at one time. (No one can contract all of their muscle fibers at the same time.) The theory of plyometrics is that when the muscles are forced into powerful eccentric (lengthening) contractions, more muscle fibers are being called into the contraction. (Eccentric is pronounced "ek•SEN•trik," not "EE•sen•trik" as is often heard.) If the muscle is immediately forced into a concentric (shortening) contraction, many of those muscle fibers will respond. So if an athlete jumps from a box 1 to 4 feet high, his calf muscles will be forced to call a great many muscle fibers into play to catch

him. If he can immediately jump upward, many of those muscle fibers will contract and help him to jump higher than he could if he had started from a standing position. The athlete should be well conditioned to strength training before he starts in a plyometric program. Also, the plyometric program should be done with relatively few repetitions and only a few days a week.

Contact

Probably the first skill that coaches should teach their players is the proper position for contact—the hitting position. The concepts learned for the hitting position are shown in Figure 11.2.

- The legs supply the power. They drive the body through the opponent.
- The back should be slightly arched. The head should be up.
- No matter how high the contact is made (whether at the knees or the chest of an opponent), the head must be higher than the

Figure 11.2 Hitting position

shoulders, the shoulders higher than the hips, the hips higher than the knees, and the knees higher than the ankles. This will enable the hitter to hit up and through the opponent.

An essential factor to get across to a player is that as he hits he must be off balance. If he is on balance, the person he is hitting will knock him backward. He must be more off balance than his opponent in order to knock his opponent back. The effective weight of the player may change during the hit if the hitter is hitting upward—making himself heavier and his opponent lighter because he will have some of the opponent's weight on his feet.

For tackling, the hitting position should have the arms out to the side or close to the body but elbows bent at a 90-degree angle, depending on which tackling technique you are going to teach. If you are teaching offensive line, you may have the players take their hitting position with their arms out in front of them, such as in the setup for pass blocking (See Figure 11.2).

Teaching how to get off balance is important because every block and tackle will start and/or end with the aggressor being off balance forward. This skill can be done in a diving drill. The players line up in a three- or four-point stance. On the coach's signal, they all dive out on the grass. It is best if they do it one at a time so that the coach can check to see that the drive is somewhat upward-head up, head above shoulders, shoulders above hips, hips above knees, knees above feet. Have players land on their chests without using their arms to break the fall. Using the hand and arm to break a fall is the major cause of broken and sprained wrists, broken arms, broken collarbones, and dislocated shoulders. Once players have learned to fall correctly, anyone who carries a ball in a game should carry a ball in this drill. He should learn to dive and fall on his side while protecting the ball with both arms. Falling on the ball can knock the wind out of him and even cause a broken rib.

When this is accomplished, the player should learn to "dive and drive." In this drill, the player dives out as in the diving drill, but after he extends his legs in the diving action he drives his legs, taking as many steps as possible, before landing on his chest. He should be off balance through this whole dive and drive action. As he becomes more proficient, he will be able to take more steps before he hits the ground. The head should never be more than $2\frac{1}{2}$ to 3 feet above the ground.

This drill is essential to every aspect of contact: the blocker scrambling in a low block, the tackler driving through his opponent, and the runner driving for extra yards. Ball carriers should do the drill with a ball in one arm, covering it with two arms just before contact with the ground.

Tackling

Tackling is the basic defensive fundamental. In the ideal tackle, the tackler has his head up, back arched, legs driving the back through the ball carrier, arms wrapping hard around the ball carrier, eyes open, and driving the ball carrier backward.

High-form tackling teaches the defender to hit with the legs, keep the back arched, keep the eyes open, and wrap the arms. In teaching this technique, the ball carrier moves into the standing tackler who is in the form tackling position (back arched, feet wide, and arms out to the side). The tackler lifts the ball carrier straight up and carries him a few steps. This teaches exploding the eyes open on contact, clubbing with the arms, grabbing cloth, and exploding upward.

Two different arm techniques can be used. The first is the wrap-around technique: here the tackler keeps his arms wide and swings them parallel to ground as he makes contact. If the ball carrier dodges the tackler, there is a good chance that the arms will still make contact with the runner and bring the tackler into the ball carrier, even if his body extension has missed the target point on the runner (see Figure 11.3).

Figure 11.3 High form tackling wrap-around technique

Figure 11.4 Upward arm drive technique

The second technique has the tackler with his arms at his side but bent 90 degrees at the elbows. The tackler drives the arms up and under the arms of the runner. This upward action completes the body extension of the tackler, giving more upward force. Also, if the arms are driven under the runner's armpits, there is a greater chance of forcing a fumble (see Figure 11.4).

When the ball carrier is 6 to 12 inches from the tackler, the tackler explodes his legs and aims his

nose about 4 inches off the center of the chest and toward the arm carrying the ball. He makes contact, extends up and through the ball carrier, and makes his arm contact—either wrapping up the ball carrier or driving him upward. He should also "grab cloth" because it gives the tackler more chance to control and hold the ball carrier.

If using the wrap-around technique, the tackler's arms must be kept parallel to the ground. (Players tend to drop their arms lower than shoulder level. This humps the back, which places more strain on the lower back muscles and reduces the upward drive of the tackle.)

This skill should be taught moving forward into the tackle, alternating hitting with the right and then the left shoulder. It should then be taught moving diagonally into the ball carrier with the right shoulder and then left shoulder—keeping the head in front of the ball carrier. It can also be taught full speed with the ball carrier 3 yards from the tackler. This skill is seldom used in a game, but it should be taught because it emphasizes all of the basic fundamentals of tackling. When it is used, it is generally in the kicking game or when a linebacker steps into a hole with only a ball carrier coming at him.

The low-form tackle is more like what will likely happen in a game. The fundamentals remain the same as in the high-form tackle, but the tackler will be off balance and lower as he makes contact. His base will be wide. His head will be up with his back arched. He will explode through the ball carrier as he drives his legs. He will finish with his body on top of the ball carrier's.

Turnovers

Bill Parcells said that the team that wins the turnover battle wins 84 percent of those games. In the Super Bowl the turnover margin has been the most important statistic in determining the winner. Where there has been a difference in the number of turnovers, the

Figure 11.5 Lift and punch

Figure 11.6 Raking the ball

team with the positive ratio has won twenty-eight and lost only two Super Bowls. This statistic carries more predictability for the winner than any other measure: total yards gained, time of possession, halftime score, who scored first, and so on.

Stripping the ball is another tactic used increasingly at the professional level. It is still not used enough at the lower levels. Remember that if a ball is stripped from the offense and recovered by the defense, it is worth at least the distance of a punt. So a stripped ball fumble would be worth at least 35 yards. Strips can be practiced during warmups.

One way to strip the ball is to lift outward on the ball carrier's elbow with one hand, then punch the ball past the elbow with the palm of the other hand. This can be worked on during tackling drills with

the second or third tackler going for the ball (see Figure 11.5).

Raking the ball is done by grabbing the ball or the ball-carrying arm and pulling it downward. This releases the ball. This technique is especially effective against players who do not carry the ball properly. If a tackler is coming from behind and cannot see the ball because the ball carrier is holding it in, this is the preferred strip. Tackle with one arm and rake with the other (see Figure 11.6).

The punch is used when you are coming from behind and you can see the ball. Tackle with one arm and punch with the other (see Figure 11.7).

Another important strip is used when coming from behind a passer who holds his elbows wide. Drive the arms inside the passer's elbows and rip out or down (see Figure 11.8).

Figure 11.7 Strip punch from behind

Figure 11.8 QB strip

DRILLS

1. Form tackling. This drill should be done with the ball carrier being tackled into the foam pits used by high jumpers and pole vaulters. Since tackling a ball carrier onto the ground often results in injuries to one of the players (broken arms and sprains are not uncommon), the risk of injury is greatly reduced by using the pit.

2. Full-speed tackling. Many drills can be used for full-speed tackling. The most common are:
   - Tackling full speed onto a high-jump pit or mattress.
   - Starting with both players on their backs with their heads touching or nearly touching. On the coach's command, the players jump up and the defender tackles the ball carrier.

3. Ball-stripping drills. One drill combines stripping with form tackling: the first player makes the tackle into the pit while a second player strips the ball by lifting the elbow and punching the ball. A second drill is to have the ball carrier chased closely by the stripper, who rips downward at the ball-carrying arm as he makes the tackle. A third player can trail then pick up the stripped ball and return it the other way.

CHAPTER 12

OFFENSIVE LINE FUNDAMENTALS AND CADENCE

"Without these there is no offense."

There is no one way to teach offensive-line fundamentals. The stance and the types of blocks you will employ will be determined by your offensive theory. If you are using a very quick hitting offense you might choose to use a four-point stance and scramble blocking (on all fours). If you are a run-and-shoot passing team, you will probably use a balanced three-point stance or even a two-point stance.

Stance

The three-point stance is used by most teams. The traditional three-point stance begins with the right toes even with the left instep. The feet are shoulder-width apart or slightly wider and are perpendicular to the line of scrimmage. From this basic foot position, the player bends the knees, squats, then aligns the outside of his right hand just inside the line of his right foot. The hand is placed about 18 inches ahead of the inside edge of the toes. The fingers should be extended, with the weight on the pads of the fingers. The back should be nearly horizontal, with the hips slightly higher than the shoulders, and the head should be up (see Figure 12.1).

Individual differences must be accounted for in placing the width of the feet and the placement of the hand. Shorter players will have their hands closer to their feet. Very big players will generally have their hands farther from their toes. It is the length of the torso that will determine just where the hand will be most effectively placed. The other

Figure 12.1 Three-point stance

arm will be held below the shoulders with an approximately 90-degree angle of the arm and shoulder and a 90-degree angle at the elbow.

Adjustments to this basic stance can be made according to the coach's offensive theory. A team that will "fire out" hard may place the hand farther forward or put more weight on the hand. A team that pulls, cross-blocks, traps, or drops back in pass protection will usually have a more balanced stance. Another adjustment might be the placement of the feet. A team that pulls and angle-blocks a great deal may be more effective if the feet are not staggered, with both feet equidistant from the LOS. It is easier to pull toward the foot that is farther back. So a right guard who generally pulls right would be in a better stance with his right foot back.

Figure 12.2 Four-point stance

Some coaches prefer the four-point stance (both hands on the ground). This allows the players to have more weight forward with less discomfort on the hands. Four-point stance teams are usually quickness teams that need to explode into the defenders fast. The farther forward the shoulders, the more weight is being carried on the hands and the quicker the player can move forward (see Figure 12.2).

As mentioned earlier, your players' stances should be determined by what you want them to do. Hayden Fry, the former Iowa coach, had his tight end in a standing (two-point) stance. His thinking was that he could see the defensive backs and linebackers better so was a more effective receiver if he stood up. In Fry's theory of offense, the little that might be lost in blocking effectiveness was more than made up for by the player's increased ability as a receiver. Coach Fry said that his ends really didn't lose that much effectiveness as blockers.

The Center Snap

The center is the most important lineman. He should be a leader, and for many teams he will be their best blocker. His stance utilizes the same principles as the other offensive linemen. If he is to

angle-block and cup-protect, he should be more balanced. If he is going forward most of the time, he should have more weight forward.

Snapping the ball is an extremely important fundamental. The method of snapping the ball will be determined by how the coach wants the quarterback to take it. Most teams have the snapper turn the ball as it moves from the ground to the quarterback's hands.

In coaching the snap, start with the ball in the quarterback's hands just exactly as he wants to take it—usually with the laces across the fingers of his passing hand. From this "perfect" position, the snapper reaches up and takes the ball from the quarterback and puts it on the ground. Note where the laces are. This is where they should be before the snap. Most right-handed centers start with the laces $\frac{1}{8}$ to $\frac{1}{4}$ of a turn counterclockwise.

Only the center can be "in" the line of scrimmage. The line of scrimmage is actually a zone bounded by two planes. Each plane extends from each end of the ball, parallel with the goal lines and as wide as the sidelines. The plane extends from the ground to the sky. Consequently any player, other than the center, who puts his head or his arm into that zone is encroaching. In high school football, merely putting any part of the body into that zone, even if the ball isn't snapped, is a penalty.

When the center comes to the line of scrimmage and assumes his presnap stance, he should adjust the ball so that it will be just the way he wants it for the snap. When the laces are properly positioned, the snapper should put his hand on the ball and slowly tip it to whatever angle he desires it for the snap. Once this angle is achieved, he should not move the ball lest a penalty be called for attempting to draw his opponents offside. The T-formation snap should be as fast as the snapper can make it. Strong latissimus dorsi and triceps muscles are necessary for a hard snap. The snapper should drive the ball hard up into his crotch, where the quarterback's hands will be waiting. The snapper should be stepping into his block as he snaps the ball. It is not "snap, then block" but rather "block while snapping." The quarterback must move his hands forward with the snapper until he knows for certain that he has the ball.

The long snap used in shotgun attacks is much more difficult to master. In this snap, the positioning of the laces in the presnap adjustment should be for the comfort of the snapper, not the quarterback. Usually the right-handed snapper turns the laces at least a quarter turn clockwise (to his right). The snapper can use a one- or a two-hand snap. On a one-hand snap, he merely passes the ball between his legs.

For a two-hand snap, he puts his nonpower hand (the left hand for right-handed snappers) on top of the ball. It is there simply to guide the ball. Using two hands usually is more likely to give a straight pass because the shoulders are forced to stay even. If only one hand is on the ball, the right shoulder may drop and the ball may drift left.

At the lower levels of football, the snapper should look at his target. It is generally best to aim the snap at the thighs rather than at chest height. During the excitement of the game, the snapper is likely to make his mistakes as high snaps. A snap aimed at the shoulders, which is 3 feet too high, may result in a large loss on the play.

At the higher levels of play the snapper may practice the blind snap in which he looks at his blocking target rather than at the target of his snap. It is even more important to aim the ball low when snapping blind.

Alignment

Depending on your theory of attack, you may want your offensive line to crowd the ball, being as close to the line of scrimmage as possible if your attack is quick hitting; or you may want the line back a foot or more if your attack is based primarily on zone blocking and pass protection. With zone blocking, you don't want the defender to be on top of you before you are in position, so being off the ball allows the lineman to take the steps needed to get into the proper position to block. With a wishbone attack you crowd the ball, but with a deep setback and zone blocking you are off the line.

The Start

The start is the first action from the stance as the player moves toward his blocking assignment. Many coaches work on "stance and start" at every practice. Since the offense knows the snap count, it should be able to get a slight jump on the defense. In fact, a well-coached team can have their bodies 6 or more inches out of the stance before the defenders begin to react to the movement of the ball. Since offensive players move on sound (snap count) and defenders move on movement, starts should be practiced with the snap count.

Cadence and the Snap Count

The snap count should be geared to getting the offensive players starting at the same instant. A secondary consideration is to fool the defense. Teams that vary their snap counts from play to play may fool the defense two ways. If they generally go on 2, the second count, they may sometimes go on 1, the first count, and catch the defenders not quite ready to play. Or they may go on 3, hoping that the defenders will jump offside on the second count—because they expected the ball to be snapped earlier.

The number of syllables in a snap count is important for the offense. While some teams use only a single syllable, such as GO, HIKE, or HUT, other teams use a two-syllable count such as HU-TWO (HUT TWO), and some other teams use a three-syllable count, such as A-HU-TWO (A HUT TWO) or RE-DEE-GO (READY GO). Research shows that the three-syllable snap count gets the offensive linemen firing off quicker.

Rhythmic and nonrhythmic cadences are also a consideration when determining your approach to the snap count. In a rhythmic cadence, the counts are equally spaced such as GO-GO-GO-GO. In a nonrhythmic cadence, the pauses between the counts will vary. Also a nonrhythmic count might be GO----GO-GO----GO. It is hoped that nonrhythmic cadences may be able to get the defense to jump offside. Some quarterbacks do this very well by varying the tones of their voices.

A number of years ago, LSU, the number one team in the nation, went on the first sound on every play of the season. The coach didn't want his players making a mistake, so he never varied the count. Remember that a major part of coaching is to eliminate mistakes. If you can eliminate all offside and motion penalties by the offense, you have made a major stride in offensive success because it is very difficult to overcome any offensive penalty.

You might use a multiple syllable cadence like Set-Down-Hike-Go. In using such a multisyllable cadence, in this case a four-word cadence, the coach might tie certain offensive responsibilities to each word. For example, the line might break the huddle and align in a two-point stance. On "Set" the offensive players would take their down-stance positions. On "Down" the offense might shift. On "Hike" motion might be used if that is part of the play. On "Go" the ball would be snapped. But if there is no shift or motion, the quarterback might have the ball snapped on "Set," "Down," or "Hike." If there was a shift but no motion, the ball could be snapped on "Hike" or "Go."

Having the offensive team start in a two-point stance has an advantage. The defensive linemen must be in their down stances because they know that the ball can be snapped with the offense in a two-point stance. The longer the defenders are in their down stances, the more cramped their muscles become and the less likely they will be able to react quickly to the movement of the offense. Consequently, having the offense set in two-point stances while the defense is down works as an advantage for the offense.

Blocking

Blocking, of course, is the basic offensive fundamental. And since most blocking is done by the offensive linemen, most of their time will be spent working on this. There are several types of one-on-one blocks, several types of double-team blocks, and a wedge block. There are two basic blocking techniques: the higher-targeted drive block and the lower shoulder block. These techniques can be used whether the blocker is blocking straight ahead, at an angle, in a double-team or combo block, or executing a running trap or lead block.

The Drive Block

The drive block is the most basic block in football. The objective of the drive block is to get the opponent moved away from the line of scrimmage, and hopefully to be knocked off his feet. The contact can be made with the heels of the hands or with the shoulder. Some coaches teach the use of the hands for most circumstances but use the shoulder contact in short-yardage situations. Others use the shoulder block all the time.

The hand-contact technique makes it more likely that the defender can be stood up and possibly be pushed on to his back (decleated). It may also allow the blocker to maintain contact with the defender for a longer period of time. It is therefore more desirable for the teams that allow their backs to "option-run"—looking for any hole that develops. This is more common for "I" formation teams.

The first step is with the foot that is farther from the line of scrimmage. The palms of the hands, with the fingers pointing upward and the wrists close together, will drive under the shoulder pads. This is called "the fit." Depending on the interpretation of the rules at your level, the player may be taught to "grab cloth" for better control (see Figure 12.3).

The eyes must be under the defender's chest and looking up at his neck. The elbows are inside the

Figure 12.3 Drive block

shoulders and pointed toward the ground. The legs supply the power. When the blocker feels that he has the leverage on the defender and is lower than him, he explodes his legs and arms, knocking the defender upward and backward. This should "decleat" the defender. The blocker continues to follow through with his block and finishes the block by landing on the defender. As far as we know, the record for "decleaters" in one game is thirty-five by Dave Cadigan of USC.

The shoulder-contact technique may be better in protecting the hole with the blocker's head. This may be preferable for teams that hit quick and have a designated hole to attack, such as a wishbone or veer team. It is also more effective against hard-charging defenders in short-yardage situations.

In this block, the blocker steps with the foot on the same side of his body as the shoulder with which he will block. This is called the "near" foot. Some coaches want a hard charge directly into the defender; others want the blocker to dip by dropping the other knee to allow him to hit more on an upward path.

The eyes should aim at the number on which the blocker's shoulder will make contact. It is important that the eyes aim at the body—then have the head slide to the side. As the contact is made, the blocker should widen his elbow so that his blocking surface is bigger. He then lifts and moves his opponent. The lift is made easier by having him "look to the sky" as soon as he has made contact. When the blocker actually looks at the sky, he can't help but drop his butt. This will give him a lifting action on the defender.

He should also "pinch with his ear" to aid him in maintaining contact with the defender. Without constant attention to applying pressure into the opponent, the opponent may slip off the block. Another aid in reducing the defender's ability to slip

---

COACHING POINTS:
The Hand Technique

- Aim under the shoulder pads.
- Hit on the sternum with the heels of the hands, fingers pointed up.
- Keep the elbows pointed down and inside the shoulders.
- Drive the hands up and through the defender's chest.
- Widen the feet while taking short, choppy steps.
- Keep the feet pointed straight ahead.
- Finish the block by continuing to drive, lifting the defender with the arms and legs.
- Drive over the defender, knocking him on his back, then landing on him.
- Stop only on the whistle.

the block is to bring the far hand across the blocker's chest and into side of the defender.

The feet should remain parallel with the direction of the block and they should widen to 2½ to 3 feet. The wider base makes it easier to maintain contact with the defender. If the blocker's feet are too close together, the defender can easily throw the blocker off him.

Keeping the blocker's feet perpendicular to the line of the block is essential for two reasons: (1) the action of the hip and knee are more effective if in a straight line, and (2) if the feet turn out, the blocker will be pushing with the inside edge of his shoe. He will have much more traction if all of his cleats are in contact with the ground. Many coaches emphasize that the blockers turn their feet inward in order to compensate for the natural tendency of most players to "toe out."

Steps should be short and choppy. If the player took long steps, he would have only one foot in contact with the ground for a long period of time and could be easily thrown off the defender.

Figure 12.4 Low shoulder or scramble block

The Scramble Block

The scramble technique is a quicker and lower method of getting to the defender, but the blocker doesn't get the effect of lifting his opponent. The point of aim of the eyes is the lower part of the opponent's thigh.

When scramble blocking, the blocker explodes on the defender in a shoulder block using the "dive and drive" technique described in Chapter 11. The near shoulder should make contact with the opponent and the opposite hand should be on or near the ground. The player then scrambles as he maintains contact (see Figure 12.4).

COACHING POINTS:
The Shoulder Block

- Aim under the shoulder pads.
- Aim at the near number.
- Explode into the defender, starting with the near foot.
- Extend your blocking surface on contact by widening the forearm.
- Look to the sky and pinch with the ear.
- Widen the base and keep the feet straight.
- Take short choppy steps while finishing the block.
- Stop only after you have heard the whistle.

The Uses of the Basic Blocking Techniques

The person being blocked will not always be directly ahead of the blocker. There are, therefore, football terms that tell the blocker who or how to block. While there may be some small variations in techniques, basically two above-mentioned fundamentals are used in any of the following situations. Usually it is up to the lineman to determine which technique he will use. Of course, it is up to the coach to see that he has ample opportunity to practice whichever of these situations he will use in a game.

The reach (hook) block is used when the defender is slightly outside of the blocker. The objective is to stop the penetration of the defender and, if possible, to move him down the line back toward the center rather than driving him into the defensive backfield. To make this block, the player can either step out with his outside foot (a position step), then make one of the above mentioned drive blocks, or he can scramble with a reverse shoulder block.

The down or cutoff block is used when the defender is set to the inside. He might be in the gap or on the next offensive player in. The first step is with the foot nearest the defender. The second step crosses the first. The block can be high or low, but in either case the blocker attempts to get his head in front of the defender to stop penetration.

Against a man in the gap who is charging hard, the scrambling reverse shoulder block may be the better technique. In this block, the player steps directly parallel with the line of scrimmage and makes contact with the shoulder that had been his far shoulder—the shoulder away from the target defender. From this point it is a scramble block. The point of aim is dependent on the speed of the charge of the defender. If the defender is quick, the blocker must move straight down the line in order to cut off the defender's charge. If the defender is slower, the angle of approach can be more toward the LOS (see Figure 12.5).

Blocking a linebacker who is aligned in front of the player is more difficult than blocking a lineman. This is because the blocker does not know where his target will be (possibly stunting) and the backer has more room to see the block and maneuver around it. If a blocker is playing a linebacker who is keying him, he may be able to fire out directly at the linebacker and the backer will charge into the blocker. But if the

Figure 12.5 Reverse shoulder block

blocker charges hard straight ahead and the backer is stunting or keying a back and moving toward the play action, the blocker will miss his target.

Many plays are designed to block the linebacker with a man farther out on the line of scrimmage in the direction of the play (called a *seal block*), or by pulling a man through the hole and blocking the backer (called a *lead block*).

Once contact is about to be made above the waist, the blocker can use either the higher drive block or the lower scramble technique. Whichever is used, it must be remembered that maintaining contact is the major concern. It is not important to actually move the backer; it is enough to keep him away from the ball carrier. An effective ball carrier can help the blocker by setting up the defender, faking one way to make the block easier, then cutting the other way. Remember also that it is possible to block from behind if a defender and blocker both start within an imaginary box 4 yards on either side of the center and 3 yards in front of the center. This is called the legal clipping zone—although the American Football Coaches Association cautions about low blocks from behind as being potentially injury causing.

The downfield block is similar to blocking a backer but is even more difficult to execute unless it is well timed. If the blocker maneuvers just ahead of the ball carrier, the runner can set up the block with a fake, with the blocker making the block and then the ball carrier cutting off the block.

Since the blocker can no longer initiate his block with low contact, it is generally easier to use the hands on the defender, just as in the high-drive block. The downfield block must start high, above the waist, but can drop low after contact or if the defender puts his hands on the blocker and wards him off. When blocking high, the blocker merely makes and maintains contact with the defender. When using this higher blocking technique, one blocker may be able to make several blocks on one play.

The double-team block is basic to power football. In double-teaming, there should be no reason for not creating a hole. There are two major methods of double-teaming—the driving block and the post and pivot.

The driving block has both blockers shoulder-blocking into the defender. The inside blocker has his head inside the defender and the outside blocker has his head on the outside. This type of block will generally drive the defender into the path of pursuing or "shuffling" linebackers, but it may open a hole for a "scraping" backer (see Figure 12.6).

The post-and-pivot block has the inside man on the double team hitting up and into the defender. This should stand up the opponent. The driving blocker then blocks into the waist of the defender and drives him down the LOS. This type of block reduces the chance of a scraping or stunting linebacker coming into the inside gap, but it doesn't cut off the deeper pursuit (see Figure 12.7).

Double-teaming a man in the gap is carried out by having the two players who are double-teaming take their first steps with their inside feet and step together. This should seal their bodies together; then they drive the defender straight back.

The key point in making any double-team block is that the two blockers "seal" their shoulders and hips so that the defender cannot split their block. The defender will try to defeat the double team by either splitting it or dropping to the ground and

Figure 12.6 Low double-team block— with a tight seal of the hips

keeping himself in the hole. The blockers must therefore get under the defender and seal themselves together in order to make the block effective.

In order to make the game safer, the Rules Committee continually makes rule changes. It was found that when one man posted the defender and the second man blocked low into the knees, more knee injuries occurred. This is called a "chop" block and is now illegal.

Some coaches prefer to teach the double team as merely the start of the block; when the blockers have started the defender backward, the inside or outside player releases and picks up the defenders in pursuit.

Figure 12.7 Post and pivot

Trapping on a defensive lineman is particularly effective when a lineman charges hard into the backfield. The trapper must get out of his stance low, turn his hips, step, and drive into the hole to be trapped (see Figures 12.8 and 12.9).

He takes an "inside angle out" into the hole. He then finds the defender outside of the hole and blocks with the shoulder closest to his own backfield. If the defender is charging aggressively it is an easy block, but if the defender plays correctly, he will be close to the LOS and will be reducing the size of the hole so it will be a very difficult block. If the defender penetrates and can't be hit, the trapper won't go after him but will turn up into the hole and block the first color he sees. If pulling to block a backer, turn the hips in the direction of the pull but keep the shoulders as square as possible while watching the backer. Mirror the backer and hit him as he approaches the LOS. If pulling both the guard and tackle, as in a counter trey, the guard pulls to trap the end while the tackle is assigned the backer.

The load block is similar to the trap but the play will be going wide, so the blocker protects the running back by keeping his head between the potential tackler and the ball carrier. The load block is generally low and is similar to the scramble technique. This type of block is used by both backs and linemen. When the blocker makes contact, he should drive his inside forearm in the crotch of the

Figure. 12.9 Pull right

defender, then turn his body upfield so that he can protect the sideline with his head.

The lead block is a block in which the blocker leads the ball carrier through the hole. It is most often a pulling lineman or a fullback. The blocker should block the man in the hole. If no one shows in the hole, he should look inside to pick up a pursuing backer. The technique will be that of a shoulder or drive block.

The wedge block is a power block, usually used in short-yardage situations. Three or more players will block an area.

The middle man in the wedge, usually the center, should get under the defender so that he can't fall down and defeat the wedge by tripping it. The players outside of the center block into the next offensive man inside of them, so the guards block into the hips or armpits of the center and the tackles block into the hips or armpits of the guards.

The wedge was a staple of the single-wing fullback buck, but it can be used very effectively by T-formation teams in quarterback sneaks or fullback bucks. It is especially effective against a defender who plays high and plays a hit-and-react technique. It is not as effective against a hard-charging penetrating lineman (see Figure 12.10).

Combination (combo) blocks are exchanges of responsibilities between adjacent players who block someone other than the man nearest them. These combinations give the linemen better angles for

Figure 12.8 Pull left

Figure 12.10 Wedge block

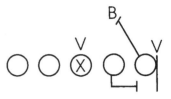

Figure 12.11 Cross block on a backer and a lineman

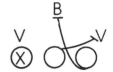

**Figure 12.12 Fold block
with linebacker on the inside**

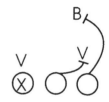

**Figure 12.13 Scoop block
between a guard and tackle**

their blocks, so the blocks are more effective than if they blocked the closest defender.

In a cross block, the outside man goes first and blocks the man to his inside, either a lineman or a backer. The inside man moves behind the outside man and blocks the next lineman out. His technique is similar to that of a trap block. This type of block is often used when the linebacker is the inside man of the two defenders near the hole (see Figure 12.11).

A fold block may be used when the coach wants the defensive lineman hit first and linebacker hit second. The second blocker moves behind the first blocker, then goes after the linebacker (see Figure 12.12).

A scoop block is used when the outside lineman bumps his man, then goes after the linebacker, who was inside him. The inside offensive lineman blocks out on the lineman who was bumped (see Figure 12.13.)

Zone blocking is a combination of a drive block, a double-team drive block, or possibly a scoop. In the inside-zone block, the blockers take a lateral step toward the play side. Uncovered linemen can then help the covered linemen. After the first lateral step, the next step is upfield. At this point, there should be four hands on the defender, but four eyes on the backer. While the defender is moved backward with the double team, the backer's action is observed. If the backer fills to one side or the other, the near lineman comes off and takes him (see Figure 12.14).

If the defender slants out, the outside blocker maintains control. If he slants in, the inside blocker has primary responsibility. Here he can use a flipper or continue to block with his hands.

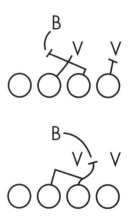

Figure 12.14 Zone block

While there are different methods of getting the two adjacent linemen onto the near-down defender, it is common to teach a drop step toward the defender, then make a crossover step to help to get the blocker square with the defensive lineman. With the blockers both on the defender, they can more forcefully drive the defender with their double team.

Pass Protection

Cup or retreat blocking is done by quickly "setting up" on the snap count.

In the setup, the blocker pops his body into the blocking position while taking a position step to be able to get an inside position on the pass rusher. If the team is using "zone" rules, the blocker will set up ready to take on whoever comes into his area. If the team is using "man" blocking, he will take the man on him no matter where that man goes. The following techniques can be used for the setup for "man" blocking (see Figure 12.15).

If the rusher is head up, the position step is to the inside with the inside leg. If the rusher is on the outside shoulder, he is already where the blocker wants him so he doesn't need a position step. If the defender is wide to the outside, the blocker steps with the outside foot and quickly slides to a position where his outside foot splits the defender (outside foot in line with the rusher's crotch).

The depth of the setup depends on the alignment of the potential pass rusher. Many coaches prefer the setup to be right on the LOS. Some coaches prefer that the blocker set up a foot or more back from the scrimmage line. The advantage of setting up on the line is that the rusher doesn't have as much area in which to generate speed and to fake. Also, by setting up close to the LOS the blocker makes the rusher fight for every foot that he gains into the offensive backfield. In addition, where the quarterback is dropping only three or five steps, he will have more clear area in front of him. If he were dropping seven or nine steps, the setup on the LOS

Figure 12.15 Pass protection setup

would not be as important. Another factor in favor of the quick setup on the LOS is that the smaller offensive men will be at more of an advantage starting close to the defender rather than dropping back and letting the larger rusher have a run at them.

If the blocker has to move laterally a step or two in order to get to his assignment, he may have to get some depth in order to be able to meet the rusher. A basic rule for most teams using man blocking in cup-pass protection is "big on big and small on small." This means that the offensive linemen will block the defensive linemen and the offensive backs will be responsible for the linebackers.

The position of the body in the setup is "hips down, head up." The feet should be shoulder-width apart and slightly staggered with the inside foot forward. The blocker should be taking continuous quick steps. The weight should be on the balls of the feet. The knees should be flexed and slightly ahead of the toes. The torso should be almost vertical, just slightly forward. (Some coaches prefer the torso to be nearly straight up so that the weight is more balanced. This is more likely to be effective if you have bigger but slower blockers.) The shoulders should remain square to the line of scrimmage. The head should be up with the eyes looking at the top of the numbers or the lower part of the neck of the pass rusher.

Depending on the rules and the experience of your players, the arms may be "locked out" straight or may be kept close to the body. If they are locked out, they will contact the rusher and maintain contact with him. (While illegal, it is very common for players using this technique to grab the opponent's jersey in order to maintain contact. NFL officials do not call holding in this situation.) With the blocker's arms straight, the rusher has a better chance of grabbing the arms and going over or under them in his attack (see Figure 12.16).

At the college and professional levels, it is common to keep the arms in closer to the body, then punch at the rusher's numbers with one or both arms. This is similar to the last 6 inches of a bench press. The elbows must start and return to the side of the rib cage. They should not be wider than the shoulders. The blocker punches, with his hands open and facing the rusher, then recoils before the rusher has a chance to grab his arms. Some coaches teach bringing the arms only 6 inches back; other coaches say to bring them farther back so that they are less of a target for the pass rusher to club or grab.

If the rusher is trying to grab the blocker, the blocker should counter by hitting the rusher's arm. The blocker must always be prepared to counter whatever moves the rusher is using to attack him.

As the rusher attacks, the blocker must remain between the rusher and the quarterback. He must also continue to keep his shoulders square to the LOS. If his shoulders are not parallel with the LOS, the rusher can more easily go behind the blocker's back and get to the passer. Most of the blocker's hitting action should be up into the rusher. If the blocker hits out too far, he will be off balance and can be grabbed and pulled by the rusher.

The feet must move continuously and never cross. They should be shoulder-width apart. If the blocker must move laterally, his steps should be short and quick. As he moves laterally, the width of his stance will widen 6 to 8 inches, then recover to the shoulder-width starting point. A key point is to

---

COACHING POINTS

- A quick setup is absolutely essential for effective pass protection.
- Feet shoulder-width apart, always moving.
- Feet pointed straight ahead; never cross the feet.
- Get position inside the rusher. Always protect the inside.
- Knees flexed and slightly forward of the toes.
- Head up. Eyes looking at the top of the numbers. Never drop the head.
- Shoulders always parallel with LOS with the torso upright.
- Weight balanced—never forward.
- Punch arms up and into the numbers of the rusher.
- Let the opponent come to you.
- Honor inside fakes but ignore outside fakes. Never get beat inside.
- Keep the rusher's hands off of you.
- Pop up at the rusher, not out.
- Give ground slowly.
- Remain up and balanced. Only if beaten will the blocker try to cut the rusher with a low block.
- After the pass is thrown, cover in case the ball is intercepted.

never get out of balance—always keep the weight centered over the center of gravity, which is in the middle of the pelvis for most people.

Countering the Tactics of the Pass Rusher

Versus the club and swim, the blocker recoils the arm being clubbed; then, as the rusher starts his swim, the blocker hits the rusher under the armpit or chest with the other arm as the swim move continues. The blocker continues to move his feet in the direction of the defensive move, then hits the rusher with his near arm and continues with his regular pass-protection technique (see Figure 12.16).

Versus the club and rip, the blocker uses a similar technique. He recoils the arm being clubbed, moves his feet in the direction of the defensive charge, and then hits the rusher under the outside of the ripping arm under the pad or, if the rip has been completed, under the armpit as with the counter versus the swim technique. If the rip is under his armpit, he can clamp his arm on the ripping arm (see Figure 12.17).

Figure 12.17 Countering the club

Versus the spin, the blocker uses whatever counter was necessary to thwart the rusher's first move; then as the rusher spins, he hits him in the back with the arm nearest the direction of the spin. He recovers his feet quickly and forces the rusher to go parallel with the line of scrimmage. The rusher must not be allowed to gain ground toward the passer while he is spinning (see Figure 12.18).

Figure 12.16 Countering the swim

Figure 12.18 Countering the spin

DRILLS

The drills that you use should fit directly into your theory of offense and the fundamentals that you employ.

1. Stance and start—should be checked daily. If your linemen are always going forward, that is the way they should go in the drill. If they pull a great deal, their start should be varied between straight ahead, right, and left pulls.

2. Stance and setup—if you do cup-protection pass blocking, you will want to work on quick steps daily.

3. When teaching any type of block, especially in spring practice, you will want to work each block in slow motion. Give the player the opportunity to "feel" the proper stance, the step with the proper foot, the "fit" into the defender, and the drive of the legs.

4. For blocking, both boards and chutes are often well-used equipment. The boards (1 × 12s— 6 feet long) are used to teach the blocker to keep his feet wide. If he allows his feet to come in too close together, he will step on the board and slip. Chutes are designed to keep the blocker's body low during the hit and drive phases of the block. Coaches can build or buy chutes.

5. Be certain to design drills for all of the defensive alignments you will face and teach the blocks or blocking combinations that you will use against them.

CHAPTER 13

OFFENSIVE BACKFIELD FUNDAMENTALS

"Get the most from your backs— while protecting the ball!"

Offensive backfield fundamentals should be designed to make and take the handoff, prevent fumbling, run with power, run with finesse, block, and catch passes. How much time you devote to any of these phases will be determined by the duties of the player in the game. So the fullback will probably spend more time on blocking and power running than the tailback, but the tailback may work more on finesse running and preventing fumbling.

Center-Quarterback Exchange

The center-quarterback exchange in the T formation starts with the quarterback placing his passing hand tight into the crotch of the center, with the back of his hand providing upward pressure. The other hand faces forward with the palm and fingers vertical, pointing at the ground. The hands should be at least at a 90-degree angle to each other. Less than 90 degrees may result in the ball hitting the lower hand on the exchange.

The wrists should touch. It is important for younger players to have the wrists touching so the ball is not driven up between the wrists, resulting in a fumbled snap. Another method of taking the snap has the top hand up, as described above, but the other hand is to the side with the thumbs touching as shown in Figures 13.1 and 13.2. Note that these photos purposely show the hands farther from the center's crotch than they actually should be, so you can see proper placement of the wrists and thumbs.

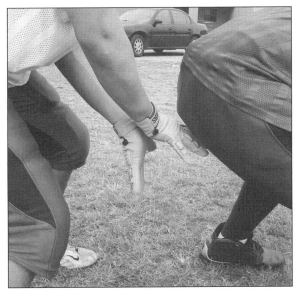

Figure 13.1

Figure 13.2

Whichever method of taking the snap is used, the quarterback must stand as tall as possible. He must also give upward pressure with his top hand against the center's crotch so the snapper can feel where he should place the ball. As the ball is snapped the quarterback must make certain to ride the center with his hands as the center charges forward. In order to do this, the quarterback must have aligned very tight to the center. For passing and zone blocking teams, pushing the snapper is not important because he will usually not be driving forward.

The first step of the quarterback depends on the type of play called. Many option teams have the quarterback's first step forward and into the line of scrimmage. Other teams have the quarterback opening up to the play or reverse pivoting and turning away from where the ball will eventually be run.

A coach should be certain to have at least three centers and three quarterbacks. Each QB should be used to taking snaps from each of the centers. How often have you seen a new center or quarterback enter the game and the first snap is fumbled?

Stances for Running Backs

A running back's stance is determined by the type of formation, the type of offense, and the individual abilities of the back (quickness, speed, and so on). It can be a two-, three-, or four-point stance. Whichever stance is used, the head must be up and the eyes forward. The back should not look to see where he is going. One of the easiest cues for a defender to spot is the glancing of a back toward his point of attack.

The two-point stance is used by teams that want their backs to be able to move laterally fast or to be able to see the defense more effectively. The stance can be nearly upright; this allows for seeing the defense well but is not a stance that allows for speed in any direction. The weight should be concentrated on the balls of the feet. One way to do this is for the player to curl his toes slightly; this places the weight forward.

One of the dangers with the two-point stance is that the player may become too eager and lean or step before the ball is snapped, resulting in a penalty.

The three-point stance is common. The amount of weight on the hand will depend on how fast the ball carrier must move forward. If speed to the inside is most important, the inside foot will be back. This is preferred in a wishbone attack. If speed to the outside is most important, the outside foot should be back. If lateral speed in both directions is important, the feet may be parallel or nearly parallel. Most teams use this stance.

The four-point stance is sometimes employed. It is most likely to be used by fullbacks on triple-option teams. It helps to get more weight forward and to hit the inside holes more quickly.

Timing Plays

Timing the play is particularly important in certain offenses. The split-T dive, the triple-option offenses such as the wishbone and the veer, and the belly series must be timed so that the fakes and the hand-off are made at precisely the right instant.

In order to "time the backfield," the coach may adjust the stance of the player (two or three point, amount of weight forward, and placement of the feet), and he may adjust the placement of the player by "cheating" him. The cheat can move the player forward or back, right or left, depending on what he is expected to do on the play.

The start for the running backs is the first step or two that the back takes after the snap. For a running back, the first step will be a lead step (moving the foot closest to the hole first) or a crossover step (foot farthest from the hole moving first.) Some coaches prefer that a running back take his first step as a crossover; others prefer that the first step be a lead step.

Some plays require precise timing, so the type of step is of extreme importance. The timing of some plays requires a lead step; others require a crossover.

For example, if the coach wanted his tailback to take two steps in one direction, then counter the other way, the first step should be a crossover. If the coach wanted to have the back cut after the third step, the first step would be a lead step (right foot), then a crossover (left foot), then a right step and cut.

The quarterback's first step depends on the type of play being run. Some coaches like the quarterback to always use an "open" pivot, opening toward the hole; others prefer a reverse pivot, turning away from the hole, then moving toward it. The open pivot gets the quarterback to the handoff point quicker on wider plays. The reverse pivot hides the ball better from the defense.

In a typical wishbone offense, the fullback is into the hole so quickly that the quarterback will always open to the hole. He must be reading the charge of the defensive tackle as he reaches back to find the fullback. On the other hand, on a crossbuck, the quarterback may be more deceptive by reverse pivoting (turning away from the hole), then faking or giving to the fullback and halfback as they cross behind him.

Handoffs

Making the handoff is also determined by the type of offense a team is running. Most teams have the quarterback hand off with one hand. Wishbone, belly, and veer teams usually start with a two-hand plant of the ball into the first back running through the line. The quarterback reads the appropriate lineman and decides whether to take the ball back or to leave it with that ball carrier.

Most teams use a one-handed give to the runner. Whether a one- or a two-handed give is made, the target should be the ball carrier's stomach. The quarterback should keep his hand on the ball long enough to make certain that there is no fumble on the handoff.

Taking the handoff is most commonly done with the running back lifting his inside arm up to shoul-

Figure 13.3 Handoff

der level. The angle of the arm and shoulder and the angle at the elbow should each be 90 degrees. The thumb of the upper hand points down. This helps to keep the elbow up (see Figure 13.3).

There are two reasons for keeping the arm and elbow in front of or inside of the shoulder. First, if the elbow is outside of the line of the shoulder, it can hit the quarterback. Second, if it is too wide, the ball carrier cannot clamp down on the ball as easily.

The runner's lower hand faces upward and is just past the midline of the body. It should be held several inches below the navel so that the target area for the quarterback is large. The runner's eyes should be on the area in which he will be running.

Pitch Plays

Making a pitch on an option play can be done with one or two hands. Some coaches teach the quarterback on option plays to look at the defender he is optioning. If the pitch is dictated, he pushes the ball away with one hand, knowing that the running back will be in the exact position to receive it. Other coaches have the quarterback look at the running back after determining to pitch. The quarterback looks at the running back and makes a two-handed pitch like a chest pass in basketball. This is the most accurate method, but it exposes the quarterback to a hit from the side. Whichever type of pitch is used, it should be aimed slightly ahead of the running back and at chest height. The pitch should be "heart to heart"—that is, chest to chest.

Carrying the Ball

Carrying the ball in the open field is done with one arm. The forward end of the ball can be controlled by straddling the end of the ball with the index and middle fingers or by cupping the ball with the hand. The runner should feel pressure in three areas: the fingers cupping the front of the ball, the ball on the inside of the elbow, and the elbow against the rib cage (see Figures 13.4 and 13.5).

Many times college and professional players carry the ball in one hand. This invites fumbling. Remember that an offensive ball carrier who fumbles and loses the ball has just cost his team a minimum of 35 yards—the yardage they would have gained on a punt.

A fumbled ball is not merely an unlucky "break" or a turnover; it is a major loss of yardage.

Many coaches prefer that the ball always be carried in the right arm. They hope that this will minimize mistakes—especially those made when changing the ball from one arm to the other. Most coaches prefer the ball to be held in the arm away from the tacklers, so on a sweep left the ball would be held in the left arm.

Very few coaches advocate changing the ball from hand to hand while running.

Running back fakes are of two kinds. The first is when the runner is not carrying the ball but has received a fake from the quarterback. He should cover the imaginary ball with two hands and plow into the line, hoping to freeze the linebacker or be tackled.

Figure 13.4 Carrying the ball—close up

Figure 13.5 Ball carrying in action

The second kind of fake is done in the open field. It will be a change in direction or a change of speed. The most effective fake is to get the defender moving one way, then to cut behind his back. It helps a great deal if the runner can get the potential tackler to cross his legs. If he can, it is a perfect time to make the cut.

The open field fake is often accompanied by another action to ward off the tackler. The straight arm or stiff arm, the flipper, a lowered shoulder, or a spin can each aid in getting past the tackler or in making a few extra yards.

The stiff arm is an open-handed punch at the opponent's helmet or shoulder pads that is designed to either keep the opponent away from the ball carrier or to push the tackler down to the ground. It can be used with either a crossover step or a spin. If the ball carrier is using a left straight arm and is cutting to his right, he will bring his left leg through fast and high as he makes his cut and drives away from the tackler. If he is using the left straight arm and wants to cut left, he will spin away by pivoting on his left leg and bringing the right arm and leg away from the tackler—spinning, then continuing downfield. He should continue to gain yards as he spins.

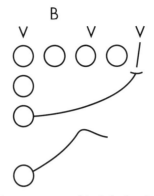

Figure 13.6 Log block by back

Setting Up the Block

The runner should use and help his blockers. Experienced runners who could outrun their blockers will usually slow up and run under control so that the blocker can do his job. The most effective place from which to set up a block is 2 to 3 yards behind the blocker. A simple step right will force the tackler to honor the fake and move in that direction. The blocker will take the defender in either direction.

Blocking

Backs block with the same techniques as linemen (see Chapter 12). The differences are that the backs get a run at their targets so they can deliver more of a blow, but their targets are harder to hit because the defenders have more time to maneuver.

The running play blocks most often used are the lead block through the hole (such as an isolation block) and the log block, in which the blocker blocks a wide defender on a sweep by placing his head between the tackler and the runner. He may also use a trap type of block on an off tackle play or aid a lineman on a double team.

The blocks of the backs are made easier if the coach has designed the plays to freeze the defender and if the ball carrier fakes to set up the block (see Figure 13.6).

Power Running

Whether running through the line or driving into a tackler for extra yardage, the ball carrier must change his running style. He should widen his legs. (Some power runners keep their feet over 2 feet apart.) This helps in preventing the ball carrier from being easily knocked off balance when hit from the side.

He must also run low with a lot of body weight forward. He should be ready to explode into the tackler. Some runners run so low and with so much power that if they are not hit at the line of scrimmage they fall—after gaining about 5 yards. This is the kind of running needed in short-yardage situations.

Running with balance is also important. The effective runner should be able to absorb hits, spin, and cut while maintaining his balance. This is another reason that running full speed is not always essential in football. The runner who is hit while running full speed will not have balance; he will have momentum. The runner who is under control will be better able to set up blocks, fake, and cut. So there is a place for both controlled running and for all-out speed. The effective runner knows when to use each.

DRILLS

1. Center, QB, running back. Center snaps the ball. The quarterback takes the steps necessary for that play, such as an I-formation pitchout or a veer dive.

2. Handoff drill. Ball carriers line up in two lines facing each other. The player in the first line has a ball. He runs at a player in the other line and stays to his right. He hands off with his left hand. The receiving player has his inside (left) arm up. The receiving player then hands to the player in the next line. This continues until the coach stops the drill. It is then repeated with the first player running to the left of the player running toward him. The handoff is now made with the right hand and the receiving player will again have his near right arm up.

3. Load blocking on dummy. Offensive back drives at dummy and blocks, keeping his head on the side opposite the LOS. (See shoulder block technique in Chapter 12.)

4. Trap blocking on dummy. Back runs at dummy and slides his head to LOS side.

5. Stiff arm and crossover drill. Hit dummy with left stiff arm, cross over left leg. Repeat with right stiff arm and right crossover.

6. Stiff arm and spin. Hit dummy with left stiff arm, spin to left. Repeat with right stiff arm and spin right.

7. Three-steps-and-cut drill. The back takes three steps one direction, then makes a 90-degree cut, then takes three steps the other way, then cuts. The speed and the angle of cut can be increased as the back gets more proficient at the technique.

CHAPTER

14

FUNDAMENTALS OF PASSING AND CATCHING

"At the highest levels, these are art forms."

Nearly all teams use the pass as an integral part of their offenses. As the pass has become more important, the fundamentals of the passer and the receiver have become more specific and detailed. Consequently, there is much more to practice today than there was a few years ago. As with other fundamentals, skills as common as passing and catching must be practiced correctly every day—even at the professional level.

Passing

The quarterback must adjust his stance to the height of the center's crotch. The quarterback's knees must be flexed so that he can get his hands into the crotch without bending much at the waist. The snapper should never be asked to adjust to the height of the quarterback. After being certain that he has the snap, he brings the ball to his chest with both hands. His first step will be determined by the type of play action he will use: drop back, sprint out, roll out, bootleg, waggle, play action, and so on.

The dropback can be either a backpedal or a crossover and run. In the backpedal, the quarterback pushes off as he rides the center. He can step with either foot, but most prefer stepping first with the passing side foot. He pushes off hard with his toes and moves back quickly as he watches his defensive keys. This type of action is more difficult to learn and slower in getting to the setup area, but it affords good vision of the entire defense. It is

especially important to use the backpedal drop when a blitz is expected.

Coaches who use the crossover step gain speed getting to the setup area and have an easier job teaching, but the quarterback sacrifices good vision of the backside defenders since his back will be toward them. In the crossover drop, the passer steps with the passing side foot, crosses with the other leg, and runs back to the passing spot. Both types of drops should be learned by quarterbacks whose teams use a sophisticated pass offense.

The setup spot, the spot from where the pass will be thrown, may be 1, 3, 5, 7, or 9 yards back, depending on the depth of the pattern. The one-step is used on such plays as a quick slant. The three-step is used on hitches and other patterns that break at about 5 yards. The five-step drop is used on longer patterns, such as those breaking at 8 to 12 yards. The seven- and nine-step drops are used for long curls and deep patterns. The coach must select the proper distance back to give the passer a chance to make the proper reads and to give the receivers time to make their cuts or get to the proper area.

The grip should be nearly correct as the ball arrives in the quarterback's hand from the snap (see Chapter 13). However, as the passer drops to his spot, he should make the final adjustments of his grip.

The size of the passer's hands makes some difference in exactly how he will grip the ball. The smaller-handed player will have to grip the ball a bit farther back in order to be able to control it and to get the maximum amount of power on the ball without it slipping out of his hands. The most commonly accepted grip has the ring finger and little finger, and sometimes the middle finger, on the laces. The index finger will be 1 to 2 inches from the end of the ball and on the seam. The thumb will be 2 to $3\frac{1}{2}$ inches away from the tip of the ball. The ball is gripped by the pads on the ends of the fingers and thumb. The palm should not put pressure on the ball and passers with larger hands may have no contact between the ball and the palm of the hand.

The nonpassing hand should be lightly touching the far end of the ball. This helps to keep the grip and prevent fumbling. If the passer is hit before releasing the ball, having two hands on it can greatly reduce the chance of the ball popping out of the passing hand. The ball should be carried in both hands at chest height while the passer is dropping back and held until the passing action starts (see Figure 14.1).

Quick feet are essential to the elite passer. As he drops to his spot, stops his backward movement, and steps up into the pocket, his feet should be moving fast. This allows him to move to face the receiver, who should be open. Once he has made that quick move toward his target, he will step with the nonpassing leg directly at the target and throw the ball.

Figure 14.1 Grip for pass

The throwing action begins with a step and a weight shift, a turning of the hips, and a rotation of the shoulders. This is followed by the forward movement of the upper arm, then the elbow extension, then the wrist rotation. All throwing and hitting movements start from the feet and end with the fingers.

The stride forward should be long enough for an effective weight shift forward. Average is $2\frac{1}{2}$ to 3 feet. The length of the stride depends on the height of the passer and the distance of the throw. Long passes generally require a longer stride. The toes of the leading foot point directly at the target. As the stride starts forward, the throwing arm starts back. The hand should be drawn back close to the head.

The ball stays close to the ear for most passes. For long throws, the passer may allow the ball to go farther back so that power can be applied to the ball longer. Keeping the ball close to the head rather than allowing it to drop far behind the shoulders, as a baseball pitcher would do, allows for a quicker release. The football pass is more like a catcher's throw than a pitcher's throw.

After the step, the passer shifts his weight to the forward foot. As this happens the hips open toward the target. This is followed by the shoulders rotating into the pass. The muscles of the upper chest are stretched as the shoulders rotate. This gives the upper chest muscles more potential power because the stretch reflex increases their readiness to contract.

From this position, the arm starts forward. The chest muscles bring the upper arm forward. The forearm lags behind the elbow. This stretches the triceps muscles so they will be able to develop more power. Next, the triceps contract and the ball starts forward. The speed of the forearm is important in keeping the nose of the ball up; this makes it easier to catch. The index finger is the last part of the hand to touch the ball.

The follow-through has the palm of the hand turning down and the fingers pointing at the target. After the arm has followed through straight with the palm of the hand down, the arm can cross the body as it completes the follow-through (see Figure 14.2).

Figure 14.2 The follow-through

Passing while running, as in a sprintout or boot-leg, requires that the passer get his shoulders parallel to the line of scrimmage. The ball should be held in both hands. Many coaches attempt to get their passers to step into the pass, just as if they were in a dropback mode. A passer running right and cutting forward on his right foot could pass on his first or third step—as the left foot lands. Going left, for a right-hander, with a cut on the left foot would require that the pass be made on the second or fourth step—as the left foot is landing.

Passing while scrambling might not let the passer step correctly or even use the proper arm action. It is important, however, to get the shoulders perpendicular to the line of flight of the ball.

The target varies with the type of pass. It isn't enough to just throw the ball to another player; the pass must be aimed so that it reduces the chance of an interception. For that reason, short passes are generally thrown low. Out patterns are thrown low and outside. Fade patterns should go over the outside shoulder of the receiver. A major difference between a "thrower" and a "passer" is that the passer will pass the ball where only the receiver can get it.

Receiving

The effective receiver must know how to get to the proper area, make the catch, tuck it away, then run with the ball.

Catching the ball starts with the eyes. The eyes should focus on the ball, even seeing the ball spin. Concentration is the key. It is common for players, even at the pro level, to take their eyes off the ball at the last second to look for running room.

The position of the fingers depends on where the ball will be caught. The surest catching position is with the thumbs and forefingers touching or nearly touching. (For hard-thrown balls, the fingers and thumbs can overlap, because the speed of the ball will separate them.) This hand position should be used even on deep balls. The receiver can turn back toward the passer and make the more certain catch (see Figure 14.3).

If the ball is lower than the waist, the hands can be held with the little fingers in and the thumbs out. This same "little fingers in" hand position is also used on overthrown balls. Whatever the hand position, catch the near end of the ball—the end farthest from the passer. Some coaches teach to catch the near stripe.

Figure 14.3 Catching high ball or low ball

The receiver should cushion the ball as he makes the catch. The arms should act as shock absorbers to take speed off the ball. The receiver should keep looking at the ball as he tucks it in. A common error, often made at the pro level, is to look away before the ball arrives to see where to run. Coaches should teach receivers to watch the ball until it is tucked away before they run.

For a very low ball, the receiver should get his arms under the ball so it doesn't touch the ground. This is the technique used in diving catches (see Figure 14.4).

Getting off the line of scrimmage is often difficult because the defenders are trying to hit potential receivers and delay them, thus changing the timing of the patterns. A receiver should avoid being rerouted along the line of scrimmage. He must fight to get directly behind the defender through either a fake or a deflection technique.

The simplest fake is a "head bob." This is merely a movement of the head in one direction as the receiver takes his first step straight ahead or in the opposite direction.

A variation of this is the head-and-shoulder fake. In this action, the receiver steps one way as he moves toward the defender; then he cuts quickly

Figure 14.4. Diving catch

the other way and gets behind the defender. Sometimes a double fake is needed. If the single fake has worked well, the defender will learn to counter it so the receiver can fake one way, fake the other way, then get behind the defender.

Deflection techniques are used by the receiver when he wants to knock the defender's hands off him. One method is to rip the closest arm up and through the defender's arms. If the receiver is cutting right, it will be the left arm that is ripped up. Another technique is the "swim," in which the receiver brings his inside arm up and over the defender's arms, knocking them downward. These techniques can be used in combination, such as a head fake one way, then a rip up as the receiver makes his cut.

Another technique, used often by tight ends, is the fake block. The receiver comes out low and makes contact but slides off the defender and continues downfield.

Getting open must be done within the theory of the offense. Some coaches have receivers run disciplined routes so that the passer knows where they will be as he makes his reads. The design of the pattern should get at least one receiver open. Other coaches just want the player to get open any way he can. If they work together, the passer will be able to anticipate how the receiver will get open versus different types of coverages. In hook and curl passes, the receiver is generally just asked to get between or in front of the defenders in the underneath zones.

Running the route is dependent on the coach's theory. The traditional way is to run to a point, such as 5 or 10 yards, come under control, and make a cut. The cut can be 90 degrees, sharper than 90 degrees (on a sideline pattern), or less sharp (post, corner, and so on). The player may make a fake before cutting. Of course, against a team playing a true zone defense, the fake should not be effective.

In this angular pattern, the player plants the foot away from the cut, then makes the hard cut and accelerates. If he is cutting right, he will plant the left foot. On more angular cuts, 90 degrees or more, the player must be very much under control, even stopped, as he makes his cut. The objective is to put distance between the receiver and the defender by getting the defender moving back, then stopping and cutting away.

A second method is to run faster at the defender but to run in a slightly "S"-shaped pattern—a "weave." The receiver tries to get the defender moving back fast and get close to him; the cut will be more of a curve. The hope is that the receiver will get distance between him and the defender through speed.

Bill Walsh's theory is that the catch is 40 percent and the run after the catch is 60 percent. The receiver must think about doing each of these perfectly: (1) reading the defense, (2) his release, (3) running his route, (4) catching the ball, (5) securing the ball, and (6) running after the ball is secured.

On a hook pattern after the catch, most receivers take two steps toward the sideline, with the body low to the ground to avoid the defender who is approaching with evil intent. After two quick, long, low steps, he heads upfield. This one move is enough for most people, but some pros are now using an inward two steps to add another method for avoidance. If you are in the open, use the same moves as a running back—get the defender moving one way, then cut behind.

Getting loose in man-to-man coverage is best done by changing directions (such as a hook and comeback, in and out, hook and go, out and up); getting the defender's legs crossed, then cutting the other direction; or getting close, then leaning into the defender and breaking the other way.

PASSING DRILLS

1. Start on both knees. The coach checks the grip, the ball kept near the ear, and the follow-through straight at the target.
2. Do the same drill on one knee—first with the right knee down, then with the left knee down.
3. Drop back to the proper depth (one, three, five, or seven steps) and throw at a target.
4. Run in a circle to the right with another passer and throw to him. Check that the shoulders are square.
5. Run in a circle to the left with one other receiver.

RECEIVING DRILLS

1. Play catch, with ever-increasing velocity on the passes; throw high, low, right, left. Check hand position.
2. Have receivers run at the passer. The passer throws high, low, right, left.
3. With the receiver running in place and facing away from the passer, have the passer throw softly five to ten passes in each of these areas (this drill is used by most pros):
   a. Receiver looking over right shoulder, balls thrown high to right.
   b. Low to right.
   c. Low to left (receiver must turn back toward the passer).
   d. High to left (receiver must turn away from the passer, see the ball over his left shoulder, and make the catch).

Repeat the same drills with the receiver looking over his left shoulder: ten passes high left, ten low left, ten low right, ten high right.

CHAPTER 15

DEFENSIVE LINE FUNDAMENTALS

"Stop the run first."

Many coaches believe that defense is the most important part of the game of football—and defensive play starts with the play of the line. This is the first opportunity we have to stop the run and the pass. As with the offensive line, stance, charge, and reaction are important. However, while the offensive blocker knows where the play is going and how he will block for it, the defensive lineman must neutralize the blocker, react to keys that the offense gives him, and then pursue the ball and make the tackle. In the past, the defenders' primary advantage was that they could use their arms. This advantage has been reduced since blockers can now use their hands in their blocks.

The stance for a defensive lineman will generally have more weight forward than the offensive lineman's. This is because a good offensive lineman will have moved about 6 inches before the defensive lineman can begin to react to the movement. The offensive lineman therefore has more weight forward than he had while in his stance. Having more weight forward helps the defender better equalize the momentum of the offensive player.

The defensive stance can be a three- or a four-point stance. If there is a great deal of weight forward, the four-point stance may be more comfortable. Players who slant and loop (defensive lateral movements) may use stances that do not have as much weight forward as those of players who are hitting directly into the blockers. So the type of stance is often adjusted depending on the defensive theory of the team or the assignment for that particular play.

Figure 15.1 Four-point defensive stance

If forward momentum is important, such as in a pass rush, the feet should be staggered. If lateral movement is important, such as in a looping charge, the feet should be parallel. The back should be straight. The hips can be higher than the shoulders. The shoulders should be even. The head should be up. The eyes should be focused on the man ahead (see Figure 15.1).

The alignment will be head up, inside or outside shoulder, or in the gap. If the lineman's responsibility is the gap, he may play very close to the line of scrimmage. If he has to control a man and is being defeated, such as the nose guard in an odd man front or the defensive guards in a wide tackle six, he may back off the line to give himself more time to read and adjust to the block.

Presnap cues may help the defender make an educated guess as to where the ball will go. He can use his intelligence and observational ability to give him hints about where the play will attack. Prior to the snap, he can glance at the position of the backs. Have they "cheated" into a different position from which the scouting reports have noted that a special play will be run? Is a back wider—possibly signaling a quick pitch? Is the back cheated up—maybe signaling a dive or trap? He can also look at the backs' eyes. Often backs look at the area they will attack, either as a ball carrier or blocker.

The blocker in front of him may be peeking laterally, possibly signaling a cross block or pull. He may also be leaning in the direction of the pull. He may have more weight forward than normal. This may be signaled by a change in color of his knuckles to whiter than normal. Less weight on the hands may signal a pull or a pass block.

The charge begins on the movement of the ball (the snap) or the movement of the offensive player. Both should occur at the same time. The target of the charge can either be a man or a gap. If charging into a man, the blocker must be beaten by neutralizing him. If charging into a gap, the defender must beat the blocker by avoiding him.

The charge must be low; remember that the low man nearly always wins in football. The defensive lineman must hit hard enough with his legs to be able to stop the offensive blocker's charge. He must also get under the offensive blocker and lift him.

His initial charge will be with leg power, with the back arched slightly and the head up. Defenders are allowed to use their hands and arms more than are the offensive blockers. This makes it easier for the defender to ward off the block and get under the blocker.

Block protection is the term used to denote the type of hand or arm action used to ward off and control the blocker. There are several types of block protection. The terminology for block protection varies with several types of names for each technique. The choice of technique depends on the player's build and his assignment; a shorter player will probably be able to get under a taller player

with a hand shiver. Any player can use the forearm rip or the other techniques mentioned below.

The hand shiver (jam or forearm shiver, in older terminology) is the most common use of the hands. In the hand shiver, the defender hits up and into the offensive blocker. He drives his hands into the blocker's chest or the lower part of the shoulder pads. The "fit" will be the same as if he were using his hands blocking—heels of the hands under the shoulder pads, fingers pointed up, the wrists close together.

The arms should "lock out," keeping the blocker at arm's length. His elbows should be under his shoulders as they start their lift. If his elbows are wide, the blocker's legs can overpower the arms (triceps) of the defender and the blocker has a better chance to get into his body. If the defender makes his arm movement with his elbows down, even if he can't lock out his arms he will still have his forearms between himself and the blocker (see Figure 15.2).

The arm lift (jam) is a one-handed shiver used primarily when the defender is protecting a gap different from where he lined up, such as controlling the outside gap from an inside shoulder alignment. The player steps with the foot farthest from the way he is moving (the "far" leg) and hits upward with the "far" hand lifting under the pads as in the two-

Figure 15.2 Hand shiver

hand shiver. The near hand is then free to play the outside of the blocker. So, if moving to the right he would step laterally with the left foot, he should hit with the left hand, then keep the outside leverage with the right arm and hand.

The forearm rip (forearm lift or forearm flipper) is a second type of shiver. In the rip, the defender makes a hard charge with his shoulder into the blocker. As he makes his shoulder hit, he rips his arm up and through the defender. The arm should have a 90-degree angle at the shoulder and elbow. The power comes from the shoulder muscles (deltoids). As the forearm hits under the blocker's pads, the defender's back arches more, the hips drop, and the legs assist in the lift. By this time, the blocker must be defeated (see Figure 15.3).

This move is not as effective as it was in the past because the blockers can now use their hands; it is more difficult to get close enough to the blocker's body to rip into it. On the other hand, the forearm rip can get the blocker's hands off the defender's body and the defender will still have one arm free. This technique can therefore be used in a gap-control defense or when slanting or looping.

Once the blocker is defeated, the defender carries out his assignment. Most teams today use "gap responsibility," meaning that the defender neutralizes his man, then protects a gap. Once it is certain that his gap is not the hole the offense is attacking, he can pursue the ball.

The forearm block (arm bar) is used to control one side of an offensive lineman. It is generally employed when controlling the gap to the side that he is aligned. It can be used to help to open a hole for a stunting linebacker to rush a pass or kick.

If controlling a gap for a pass or run, he should align so that he can hit with the arm farthest from the gap. In this move, the defender drives his forearm into the area between the blocker's shoulder and neck. If controlling the outside gap, he steps with his outside leg and uses his inside forearm. If controlling the inside gap, he steps with his inside leg and uses his outside arm.

Figure 15.3 Forearm rip

If using this move to open a hole for a stunting linebacker, especially a kick blocker, he can hit with the arm farthest from the blocker and drive the blocker away from the hole by turning the blocker's head and body away from the hole.

The butt and control (or blast and grab) is used against blockers who aim high. The defender drives his face into the blocker's chest, with his hands hitting near the low part of the blocker's numbers. He grabs the opponent's jersey and hand—shivers him as he neutralizes his charge and fights the pressure. This technique allows the defender to get a great deal of power from his body. He then fights the pressure and disengages.

Varying the Charge

The defensive lineman may not always hit the man in front of him. He may angle into a gap or may hit an adjacent man rather than the one on whom he was lined up.

The slant charge is a direct charge at an angle from an alignment on a man to an adjacent gap (a penetrating charge) or into the next offensive man (a controlling charge). If it is into the gap (the more common slant), he should align on the LOS. He steps diagonally with the far foot (the left foot if going right), then with the near foot. He protects himself from the nearest blocker with his far hand, the hand which was farthest from the blocker when he started his charge, as he charges into the gap. He aims at the near hip of the adjacent offensive lineman.

Some coaches use a slant into an adjacent man. This may be done from a gap alignment or from a position about a foot off the line of scrimmage and on a man.

The charge is the same except that the target of the charge is the near shoulder of the adjacent man. He shivers the man, usually with a hand shiver, and reacts to the pressure.

The loop charge is made around the adjacent man. It may be from an inside position on a man, around his head, and into a gap that he penetrates. It can also be made from the adjacent man to the next man on the line of scrimmage, in or out. If looping, the defender will need more distance from the LOS—as much as a yard, depending on the width of the line splits and the abilities of the blockers.

The charge is started with the far foot stepping laterally, then the near foot. The far hand must offer block protection. If the target is the gap, the defender penetrates. If it is the adjacent man, he hits and reacts to the pressure.

The goal line charge starts with a stance that has the feet close to the LOS and a great deal of weight on the hands. On the snap, the defender dives through his man or through his gap at about knee height. He then brings his legs up quickly and continues his penetration into the backfield.

Reading the first step of the blocker can assist the defender in knowing how to react as he is making his initial charge. Many coaches teach their blockers to step with the foot on the same side as the shoulder with which they will hit. This can give the defender a jump on his reaction. He can start his lateral movement before seeing which way the blocker's head will move.

If the blocker pulls, the defender may be taught to follow the pull. However, if a team uses the "influence trap," he must be aware that a trapper may be coming from the other side and block him from behind. This is more likely to occur if his man pulls outside and a guard from the opposite side of the center traps him.

If the blocker moves toward the next man in or out, the defender must hit him to slow up the blocker's charge. With the blocker blocking away, the defender can expect a similar block on him or a trap. If he is blocked by an adjacent man, he must fight the pressure; however, he must also expect a trap. The scouting report can give him an idea as to what type of blocking scheme he must counter. Most traps come from the center out, but some teams now trap from the outside in.

Playing the angle block can be expected if the offensive man lined up on the defender blocks the next man to either side of him. If the man on him blocks to the defensive right, he can expect a blocker coming from his left, a cross block coming at him from the right, a trap block from the right, or a lead block from a back. The defender must fight the pressure of the blocker and not be driven off the line of scrimmage.

The first move he should make is into the blocker in front of him keeping him off his assignment. This does two things. It helps the defender regain his balance while he recognizes who will be attacking him and it slows up the blocker who had aligned in front of him and reduces his effectiveness in blocking another defender. After seeing or feeling the man who is attacking him, he should hit him with a forearm rip with the arm nearest the blocker. He should then work to control him and fight the pressure with his far hand and legs. If all else fails, he should drop to all fours to create a pileup at the line of scrimmage.

The trap block is another possibility. If the blocker on the defender blocks down on the next man and he feels no pressure, there is a good chance that he is being set up for a trap block. He should then narrow the gap between himself and the blocker who is blocking down the line. He should not move across the scrimmage line but should set for the trap, being ready to play it with his outside arm, with a forearm flipper, or his hands. Some coaches teach their players to drop to the inside knee when they feel no pressure; this puts the defender lower than the trap blocker and can reduce the trapper's effectiveness.

Seeing the near back's first step may also give a hint of the type of play being run. Is he coming right at the defender as a blocker or a ball carrier? Is he moving across the center, indicating that the play will not come quickly at the defender?

On a pass play, the defender should check on the first step of the near back. If he steps out, it will probably be a pass block. However, if the fullback stays in one spot or a halfback steps inward, it will more likely be a draw play.

Protecting the gap responsibility is essential for teams that play gap-control defenses. If playing gap control, the defender hits into the blocker with his head and shoulders, then slides his head to the side of the gap that he is controlling. While doing this, he hits upward with the hands in a hand shiver, stops the offensive charge, then separates from the blocker. The defender's feet must keep moving while the legs provide upward and forward pressure on the blocker.

Fighting the pressure is the next job of the defender. If the defense is playing with "hit-and-react" technique, the defender will "read the head" of the blocker. This means that he will be aware that the blocker is trying to take him one way, opposite the blocker's head, so will fight through his head. The defender should never go around the blocker but always cross the face of the blocker going to where the ball carrier will probably run.

As he reacts to the pressure of the block, the defender must never cross his legs as he moves toward the ball. His feet must be wide so that he has lateral balance. He should move his legs quickly, taking short choppy steps.

If the blocker drops back in pass protection, this signals the defender to attack the blocker, attempt to turn his shoulders, and then take the proper pass rush lane. In this reaction, the defender should use

Figure 15.4 Fighting double-team block

his hands, not his forearms, because it will give him more ability to maneuver and whip the blocker.

Fighting the double-team block can be done in different ways. The defender can choose to whip one blocker. He can drop to the ground, reducing the effectiveness of the block. He can split the block. Or, if defeated in attempting to overpower the block, he can spin out of it. If the outside blocker is an over-powering player, he may just attack through the inside man or the gap between the blockers.

If the blockers have not been able to get under him, the defender may be able to drop to the ground and trip the blockers. This reduces the effectiveness of the double team because they can't continue to drive the defender.

In splitting the double team, the defender can drive his body into the inside man while pushing with his hands against the outside man. He attempts to "split the seam" of the block by not allowing the blockers to seal their bodies together (see Figure 15.4).

If defeated by the double-team block, the defender can spin out. If the block is high, such as into his chest, he can use the high spin out. To do this, he throws his inside arm toward his back and steps back with his inside foot. This exposes his outside shoulder to the block of the outside man. As he turns, the outside blocker will push on the back of the defender's outside shoulder, which helps him in his spin. As he completes the spin he will get low and attempt to come back into the hole.

Some double-team blocks are delayed with the initial drive block by a lineman being joined by a running back or a man in motion joining as the second part of the block. The block is played the same way as when two linemen are blocking, but the fact that the second man is a bit late and was not in the blocker's triangle makes it a surprise, so the secondary reaction may be late.

Defeating the scoop block is done by hitting the blocker on him who is either hitting him with his head outside or is faking a block, then releasing outside. On the scoop block, the blocker is higher than normal because he is trying to slip the block and attack the backer.

The reaction should be outward through the head of the first blocker. As the first blocker slips by him, he must be alert to the blocker coming from the other side. He should head upfield, making penetration, as he gets his body ahead of the second blocker. He can use the near hand or both hands into the chest of the second blocker to redirect him.

Playing the lead block is difficult because the blocking back is not in the defender's immediate field of vision. However, since the back is generally smaller than the lineman, there should be a bit of a mismatch at the collision point. If the back blocks high, the defensive lineman should jolt him by getting under his pads, lift him, and knock him backward.

Generally, the back will block low. In this situation, the defender must protect his legs. He hits the blocker's shoulder pads and knocks him to the ground and into the hole, while ready to make the tackle. If the ball carrier is a distance behind the blocker, the defender will have time to gather himself and be ready to make the tackle.

Being aware of block progression is essential for intelligent and effective defensive line play. The defender must know which players are most likely to attack him. The normal concerns for a defender are listed in the following diagrams, but the scouting report should refine these because every team does not attack with all of the potential blockers. For this reason, each scouting report can refine the progression for that week. Being aware of the blocking triangle allows the defensive lineman to read the most dangerous potential blockers.

Expected Progressions

A. Man on center (nose guard, nose tackle): (1) man on, (2) strongside guard, (3) weakside guard, (4) near back, (5) strong tackle, (6) weak tackle, (7) tight end, (8) flanker in motion. The blocking triangle is the center and both guards (see Figures 15.5 and 15.6).

B. Man on guard (defensive guard or tackle): (1) man on, (2) lineman outside (near tackle), (3) lineman inside (the center), (4) far guard, (5) near back, (6) far tackle, (7) flanker in motion. The blocking triangle is the man on and the two adjacent linemen (see Figure 15.7 and 15.8).

C. Man on tackle (defensive tackle or end): (1) man on, (2) man outside (tight end or wingback), (3) man inside, near guard, (4) near back, (5) far

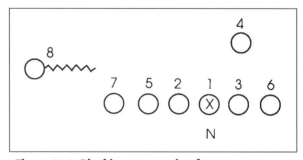

Figure 15.5 Blocking progression for man on center

Figure 15.6 Blocking triangle for man on center

guard. The blocking triangle is the man on, the man inside, and either a lineman, wingback, or inside slotback to his outside; if no man outside, the near back, flanker in motion (see Figures 15.9 and 15.10).

D. Man on end (defensive end or outside linebacker): (1) man on (the end or inside slotback), (2) man inside (tackle), (3) near back (wingback or set back), (4) near guard, (5) far guard, (6) flanker in motion (see Figures 15.11 and 15.12).

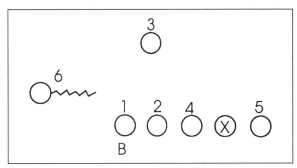

Figure 15.11 Blocking progression for man on end

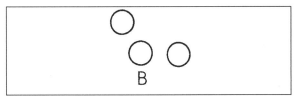

Figure 15.12 Blocking triangle for man on end

Blocks to Expect from Each
Person in the Blocking Progression

1. *Nose man*

From center—drive, scramble, hook, post on double team.

From either guard—angle, scoop, drive man on double team, wedge.

From near back—delayed double team, lead block.

From either tackle—trap.

From end or wide receiver—trap or delayed double team.

2. *Man on guard*

From near guard—drive, scramble, hook, post on double team.

From center or near tackle—drive, angle, scoop, drive man on double team, wedge.

From far guard—quick trap.

From near back—lead or delayed double team.

From far tackle—long trap.

From man in motion—trap or delayed double team.

3. *Man on tackle*

From tackle—drive, scramble, hook, double team.

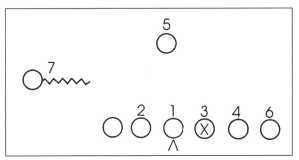

**Figure 15.7 Blocking progression
for man on guard**

Figure 15.8 Blocking triangle for man on guard

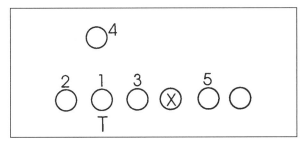

**Figure 15.9 Blocking progression
for man on tackle**

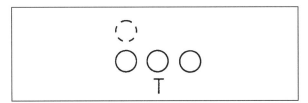

Figure 15.10 Blocking triangle for man on tackle

From end, or inside slotback—double-team drive, angle block.

From near guard—angle, scoop, cross block.

From near back—kick out or log block.

From flanker in motion—trap inside or outside.

4. *Man on end*

From end or inside slot—drive, hook.

From near tackle—angle, scoop, cross block.

From near back—(wingback) angle, double team (setback) kick out, log, delayed double team.

From near guard—trap or log.

From far guard—trap or log.

From flanker in motion—trap, log, delayed double team.

Coaches can set up their defensive reaction drills based on the types of blocks and the expected blocking progressions. For example, if no one in your league uses a scramble block or a scoop block, there is no need to practice against it. Your defenders should work on what they will encounter.

The pass rush begins with the recognition of a pass. It may be the drop step of the blocker. On play action passes, the pass will take longer to recognize. Once the defender becomes aware of it, he should yell "pass" to alert his teammates. He should then start his rush by getting his hands on his opponent's jersey at chest to shoulder level. He must charge hard to defeat the blocker. Several techniques can be used, depending on how the blocker is blocking. Does he have too much weight forward or backward? Can his shoulders be turned? Are his feet quick enough to stay with the rusher? Does he have a weakness that can be defeated?

Once the rusher has his hands on the blocker, he can charge through the blocker, overpowering him, or he can attack one side. A big defensive end attacking a smaller offensive lineman or a back may decide to bull-rush right through his blocker. If the blocker is retreating fast and has too much weight on his heels or excessive backward momentum, he may also be susceptible to the head-on attack. If the matchup is even, it is better to attack one side of the

blocker. Whatever the blocker's technique and size, there is a pass-rush technique to beat him.

As he rushes the pass, he must be alert to the draw and the screen. The draw is usually signaled by the running back staying in one position or stepping inward, rather than stepping out to block or release. The screen is signaled when the blocker lets the defender past him after fighting for about two seconds, and the passer drops deeper than normal.

Basic Pass Rush Techniques

The bull rush is used against a fast-retreating blocker whose weight is on his heels. It can also be used by a big strong defender against a smaller blocker. In this rush, the defender rushes hard at the blocker. He punches the heels of his hands into the outside of the chest or under the armpits of the blocker. He drives his legs hard as he pushes the blocker into the passer. Because the defender is more aggressive, he may be able to knock down the blocker using this charge. Linemen or big backers being blocked by smaller backs often use this type of rush to intimidate the blocker.

The jerk is used if the blocker has too much weight forward; the defender should start the charge forward, then as the blocker lunges forward, grab the blocker's jersey or pads and pull him forward as he goes around him.

Most pass rushes are to the side of the blocker. The defender should get the blocker's shoulders turned away from the line of scrimmage. As he does this, he can attack with power through that shoulder. Here are some techniques to attack through the shoulder that is turning backward.

The rip and run technique has the defender drive his far arm with a hard rip under the near arm of the blocker. So if the defender is going to his right (the left side of the blocker), he hooks his left arm under the left shoulder of the blocker. As he does this, he rips against the ribs and lifts up on the shoulder as he charges. This technique eliminates the blocker's hands as weapons, turns the blocker's shoulders, and

Figure 15.13 Rip and run

Figure 15.14 Wrist club and swim

eliminates the blocker's ability to cut-block him as he moves past him (see Figure 15.13).

The wrist club and swim is another technique that is used to the side of the defender's initial charge. The defender steps with the far foot and moves to the side of the blocker. When he is close to the blocker, he grabs the blocker's hand or forearm or hits it with his forearm. He can also slap the hand down. (If going to the right, he hits the blocker's left hand or forearm with his right hand.) This action knocks the blocker's arm off the rusher and creates a path for the rusher. Then he swings his far arm over the near shoulder of the blocker in a swimlike move (see Figure 15.14).

The shoulder club and swim has the rusher hit into the shoulder of the blocker, then use his swim move. If going to the right, he hits the left shoulder of the blocker with his right hand (see Figure 15.15).

The shoulder club and slip-or-rip move has the rusher hit the blocker with a hard blow of his hand into the blocker's shoulder pad or upper arm. The blocker's shoulder should be lifted in either case. The rusher then drives his far shoulder under the blocker's

Figure 15.15 Arm lift and charge

armpit. This is a good technique for shorter players working against taller blockers. In this case, the rusher can grab the area near the blocker's elbow and lift as he charges under the arm.

The bull rush and slip is slightly different. The defender starts forward in the bull-rush technique, but as the charge continues, the defender lifts one shoulder of the blocker, then brings his far arm under the blocker's shoulder and drives past him.

Another method of pass rushing is to start the blocker's shoulders turning one way, then attack the other way. Do this after the blocker has overcompensated for the outside rush and is somewhat off balance.

The pull and swim technique has the defender start in a hard rush to one side with his hands on the blocker's chest. As the blocker turns his shoulders in one direction, the rusher either grabs the blocker's jersey or reaches behind his shoulder and turns the close shoulder toward him as he swims over it with the other arm. So if the rusher is charging to his right and the blocker's shoulders turn in that direction, the defender grabs the blocker with his left hand, pulling the right shoulder toward him as he swims his right arm over the blocker's right shoulder. This works well for taller defenders.

The reverse club and slip is used by shorter players. Start the rush to one side while turning the blocker's shoulders in that direction. As the shoulders turn, the defender reaches up with his trailing hand and grabs the blocker's elbow or upper arm, pushing it upward, then ducking under it by driving his far arm under the blocker's upraised arm. If starting to the right, the defender lifts the right arm of the blocker with his left hand, then ducks under the blocker's right shoulder.

The club and spin is another technique to reverse the rusher's charge. The rusher starts his normal rush, but with the pressure to the outside, the rusher hits hard into the blocker's midsection with a hand or forearm and whips his other arm behind him, spinning to the inside. The spin must bring him closer to the quarterback, not back to the line of scrimmage or parallel with the LOS.

The arm lift and charge is perhaps the most effective pass rush technique; however, very few players have the strength and skill to use it. In this technique, the rusher grabs the blocker's wrist with one hand, then raises it over the blocker's head. He hits the blocker's chest with the other hand and raises him as he charges directly through the blocker.

The rushing lanes are important to understand as the defender moves past his blocker. As the defender makes his move against the blocker, he must be aware of where the passer is moving and of his own responsibility for the rush. The outside rushers usually take responsibility for containing the passer—making certain that he does not get outside of the rush.

The inside rushers can then be more flexible in the rush they take. However, they must be aware of the possibility of the draw play.

If the passer escapes the contain of the outside rusher, somebody must assume that responsibility in order to stop the passer and rush him again. If the passer is allowed to run unimpeded outside of the rush, he gains much more time for his pass, or he can run. It is therefore essential that he be contained in the pocket by the outside rusher.

Stunts

Stunts or blitzes are designed to confuse the blocking assignments of the offensive line. They are designed to make the big play, either a sack on the passer or a loss by a running back. The stunts may involve linemen, backers, and defensive backs. Two or more players may be involved in any stunt.

Since stunts involve a guessing game, the defenders must be alert to plays that could have been called that would have defeated the stunt. For this reason, the man who is expected to break free into the backfield should check the play as he starts his stunt. If the play is coming at him, the stunt can be scrapped. Often a team that stunts when it expects a pass is fooled when the offense runs a play right at the spot vacated by the defender.

Another important factor is that the stunts should take place on the offensive side of the line of scrimmage. They must be aggressive charges.

Twists involve two linemen. The first defender moves across the face of one or two blockers while the second goes behind and moves into the seam created by the blocker's attacking the first man. As the linemen move, they must be able to protect themselves with the block-protection techniques described earlier.

As the defenders cross, they should be aware of the movement of the blockers.

If the blockers move with them, it is a man-to-man blocking scheme. If the blockers stay, they are in a zone scheme. Stunts work better against the man schemes.

Stunts against a zone scheme are usually more effective if the zone is overloaded with a three on two attack.

Pursuit

Pursuit to the ball is the next job of the defender. If the defender is not directly attacked, he must quickly discover where the ball is going, then take a path that allows him to intercept the ball. If it is a pass, the rusher must follow the ball and get to where he can make the tackle if the receiver is delayed or runs laterally.

In taking the pursuit path, a cardinal rule is to "never follow your own color." Every defender must take a route that will get him to the ball carrier without having to run over his own man.

Trailing the play is the responsibility of one of the defensive linemen—usually the widest man away from the play. He should be alert to counters, reverses, bootlegs, play-action passes, and cutbacks. His path should be as deep as the deepest man.

DRILLS

1. Shiver drill. This can be done into a bag, an arm shield, or a sled. The player explodes his body, makes the desired shiver (hand or forearm), then drives his legs. In the beginning, this drill may be done with the defender on his knees, popping his shiver into a blocking bag. The coach looks for proper technique—elbows and shoulders at a 90-degree angle for the forearm shiver; elbows in and down for the hand shiver.

2. Pass rush contain drill. This drill is performed with four rushers against five blockers and a quarterback. The rushers start attacking in their lanes. The quarterback drops, then attempts to escape outside the contain rusher. If he escapes, the next rusher to the inside loops back and outside, then becomes the contain man and the rush continues.

3. Pursuit drills. These drills should be done in different parts of the field and in different phases of the game (scrimmage play, punt coverage, and so on.)

CHAPTER 16

LINEBACKER FUNDAMENTALS

"Mobile and hostile"

Linebackers are the backbone of the defensive team. They must be sure tacklers. They must be prime run defenders, but they are also prime pass defenders. Offensive strategies and tactics are often devised to fool the linebackers. Faking the run, then throwing the short pass; faking the dropback pass, then running the draw; starting the play one way, then countering opposite—are all ways to fool the linebackers.

When coaching the backers, it is important that they be disciplined in their responsibilities, but they should not be robots. They should be able to play recklessly within the scope of their assignments.

Inside Linebackers

Stance for linebackers is a two-point stance. Inside backers can be more upright because they will be farther from the blockers. The feet should be perpendicular to the LOS and the feet $1\frac{1}{2}$ to 2 feet apart. The knees are flexed. The torso flexes forward and the head is up. The hands are at about chest height if a blocker is an immediate threat. If the blocker is $1\frac{1}{2}$ yards away or more, the arms can be dropped comfortably in front of the body. The weight should be on the balls of the feet (see Figure 16.1).

Movement of the linebackers is primarily lateral while remaining in the hitting position. Once the blocker knows where the ball is, he must attack with an inside-out force. The backer should shuffle sideways (not crossing his feet) while keeping his shoul-

Figure 16.1 Stance

ders parallel to the LOS. It is only as a last resort that the backer would turn and run. Plays such as a quick pitch or a spot pass to a wide receiver are such situations.

Keys for inside backers are essential so that they cannot be easily fooled. Linebackers may key a lineman or a back or read through a lineman to a back. In some cases, they can key the spin of the quarterback—if the basic plays (not the counters) always go to the side toward which the quarterback opens, the linebacker can start in that direction. Some teams always reverse-pivot so the backer can start to the side away from which the quarterback turned.

Keying the guards is standard in the Okie 5-2 or pro 3-4. The backer "mirrors" the action of the guard. If the guard attacks him, he attacks the

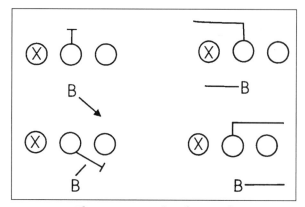

Figure 16.2. Keying the guard

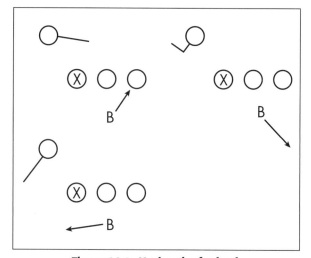

Figure 16.4. Keying the far back

guard, then pursues. If the guard drops back in pass protection, the backer drops into pass coverage. If the guard pulls behind his linemen, the backer moves behind his linemen. If the guard blocks the next man in or out, the backer steps into the same area in which the guard moved (see Figure 16.2).

Keying a near back is done similarly. If the back crosses the center, so does the linebacker. If the back attacks on his side of the center, the backer moves to that area.

Generally the backer will key only the first step, but sometimes, in order to pick up counters, he will key for two or three steps. A "near-back key" is used when the offensive team does not cross its backs (see Figure 16.3).

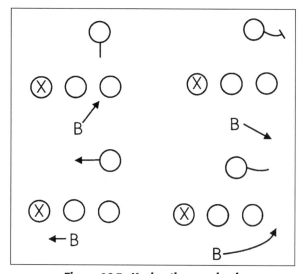

Figure 16.3. Keying the near back

Keying a far back (crosskey) is often used when the offensive team crosses its backs, such as in a crossbuck or a belly series counter. The same principles apply as in keying a near back. If the far back comes at the backer, he holds and protects his responsibility. If he moves in the other direction, the backer pursues (see Figure 16.4).

In playing against an "I" team, the backer may be coached to key the fullback or the tailback. Usually he keys the back who is most likely to run a counter.

Reading through a lineman to a back is more complicated but is often much more effective because it can pick up counter plays in which a lineman leads. There is no reason to key linemen's pulls unless they lead in counters.

Reading through the near guard to the near back is the easiest read. However, it should not be used if the offense crosses its backs. When reading guard to near back, the backer should look through the guard to the near back. If he sees lateral movement from the guard (a pull), he honors that and starts laterally. If the guard moves forward, even at an angle, he disregards the guard and keys the back.

If a team crosses its backs and pulls one or both guards on counters, the backer should read through the near guard to the far back. He uses the same principles as above—lateral movement by the guard is primary, if no lateral movement, key the back.

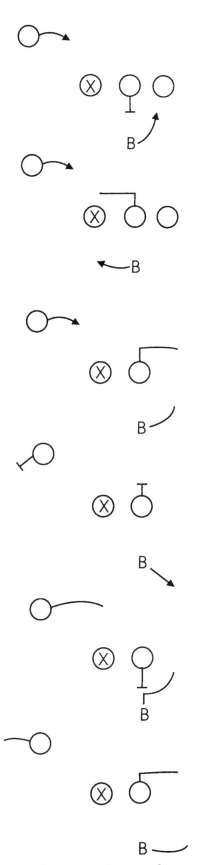

Figure 16.5. Cross reads

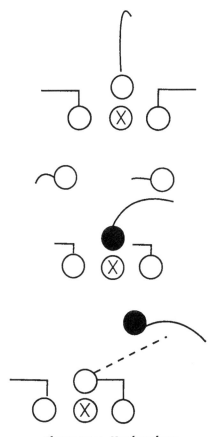

Figure 16.6. Key breakers

If a team uses a heavy keying defense, this read through the lineman to the far back is the "universal" read. It works against any offense, but it is the most difficult to master (see Figure 16.5). The only exception to its success is when a team employs key breakers, such as false-pulling a guard or running the far side back away from the point of attack, both of which are highly unusual (see Figure 16.6).

With practice this can be performed effectively, but it is not a technique that can be mastered the week of a game. A heavy keying defense, if it is to be used, must be practiced all year.

Another type of key is reading a triangle. The triangle may be the guard, center, and near back or the guard, tackle, and near back. Some coaches prefer the guard, quarterback, and near back. In this read, there is more emphasis on the blocking pattern of the linemen than the movement of the back (see Figures 16.7a and 16.7b).

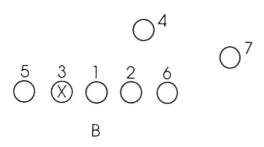

Figure 16.7a Blocking progression for inside backer

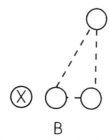

Figure 16.7b Triangle for inside backer

Another possible assignment for the backer can be to "get" a back. In this assignment, he will be responsible for stopping one back, whether it is a run or a pass. This assignment may be used when the defense called is a man-to-man pass defense, or it may be used when one offensive back is a controlling type of player. When this is the case, one or both inside backers may be told that their only responsibility is to stop that player.

Playing the Block

The blocking scheme will give the inside backer an even better idea as to where the play is heading. There are several ways that the blockers can attack the inside backers. The backer must focus on the potential blockers rather than looking at the back. He may read his key, then look at the blockers; but if he looks for the ball carrier, he is likely to be blindsided by a blocker and knocked out of the play. So he should concentrate on the blockers first.

The drive block by the lineman head-up on him should be met with a shoulder charge and forearm rip by the inside shoulder and forearm. The inside leg is forward. The target is the inside number of the lineman. From the snap of the ball, he should be checking the flow angle of the backs to tip off an inside or outside attack. Still, he must defeat the block before he moves right or left.

If the backer is playing on the guard, as in an Okie or a 3-4, he should squeeze the guard toward the center with his outside arm. Don't let the guard's head get past the backer's outside hip. If the ball goes outside, react and make the play from the inside out (see Figures 16.8 and 16.9).

Figure 16.8 Playing drive block

Figure 16.9 Playing drive block—close up

The cut block is a block aimed at the backer's knees or lower. If he is not looking at the blocker, this can be an effective block. However, if he sees the blocker coming low, he merely has to keep his feet back, put his hands on the blocker's back (helmet and shoulder pads), and push him down while slightly giving ground.

In the reach or hook block, the lineman steps outside to get an outside position on the backer. The backer must step wide with his outside leg in order to meet the blocker head-up. He then plays the same technique as in the drive block.

The scoop or slip block has the lineman on the backer blocking the next defensive lineman toward the flow. The offensive man toward the flow is then free to slip his man and get a better angle on the backer. A key is that the offensive lineman on the backer moves directly down the LOS toward the backfield flow.

The backer must step in the same direction and be ready to meet the next blocker. He must meet the blocker with the inside forearm and shoulder, using the outside hand to help control the blocker. Be ready for the cutback. If no cutback, he should take the best angle of pursuit—to either side of the blocker.

The cross block is expected when the lineman blocks down. The backer steps with his inside leg at a 45-degree angle toward the man who is attacking him. He makes the same type of hit (inside shoulder and forearm to inside number), squeezes the blocker into the hole with his outside leverage, and then reacts to the ball carrier.

The down block is met with the outside shoulder and forearm into the outside number of the down-blocking lineman. Watch for cutback, then pursue.

The trap block is keyed when the lineman on him blocks down. The backer looks inside, expecting a pulling lineman to attempt to block him out. He meets it as with his inside shoulder and forearm to inside number of trapper. Squeeze the trapper into the hole. Don't let the trapper's head get past the outside hip. Make the play bounce outside.

The fold block requires the backer to take a lateral step in order to meet the blocker head-on. Meet the blocker with the near shoulder and forearm. Pursue across the blocker's head.

The isolation block is keyed when the lineman blocks down or out and the near back is coming into the hole. It is played the same as a drive block—inside shoulder and forearm to inside number. Squeeze the back to the inside to make the play bounce out.

The pull-and-seal by the lineman is played by stepping laterally, hitting with the near shoulder and forearm, and checking for a blocking back or the ball carrier.

Blocking Progression

The inside backer must be aware of blocks coming from several areas. His concerns are (in this order): (1) man on, (2) man outside, (3) man inside, (4) near back, (5) far guard, and (6) near end, tackle, or flanker.

The blocks he might expect are:

- From man on—drive, scramble, cut, double team, zone
- Man inside or outside—angle block, scoop, fold, double team, zone
- Near back—lead, delayed double team
- Far guard—trap
- Near end, tackle, flanker in motion—seal

The pursuit path of the linebacker can be based on the instinct of the player or can be planned. If his only assignment is to make the tackle, the onside backer should pursue, keeping the runner on his outside shoulder. The offside backer should keep the runner about a yard ahead of him to prevent a cutback.

When his pursuit angle is planned as part of the defensive assignment it, can be into the line or behind the line. When the backer's responsibility calls for him to move into a hole in the line, it is

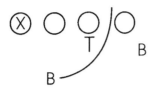

Figure 16.10. Scrape off hole created by alignment

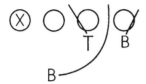

Figure 16.11. Scrape off hole created by charge of the linemen

called a *scrape*. If he must stay on his side of the LOS until he has a clear shot at the ball carrier, it is called a *shuffle*.

Many defenses are designed to have the onside backer scrape into a hole created by the placement or the charge of the defensive linemen. This is really a controlled stunt. The backer doesn't know where he will penetrate until he reads his key. As he moves into the hole, he must spot the ball carrier, stay slightly behind him to eliminate a cutback, then attack the ball (see Figures 16.10 and 16.11).

The shuffling linebacker moves behind the LOS, staying about a yard behind the ball carrier. When he sees an opening, he can move across the line and make the tackle. In shuffling, keep the shoulders square to the LOS and move without crossing the legs for as long a distance as possible.

Playing off blockers is often essential to get to the ball but the backer should remember that his job is to make the tackle, not to play off blockers. Fighting the pressure is easier for linebackers because they have more room to maneuver. Most defensive assignments expect the linebackers to have an outside responsibility; because of this, they will generally use one of two techniques.

The backer may play the blocker with a forearm flipper, using the inside forearm and keeping the outside arm free to control the outside of the

blocker. This is more often used if the blocker is upright.

Versus lower blockers or those coming at an angle, the backer may use his hands to ward off the blocker, always making certain to control the outside of the blocker. The hands should control the shoulder pads as the backer concentrates on the blocker while "seeing" the ball carrier. As with defensive linemen, the backer should fight through the blocker's head. It is permissible for a backer to give a little ground as he plays through the head and continues his lateral movement.

When the blocker is coming from directly in front of the backer and the ball carrier is directly behind the blocker, the backer must defeat the blocker while not taking a side. The forearm rip is generally the most effective technique to use. He should straighten up the blocker, push him away with the free (outside) hand, and make the tackle. He should never spin in this situation.

Outside Backers

Stance for an outside backer playing on a tight end or an inside slot back is usually lower than an inside backer's stance so that he can meet the potential block of his nearest opponent.

Alignment is closer to the line of scrimmage, usually as close as possible if there is a blocker who is an immediate threat, such as a tight end or slotback. If he is playing wider, such as in a walk-away position, he may drop off a few yards.

Keys for outside backers usually start with the nearest two linemen, then the near back. If the backer is playing on a tight end, he reads the end and tackle, then the near back. If the end releases, it is likely to be a pass or a run away from the backer's side. The end is the major key.

Before the snap, the backer will recognize which types of plays can be run at him from the backfield set. A wide halfback gives the offense the possibility of a quick pitch. With this possibility, the backer

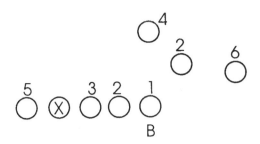

Figure 16.12a Blocking progression for outside backer

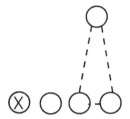

Figure 16.12b Triangle for outside backer

must be alert to the pull of the tackle leading the pitch. With backs in a veer set, he should be alert to the veer attacking his area, then play his responsibility—either the dive back, the quarterback option, or the pitch, whichever his coach has assigned on that defense.

In looking at his triangle, he must be alert for the end and tackle blocking down—this probably indicates a trap. If it is a veer set or a wishbone, he must be ready to play the option if the linemen block down (see Figures 16.12a and 16.12b).

Most coaches assign the linebacker on the tight end to keep the end off of the middle backer, to be able to fight off a seal block, and to slow up the end on pass plays.

The outside backer must be alert to several types of blocks and plays aimed at the off tackle area or wider—the drive block, kickout block, and reach block from linemen. He must be aware of a block from a back that can be designed to take him in (log) or out. He must also be alert to the sweep, pitch, and option. Generally, the outside backer will react to the step of the tight end. If he is a weak side

backer with no one on him, he will have more time to read keys and react.

Playing the drive block is done by stepping with the inside foot, striking under the shoulders with the hands or forearm, then bringing the hips closer to the blocker so that the blocker can be lifted. If using the hands, he should lock out the arms, then react to the pressure or the keys. He should control the LOS and not be driven back. The blocker should be controlled with the outside hand to squeeze him inside thus reducing the off-tackle hole. By keeping outside leverage, he can pursue wide from the inside out.

Playing the reach block is done by stepping laterally as the tight end steps laterally to get an outside position. The backer hits with his hands into the end's shoulder pads and keeps the end's shoulders from turning him inside. An effective outside backer turns the blocker's outside shoulder away from the line, making it impossible to be hooked in. The end must not be allowed to get an angled position on the backer and wall him off from an outside play.

Playing the cut block is done by stepping inside as the end steps inside. He must maintain outside leverage with his hands or with a forearm rip with his inside arm and control with his outside hand.

Playing the pulling lineman is done by stepping into the end, who is blocking down, and controlling him with a hand shiver, knocking him off of the defensive end. The backer should check the flow of the backs and the depth of the pulling lineman to determine if they are attempting to run off-tackle (to his inside) or wide. Guards pulling deeper or a back taking a looping path toward him (to log him in) indicate wide plays.

If the play is designed to run inside, he should control the end with his inside forearm and outside hand or both hands. He should close the hole down from the outside. If the play is going wide, he must avoid being logged in by a back or pulling lineman by using his hands and keeping his feet free as he strings the play out.

Playing the cross block of the end and tackle is done by controlling the end, keeping him off the inside defender, then closing the hole and meeting the tackle with the hands or an inside forearm. This block is recognized by seeing the tackle come directly at him from over the hip of the down-blocking end.

Playing the tackle log or hook block is done by controlling the end as in the cross block. If he sees the tackle looping deeper, he can expect a log type of block, pinching him inside, so he steps laterally to gain a head-up position with the tackle, hand-shivering him, avoiding being hooked, and controlling the LOS.

Playing the inside-out (kick out) block of a back is done after controlling the end who is probably blocking down. The backer should approach the back at a 45-degree angle. The back should be hit with the inside shoulder and forearm but controlled from the outside with the outside arm. The hole should be reduced, forcing the ball carrier to bounce wide.

Playing the load block (arc block) of a back is recognized by seeing a wider, often arcing, pattern that allows the back to get outside. Hit the back with an inside forearm rip or with the hands—always making certain that he has outside leverage.

Blocking Progression

The backer's concerns are man on, man to either side, near guard, near back, far guard, and flanker.

Blocks to expect:

- From man on—drive, cut, hook (reach), zone
- From man outside—double team, angle
- From man inside—angle, zone
- From near guard—trap
- From near back— lead, log, delayed double team
- From far guard—trap, log

Playing the release of the tight end requires that the backer hit him to knock him off his path. If he releases inside, the backer should step down with him. The height of the end's head may tip off the type of play (low for run or high for pass). An outside release may signal pass, an option play, or a run to the other side. The backer hits the end, then looks to the inside to find the ball.

Playing the option depends on the theory of the defense being used. In some defenses, the backer attacks the quarterback, making him pitch quickly. In other defenses, he may be required to "slow-play" the quarterback. In slow-playing him, the backer remains on the LOS in a position where the quarterback will have trouble cutting back on him. The backer strings the play out as the defensive pursuit forms and the ball approaches the sideline.

General Responsibilities of Backers

Stunts (or blitzes) give the linebackers opportunities to make big plays. In a stunt, the linebacker attacks the assigned area on the snap. He can continue through the hole or make a read as he attacks and adjust his charge based on the read. For example, if the stunt was designed to work against a drop-back pass but the offense ran a quick pitch, he would adjust and get into a proper pursuit path rather than continuing toward the quarterback.

The stunting backer should not tip off the offense that he is blitzing. He must start on the snap and charge toward his hole responsibility. As he approaches the hole, he should adjust to the line's movement or the backfield action. If the guards pull, he should follow. If they set in pass protection, he should attack and use the techniques of pass rush described in the chapter on defensive line play. He should know whether he has an inside rushing lane or has outside contain on the pass.

Pass defense is a prime responsibility of the linebackers. They may drop into a specific zone or play man-to-man defense. Here are some concerns for the backers playing zone defense.

Zone Defense

Pass drops begin when the backer picks up his pass key. Most coaches teach to turn to the outside and run back to the assigned zone while watching the quarterback's eyes. Coaches generally also ask the backer to peek at the near receivers to get a tip on the pattern that will be run. If he sees a wideout starting to curl in, the backer may adjust to a wider and deeper spot than he had anticipated. If he sees the wideout running a quick slant, he may adjust to a shorter and wider position.

The most important concern should be the quarterback's eyes or jaw. For this reason, some coaches don't let their players peek at the potential receivers; they merely get their keys from the passer's eyes. Few passers at the high school, or even the college level, do a good job of "looking off" the backers. This is especially true if there is an effective pass rush. Another key many coaches use is the QB's shoulder. It is a key that develops later than the eyes, but if a QB is adept at looking off pass defenders, the eyes are a less valuable key. The shoulder will not lie.

When reading the eyes, the backer starts to make his drop, but adjusts his drop depending on where the passer looks. By watching the eyes effectively, four short defenders at a 10-yard depth should be able to cover the entire width of the field. The problem, of course, is to be able to get to the proper depth.

Traditionally, the proper depth has been 10 yards. However, as 15- to 18-yard patterns have become more common, the drops have often been adjusted to compensate for these patterns. Some coaches have their backers drop immediately to the 10-yard depth, then count 1001, 1002, and start drifting farther back. The thinking is that if the pattern were a 10-yard "hook" or "in" pattern, it would have been thrown by the time the backer gets to the 10-yard depth, so the backer can drift deeper to reduce the seam between himself and the defensive backs. Another key used to adjust the drop depth is

to have a 1-yard drop on a QB's one-step drop, 3 to 4 yards on a 3-step drop, and 10 yards on a 5-step drop. This should put the backer at the approximate depth of the pass reception.

Reading the quarterback's eyes can give the backer a big jump on the direction of the pass. As with so many other factors in football, the coach must choose between having the backer peek at the receivers or reacting only to the eyes of the quarterback. It is obvious that if he is peeking at receivers, he has lost eye contact with the passer and may miss the early jump that he could have had if he had not been looking for receivers. Some coaches maintain that the backers cannot really see the eyes so they must look at the face guard or the chin of the passer.

Backers can get the jump on the ball if they move immediately as the passer looks at his target. Some coaches teach to start slowly, then run fast as the passer takes his long step. Most coaches teach the backers to run fast at the target when they see the passer look. They should keep their eyes on the quarterback while running. Some coaches teach to look at the target receiver and sprint toward him as the QB looks, so the defender can get under the receiver. Coaches must determine whether to run quickly on the passer's eye key or to protect against a possible throwback—choosing reckless pursuit or caution.

The backers should tell each other where the receivers are and who may be entering their zone. "Curl behind" or "deep cross" are examples of alerting an adjacent linebacker.

Man-for-Man Pass Defense

The backer must know whether he has deep help from the safeties or whether he has his man all over the field. If his assignment is to take away the underneath patterns (up to 18 yards), he can play more recklessly. In this assignment, he can play under the man and knock down or intercept any short passes. If he has no deep help, he must play more cautiously.

With deep help while playing a receiver wider than a tight end, he can align himself inside and at a depth of 6 inches to 4 yards. He should not let the receiver inside of him.

The backer should concentrate on the receiver, chucking him and keeping him outside. If he is playing tight to the LOS, as in a bump and run, he must slow up the receiver's pattern and knock him out of the pattern by making him run laterally rather than upfield. He must then stay on the inside hip of the receiver.

If the defender is off the ball, the backer maintains his inside position. If the receiver tries to cross inside, he hits him. He should try to remain 2 to 3 yards deeper than the receiver and a yard to his inside. He should duplicate the receiver's cuts while maintaining his "air cushion" between himself and the receiver. If the receiver gets behind him, he gets on the receiver's inside hip.

The defender must be as close to the receiver as possible, continually looking at the receiver. He looks for the ball when the receiver looks for the ball, the receiver's eyes are obviously concentrating on the ball (they usually widen), or when the receiver's hands come up.

If the backer's man is a running back, he checks for an immediate release by the back. If the back sets to block, the backer goes to him and plays him with his hands. This keeps the back occupied so he cannot help to block a defensive lineman and the backer is near his man in case the back releases for a screen pass.

DRILLS

1. Key, read, or "get" drills. The type of drill is dependent on the type of key the coach wants the backer to learn. Examples are:

   - Key guard
   - Read through guard to near back
   - Read through guard to cross back
   - Read C, G, near back triangle

2. Hand shiver or forearm flipper drill—maintaining outside leverage. Coach signals one of the linemen to come at the backer. The ball carrier can be added to the drill. Use bags to limit the ball carrier's area to run.

3. "Reading the eyes" drill. Coach simulates taking the snap, dropping and looking in each direction. The backer reacts to the coach's eyes. The coach may throw the ball on his first, second, or third look.

4. Man-to-man pass defense drill. Coach signals the receiver (tight end, wideout, or running back) to stay and block or to release inside or outside and run a pattern.

5. Pass-rush techniques. See Chapter 15.

CHAPTER 17

DEFENSIVE SECONDARY FUNDAMENTALS

"The last line of defense"

The players in the defensive secondary, the corner backs and safeties, must be intelligent, skilled players. They are the last line of defense to prevent touchdowns. Their techniques are predicated on the defensive theory of the coach—whether they play man to man or zone, loose or tight, deep or shallow. In any case they must play mistake-free football.

In order to reduce mistakes, the secondary rules should be very simple. Some coaches teach only one defense, with the defensive backs never varying in assignment. This greatly reduces errors, but it also reduces the ability to change the coverages and attempt to fool the offense. At the lower levels of high school ball, simple rules may be best. At the professional level, multiple coverages are a must. Still, broken assignments often occur at the pro level. This should make the high school and small-college coach consider a simpler defensive scheme than they see on *Monday Night Football*.

Stance is a comfortable two-point stance. A "bump-and-run" cornerback would have both feet parallel or near parallel. If taking away one side of a receiver, the bump-and-run player may play the near foot slightly closer to the receiver. Backs playing deeper may play in a similar stance but with the inside foot back.

The bump-and-run player has his hands up, ready to hit or absorb the receiver. Backs playing deeper can keep their arms more relaxed. The closer the defensive back is to the receiver, the more important is his stance.

The alignment of the backs depends on their responsibility. Some coaches prefer that they align the same on every play so as to reduce the presnap read of the quarterback and receivers. Other coaches align the defensive players so as to make their assignments easier to carry out.

The bump-and-run player will be very close to the LOS. The free safety may be 10 to 15 yards deep. The strong safety may be 2 to 10 yards deep and 1 to 2 yards outside of the tight end. The corners may be as deep as 10 yards but are usually at a 5- to 8-yard depth. The corners may play slightly outside or inside the receiver, depending on the width of the receiver and the responsibility of the defender.

Against a tight team, such as the tight T or wing T, the defensive halfbacks or corners might play 3 to 4 yards outside of the end or wingback and 4 to 8 yards deep. The safety or safeties might align only 8 to 12 yards deep.

If there is a single safety and he is required to play the deep outside zone or if the defensive halfback has to rotate up, he may play as deep as needed in order to be able to beat the widest player into the deep outside zone. If there are twin safeties who will rotate in an umbrella defense, they need only be deep enough to get to their zones ahead of any possible receiver (see Figures 17.1 and 17.2).

The responsibilities of the defensive secondary are dependent on whether they are playing a zone defense, a man-to-man defense, or a combination of the two. In the zone defense, the defensive back should get to his area while watching the passer.

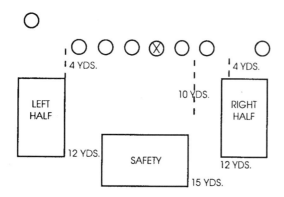

**Figure 17.1 Possible alignment areas—
three-deep secondary**

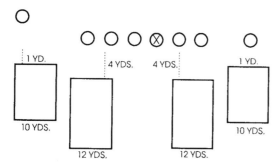

**Figure 17.2 Possible alignment areas—
four-deep secondary**

The depth he will play is determined by the zone he is assigned to cover.

In the man-to-man defense, the back's major concern is to watch his man. The depth he will play depends on whether the coach wants him to play bump and run or play off the receiver giving him a cushion of air and not allowing him to complete the deep pass. If giving the receiver a cushion, the DB will generally play 5 to 7 yards deep.

Offensive tendencies give the DB a clue as to what to expect. He must first know the down and distance and the field position. What are the offensive tendencies based on these factors? The coach should have the run-pass tendencies for the various combinations of down, distance, and field position—and possibly the score. These tendencies should then be combined with the formation potentials and tendencies. For example, a few years ago, if Green Bay came out in a slot set with the slot

off the line, we would expect him to run a quick "look in" or smash route. But if he was on the line, with the wideout off the line, there was a strong tendency to run the slot to the flat, with the wideout clearing. This was normally done with Favre sprinting to the slot side.

The corner should also be able to judge whether the offensive line is heavy (lots of weight on the hand) or light. This should provide another tendency toward run or pass. Time on the clock is also an important factor, especially late in the game when the offense is likely to reduce the number of sets and plays it will use.

The next key, particularly for corners, is to watch the wideout as he approaches his position. Is he looking at the sticks? If so, he is probably going to run a first-down depth pattern-hook or out. If he is going to crack block, he will generally look in at the safety or backers, not at the corner.

The corner then needs to check the distance the wideout is from the formation or the sideline. The distance from the sideline should be a good indicator as to whether the wideout will run an out. Generally, there is a certain distance from the sideline in which the offense will not run an out pattern. If he is close to the formation, it may indicate that he will be blocking or running some sort of out pattern. Sometimes a mannerism can be spotted during the game or in the film. Some receivers will dry their hands if they are expecting a pass, but won't bother to do it if it is a run.

The distance a flanker is off the line may also give you a clue as to what to expect. If he is getting as close as possible while still keeping the minimum distance necessary from the LOS to be a flanker, it is probably a run.

If he is back farther than the minimum 1-yard distance needed to be a flanker, it is likely to be a pass. If the corner is up in a bump or press cover, these distances are more likely to be evident. Because you want the corner to be aware of all of these things, you want him out of the defensive huddle quickly.

The quarterback will also often provide clues as to what he will do. This can be particularly important to safeties. While a few QBs will show no tendencies (Joe Montana was one of these), most will look quickly in the direction they will throw. Even the pros seldom do a good job of looking off the DBs. Does the QB lick his hands only on passes, or does he do it on every play?

You might also have your backs shift positions when they hear an automatic. If your corners are off 8 yards, an automatic will probably be a hitch, slant, or quick out, so have your corner move to a press position. If he is in a press and hears an automatic, it is likely that a deeper pattern has been called, such as a postcorner, so have him jump back to an 8- to 10-yard depth.

Once the ball is snapped, new keys become evident. If you are watching the QB, he will either turn and hand off or get into a play-action pass or he will pass drop. Always expect the three-step drop. The three-step drop will be a long step, then a short step, then the setup to throw. If his second step is long rather than short, it will be a five-step drop. On the three-step drop, you expect hitch, quick out, slant, fade, or screen. On the five-step drop, you have eliminated these routes and must play the deeper routes. Once the DB has seen the second step as short (three-step drop) or long (five-step drop), he can concentrate on the receiver and be ready to jump the routes he may run.

The depth of the corner can be on the line for bump coverage, 2 to 3 yards deep for press, or 8 to 10 for deep. DBs should be able to play the deep cover and either bump or press. If he is playing up, he needs to move with movement. If he is at 8 to 10 yards, he can wait until he reads the second step of the QB before he moves. If it is a three-step drop, he will almost always be moving up to the receiver whether in man or zone defense. His positioning should eliminate the fade being thrown. It doesn't make sense to put a defender at 8 to 10 yards, then have him immediately backpedal at the snap. He is already deep enough to disallow any one- or three-step pattern from getting behind him. For this reason, few pros backpedal until they read a five-step drop.

Playing deep gives the defender the advantage of being able to read the quarterback's second step before shifting his attention to the receiver's moves. If the DB is tight, he can concentrate only on the receiver's moves.

Always take away the inside or the outside—never align head-on. This allows the receiver to have the advantage no matter which way he breaks. So, generally take away the outside if he is close to the formation and inside if he is wide.

Zone Defense

Zone responsibilities require that either two or three defensive backs cover deep. If three backs are used, they generally play the three-deep zones if it is a drop back-pass.

They may rotate into a two deep on a long sprintout or rollout pass if the corner on the side of the flow is given the assignment of the flat zone. With two safeties and two corners, many combinations are possible to cover two- or three-deep zones.

If flow goes away from the defensive halfback (three deep) or the corner (four deep), he should remain cautious of the bootleg, reverse, reverse pass, counteraction, or play-action pass. His rotation should not continue until he is certain that there is no possibility of a play coming back to his area.

Zone techniques start with obtaining whatever depth is necessary to get to the proper zone. This must be done prior to the snap of the ball. If a safety in a three-deep alignment is required to cover the deep outside zone in a rotation (against a sprintout or rollout) he may start 12 to 15 yards deep. On the other hand, a corner who is required to cover the deep zone behind him may be able to line up 6 to 8 yards deep and still have plenty of time to get to his zone.

The first steps of the defensive back in most defenses are back. Some teams have the defender turn and shuffle or start to run into his zone. This gets him there more quickly. Today, more teams have him backpedal toward his zone. In either case, he reads his keys for run or pass as he takes his first steps. If a certain run key is read, he can forget his zone and play his run responsibility. If he is in doubt, he plays the pass.

If running backward into the zone, the defender must have the agility to turn right or left whenever the quarterback looks in that direction. (See the analysis of this technique in Chapter 11.)

Backpedaling is the most common technique used today. The backpedal is preferred because

- It allows the defender to keep his original alignment and leverage on the receiver.
- It keeps the defender's shoulders parallel to the line of scrimmage and allows him to move forward, right, or left quickly.
- It is more effective than the shuffle if playing a loose man-to-man coverage.

The technique of the backpedal requires that the defender keep his torso forward with his chin over his toes and his shoulders over his knees. Keep the head down and the elbows bent at 90 degrees. The defender steps back quickly while driving his arms hard. By keeping his head and torso forward, he remains balanced and able to stop and break forward for any short pass. His feet should be no wider than his hips. The player should concentrate on "stepping back" rather than "pushing off" because emphasizing pushing back may force him to lean back on his heels and make him stand up straighter, both of which will slow him down.

The defender should backpedal at three-quarter speed. If he were at full speed, he would not be able to change directions as fast to come up for a run or to break for a short pass. The steps should be small to medium in length. The feet should stay close to the ground. The knees should be bent to allow the feet to reach back. The arms should pump forward and back, not across the body. He should think of pulling himself over his feet.

As he backpedals, he should remain in the proper leverage position, usually outside, in order to take away one of the receiver's options in cutting. Once the receiver cuts, the defender should whip his near arm toward the direction he will be running. This helps him to change directions more quickly.

The defender should be able to keep his leverage on the receiver for about 15 yards before he has to turn and run with him. This occurs when the receiver is about 3 yards from the defender. Receivers want to get to the defensive back as quickly as possible and force the back to turn and run. They also want to get head-up with the defender. Backs therefore must work on staying in the backpedal as long as possible while keeping the shade on the receiver.

Defensive backs should work on backpedaling straight back and on backpedaling both in a weave pattern and at 30- and 45-degree angles to their initial straight drop. They must continually work on keeping the cushion (at least 3 yards) and the shade (at least 1 yard) on the receiver.

The speed and depth of the drop is dependent on the coach's theory. Some coaches prefer that the defensive back be much deeper than the receivers. If using this theory, the back is much more likely to be able to intercept the long ball or to react more effectively laterally to any long ball. It should be noted that a long pass released when the receiver is 12 to 15 yards downfield will be caught after the receiver has run an additional 20 to 30 yards. So it is not important to be close to the receiver if he is running a long pattern. (On quick-in patterns, the receiver will run about 6 yards to the reception point after the ball is thrown. On quick-out patterns, he will run about 10 yards.)

The deeper the defender is before the release of the pass, the more he can come under control as the passer sets, and the greater lateral distance he can cover when the ball is released. Of course, if he is deep, the seam between him and the undercoverage will be greater. The advantage to playing closer to the receiver is that the defender will be closer to the target area if the pass is thrown into the intermediate zone of 15 to

22 yards. The coach must therefore decide whether he wants a more effective coverage of the long pass or a compromise in which there is more help by the deep backs in the intermediate coverage.

Whichever theory is utilized, the defender must watch the quarterback. While many coaches have the defender peek at the receivers in his area, doing so may take away the defender's ability to react quickly to the passer's eyes or arm. It generally takes more than a second to change focus from peeking at a receiver to establishing contact with the passer's eyes.

Some coaches have the defensive backs turn their bodies and even move a bit toward the direction that the passer is looking. However, the main key to release the defender to go to the ball is the "long-arm action."

Most passers fake a pass with a short-arm action and a short step. When passing long their arms come back farther and they take a longer step. By watching the passer's "long-arm" action of the passer, the defender can start to go in the direction of the pass before it is thrown.

Once the ball is in the air, the defender should move to the area in which he can intercept it at the highest point. Since he will have a greater depth than the offensive receiver (at least 5 yards), he should have more room to maneuver for the ball than will the receiver who is running at top speed to the point of reception.

Playing through the receiver to get to the ball is essential. Once the ball is in the air, it belongs to either team; neither team can interfere with the other. Interference occurs only when one player plays the man rather than the ball.

Catching the ball should be done by squaring the shoulders to the ball, reaching or jumping high (catching the ball at its highest point), looking the ball into the hands, and catching the near end of the ball. If the defender concentrates on catching the end of the ball, it won't go through his hands. If it were to bounce out of his hands and forward, he would still have an opportunity to catch it after he had stopped it.

After making the interception and tucking the ball under his arm, the defender yells "fire" to alert his teammates that he has intercepted and that they should block for him.

Verbal communication on the pass is essential. The sequence is:

1. "Pass" when it is recognized that a pass play is coming;
2. "Ball" when the ball is released.
3. "Got it" when the defender knows he can intercept it. This alerts his nearby teammates to get ready to block for him or to be ready for a tipped ball. Without this call, occasionally two defenders are in position to intercept and they hit each other, knocking each other off the interception.
4. "Fire" when the defender has made the interception and tucked the ball away. This alerts all of his teammates to block.

In addition to the above, the backs should call out the patterns in front of them as they unfold. By calling "slant," "hook," "out," "in," "comeback," or "curl" the backers have a better chance of adjusting their drops and making the interception or knocking the ball down.

Man-for-Man Defense

Responsibilities vary according to the theory of the defense. Bump and run requires a tight defense geared to take away the short and intermediate area passes. Deep man-for-man coverage is designed to take away the intermediate and long passes.

Man-for-man responsibilities can be either bump and run, a press technique, or playing off the receiver with a cushion of air. In a bump-and-run technique, the defensive back takes away the underneath patterns by playing between the passer and the receiver. This is called "trailing." The long pass is taken away because of the defender's speed. If the team is playing bump and run with the deep zones covered, the speed of the corner is not as critical.

Bump-and-run coverage is designed to slow up the pattern by hitting or absorbing the receiver on the LOS and making him move laterally before heading upfield. The defender is nearly always asked to take away the inside of the receiver.

The defender lines up just outside or slightly inside the receiver. The stance is parallel to the LOS so that the defender can step with the receiver, hit him, and block his release downfield. He should align as close as possible to the line of scrimmage.

In the "press" technique, the defender plays up to a yard and a half off the receiver. He backpedals with the receiver; then, as the receiver makes his cut, the defender hits him with his "far" arm (the arm away from the direction of the cut). This hit should slow up the receiver a bit and will also help to turn the defender so that he can run with the receiver.

When using the press technique, many coaches teach that the primary responsibility is inside. If a receiver has cut inside and then outside, the defender is told to honor the inside fake; then, on a double-cut pattern, turn away from the receiver, getting depth as he relocates the receiver on his outside. Double-cut patterns such as post-square-out (a "dig" pattern) or a post-curl-out will leave the receiver open. However, the more dangerous post corner has a good chance of being well covered.

If the defensive theory is for the defensive back to play off the line, he will not have as much responsibility for the very short passes but will be asked to take away the intermediate routes and still play the deep routes.

However, he may also have a safety behind him for the deep routes so he can play the intermediate routes more aggressively. When playing off the line, many coaches require the defender to "shade" one side or the other—playing about a yard inside or outside of the receiver and taking away one possible cut. Most often they take away the outside cut, inviting the receiver to cut into the middle of the field, where the linebackers may help out.

In playing man to man, the cardinal rule is to never take your eyes off your man once you have focused on him. Don't look back for the ball. If you have started deep and watched the QB's eyes for the first two steps, then switched to your receiver, don't take your eyes off him again.

Jamming the potential receiver is a technique used in man-to-man bump-and-run defense and in some zone defenses, if the corner has a shallow zone-pass responsibility. The two-hand jam technique is similar to the hand shiver used by defensive linemen but is generally made from the inside out or the outside in. The hit should be made with the palms open and the thumbs up. The blow should be struck from low in the numbers up and through the receiver. By straightening the receiver up, he will be thrown off his path and the timing of the pass may be hindered.

Most coaches teach to bump with one hand only. This stops the defender from overextending into the hit. There are two schools of thought on this: One method is to hit with the hand that is farthest from the direction that the receiver is moving. This allows the defender to open up in the same direction that the receiver is moving. A second theory is to hit with the hand nearest the direction that the receiver is moving; then, when the receiver starts to clear, to throw the far hand into the nearest shoulder of the receiver. This helps the defender turn into the receiver. The receiver's movement actually helps the defender to turn toward his opponent and run with him (see Figures 17.3 and 17.4).

Since the defensive back should be able to maintain his balance, he should not overextend into the hit; he must keep his balance. However, when he knows that he has effective help in the deep zone, he can really unload on the potential receiver as long as he can keep his balance.

Some coaches, afraid that the bump-and-run player will overextend while hitting, have their players "absorb" the body of the receiver. To do this, the defender stays in front of the receiver, puts his arms out, and allows the receiver to make some forward

Figurre 17.3 One-hand bump

Figure 17.4 Reach across

progress. This softer approach to "bumping" allows the defender to stay more balanced and to keep his body in front of the receiver longer.

Some coaches teach that if the defender is inside of the receiver, he should bump him only on an inside release. Playing the inside is much simpler and more effective for most players playing man-to-man defense because they can prevent the quick inside release and still maintain the preferred inside position on any outside release patterns. The major

difficulty with this arises against a team that is proficient in completing a fade pattern.

The defender should try to run the receiver out of his route and slow up the timing of the pattern. Since the receiver will be trying to get into his planned route, the longer the receiver is delayed the more the overall pattern is disrupted and the greater chance there is for a sack. So if the receiver is forced to run along the line of scrimmage, he has been effectively delayed.

On the movement of the receiver, the defender should move his feet quickly, mirroring the receiver's feet. This keeps him in front of the receiver. He then either absorbs the receiver or steps into him and hand-shivers ("chucks" or "jams") him on the chest or shoulders. Make the receiver run laterally as long as possible to throw off the timing of the play. When the receiver has released, he should "get into his hip pocket" and run with him, duplicating the receiver's moves.

The objective is to keep the potential receiver on the LOS as long as possible; then once he has escaped the bump, the defender must keep an inside position on him if he is playing man. He should be watching the back numbers on the jersey and sprinting to catch up. When the receiver's numbers turn away, his eyes look up, his hands go up, then his arms go up. The defender can then turn away and look up for the ball. Look up, not back, for the ball. The exception to this is when in the red zone and a fade is being run: then definitely turn toward the receiver because the ball will be thrown high and outside.

Watching the receiver's head and hands tells the defender when to look for the ball. Some coaches have the defender concentrate on the turn of the head and the focusing of the receiver's eyes. The eyes may open wider as the ball approaches. Other coaches have the defender watch the hands and arms. As the arms come up in preparation for the catch, the defender turns and looks up for the ball. The defender should be aided by his teammates calling "ball" as the ball is released.

Once the ball is in the air, the defender plays the ball. His inside position gives him an effective advantage in intercepting or batting down the ball—if he has remained close to the receiver. If the defender does not turn to play the ball and the ball hits him, he may be called for pass interference because he was playing the man rather than the ball. This is particularly true if the defender sees the arms raise and he raises his arms to block the receiver's vision without looking for the ball.

When a defender turns to look for the ball, he often unconsciously moves closer to the ball and away from the receiver. Because of this, the man-to-man defender should be coached to lean in the receiver's direction as he turns. This reduces the chance of a completion over the defender's head.

A newer technique used by many teams is to have the defender watch the arms of the receiver. As they come up, he grabs the far shoulder with his near hand and rips through the near elbow with his far hand. (If the receiver is to the right and outside of the defender, he would hit the left elbow of the receiver with his left hand and grab the right shoulder of the receiver with his right hand.) Normally, the ball will have hit the receiver's hands just before the defender hits him, so the receiver is playing the ball, not the man.

The man-for-man defender must be particularly conscious of the types of patterns that should work most effectively against him—the out and up, the hook and go, the post corner, and the lean-in (on the defender) and breakout.

The double fake is better countered by watching the eyes. The adept receiver may raise his hands on a fake (the hook, the out, or the post move of the double-cut pattern), but his eyes will not bulge in anticipation of the catch.

The next responsibility begins when the defender recognizes that the play is not a pass or when he sees that the pass is thrown out of his area. When the ball is snapped, the defensive back, who is playing a zone defense, thinks "pass" as he reads his keys. If the key definitely shows "run," he adjusts his backward movement and begins his movement forward or laterally into his proper rotation or pursuit path.

The man-for-man defender must listen for verbal instructions from his teammates to alert him for "pass," which he is covering, or "run," which will take him out of his pass-coverage responsibility and get him into a pursuit path. If he is covering the pass and hears "ball," he can look for the ball and play it rather than play his man.

When the pass is thrown into another area, the defender must sprint to that area in the hope of

1. making the tackle if the pass is complete;
2. catching the tipped ball if it is short and tipped by a linebacker, or long and tipped by the receiver or the covering back;
3. stripping the ball if it is caught by the receiver;
4. recovering a fumble if one occurs; or
5. blocking for a teammate if he has intercepted the ball—the receiver should be the first target for a block.

Stripping the ball from the receiver can be done as he is catching it or after it has hit his hands. When the receiver has his back to the defender, such as in a hook pattern, the defender can bump him hard with his chest while bringing his hands under the receiver's elbows and ripping the arms outward and upward. This is called "playing through the receiver." The defender's contact should occur just as the ball contacts the receiver, not before (see Figure 17.5).

Another type of strip on a hook or comeback type of pattern comes from top to bottom, with the defender bringing his arms around the receiver and downward, attempting to make contact with the ball and forcing it downward (see Figure 17.6).

When stripping from the side, the defender should grab at the receiver's far arm with his own far arm (so going to the right he should grab the receiver's right arm with his right arm). The reason to go for the far arm is that it is the hand on the far arm that is primarily responsible for stopping the ball on the catch.

Figure 17.5 Out and up strip

17.7 Near arm strip

Figure 17.6 Up to down

If the far arm of the receiver cannot be reached, the defender can reach with his near arm for the near arm of the receiver while wrapping up the receiver with the far arm and making the tackle. If he is moving to his right and the receiver is moving and ahead of him, he can reach for the receiver's left arm with his left arm while wrapping up the receiver with his right arm. This is more effective if the ball is thrown ahead of the receiver and he is reaching for it (see Figure 17.7).

Supporting the run responsibilities are dependent on the defensive theory. The cornerback may

have the wide responsibility on a sweep or option. However, that responsibility may be given to a safety, who might be able to read the run more quickly because he is more likely to be playing a zone or, if in a man-for-man defense, watching the tight end on his side (see Figures 17.8 and 17.9).

A "hard corner" may take an "outside-in" support movement, attempting to stop the flow and turn it in to the linebackers.

More often, however, the defensive backs use the sideline as a twelfth man and take an "inside-angle out" on the support. The backs away from the point of attack should take the path necessary to make certain that they can make the tackle if necessary.

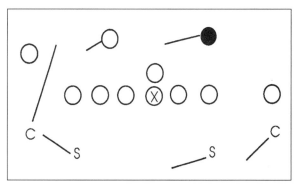

Figure 17.8 Corner supporting the wide run from wide position, safety rotating

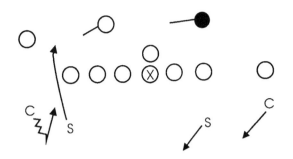

Diagram 17.9 Safety supporting the wide run, corner in a secondary support resposibility

This requires a deeper angle for the backs farthest from the point of attack.

Defensive backs must never be knocked down. They have plenty of room in which to maneuver and should use their hands to play off the block.

Playing the blocker is another skill that defensive backs must master. Often the defensive back will have room to maneuver around the blocker who is moving fast. A simple fake one way and a move the other may be sufficient to get the blocker out of the way and be ready to make the tackle. This can be used if the ball carrier is some distance from the blocker.

If the blocking is well timed and the ball carrier is close to the blocker, the defensive back must meet and defeat the blocker.

When this is necessary, the defender must drop his weight over the leg with which he will make his lift (usually the inside leg). He anchors his back leg to absorb the blocker's hit. He gets his pads under the blocker's.

He rips with the arm over the forward leg. The other arm, usually the outside arm, punches up through the blocker's shoulder. The elbow must stay close to the body and under the shoulder. The palm and fingers should be up.

Tackling must be "sure" in the secondary. For this reason, the defensive backs may tackle high. They should be adept at working the high-form tackle. They must be able to slow up the ball carrier to allow the pursuit to catch up.

When tackling, the defensive back is not concerned with knocking the ball carrier backward but with "wrapping him up" with his arms or forcing him out of bounds. The defensive back should never allow the ball carrier two ways to go; he must always take away one path, then make the tackle.

Be alert for the pass at all times. Teams are often apt to pass

1. after a time-out;
2. after penalties on the defensive team;
3. at the end of the half or game, if behind;
4. after a substitution;
5. after a sudden change of possession (fumble, interception, long kick return);
6. on first and ten, especially in four-down territory;
7. on second and short;
8. on third and long;
9. after an injury to a defensive back or linebacker.

Goal Line

The closer the offensive team moves to the goal line, the closer the defenders must play the receivers. Most defenses call for a tight man-to-man, even a bump-and-run, type of defense in this area. Because of this, the defensive secondary must be aware of pick plays with a flanker and tight end or two tight ends crossing.

DRILLS

1. Three Steps and Turn—see Chapter 12.

2. Running Backward and Reacting to the Ball. This drill can be done backpedaling or running. The player gets to his zone and continues backward. As the passer looks, the defender turns his body in the direction that the passer is looking. When the passer makes the "long-arm" action of the pass, the defender breaks for the ball in the direction that the passer is stepping.

   A variation of this is the Three-Passers Drill. The deep-three defenders each have a passer to watch. The coach tells each of the three passers to do the same thing (three-step drop, throw right corner; roll right, throw back left; boot left, and so on). With this drill, all the rotations can be practiced and three defenders get work at the same time.

3. Backpedaling. Once the technique of backpedaling has been learned, the player is taught to weave, running a serpentine or "S" pattern and backpedaling at 30- to 45-degree angles.

   Another backpedaling drill is to align the defensive back 5 yards from the receiver. On the signal, the receiver runs at the defensive back to tag him. The defender works on speed of backpedaling.

4. Backpedaling and Reacting to the Ball. Defender starts in his backpedal, watching the coach's eyes. The coach looks to an area and throws.

5. Running into the Ball (Interception Drill). This drill gives the defender practice on catching the ball when moving into it. The speed of the pass can be increased as the defenders become more adept at catching. They can improve their ability to catch by softening the catch (reaching for it and giving with it to cushion it).

6. Line Drill. Start with one receiver on each hash mark and a defender in the middle of the field. The receivers start downfield while the defender retreats. The coach can throw to either receiver. This shows the defensive back that he can cover a wide lateral area if he has sufficient depth and reacts on the passer's long-arm action. The drill can also be performed across the field, with the receivers running on yard lines 20 yards apart and the defender on the yard line between them.

CHAPTER 18

KICKING FUNDAMENTALS

"Making the breaks that win."

Perfecting the fundamentals of the kicking game help you to protect against the game-breaking miscues that often occur in the kicking game.

The Long Snap

The punt long snap is one of the most important skills in football. It is often difficult to find a good long snapper. Professional teams often draft a lesser player if he is an effective long snapper.

Legendary coach Paul "Bear" Bryant estimated that 98 percent of blocked punts occur because of a poor center snap.

The long snapper need not be your center; some teams use a reserve quarterback. With so many teams using the spread punt (with the punter 12 to 15 yards back), there is not as much need for the center to block, just to snap fast and accurately.

The snap should take .7 seconds to get the ball back 10 yards, .75 seconds if the punter is 13 yards back, and .8 seconds if the punter is 15 yards back. The snap can be made directly from the ground or by picking up the ball, then snapping it. The snap directly from the ground is fastest and is definitely the preferred method.

The snapper's stance should be such that his feet are a good distance from the ball so that he can reach out comfortably.

The feet should be even, with the toes equidistant from the line of scrimmage. If one foot is back, it may cause the ball to drift to the other side. Most

Figure 18.1 Snapper stance

of the weight should be on the balls of the feet; little weight should be on the football.

The strong arm takes a grip as if the ball were to be a forward pass. The last two fingers usually grip the laces. The other hand can rest on top of the ball and will aid in keeping the ball straight. With both arms moving between the legs, errors that would move the trajectory right or left are minimized (see Figure 18.1).

The target should be the inside thigh or knee of the punter's kicking leg. The punter should give a target with his hands. This low target is important because snappers tend to snap too high rather than too low—especially in the heat of a game. If the snapper aims at the knees and snaps 2 feet above the target, the ball will still come to the punter's waist. He would have to miss the target by 6 feet or more in order to snap it over the punter's head. (Many punters give a target at chest or shoulder level. When the snap is 2 or more feet above this high target, the punter must reach or jump and will lose his rhythm.) The snap count should be up to the center.

The snap should be hard at the target. The presnap movement of the center's hips should be minimal. Most snappers raise their hips just before starting their backward snapping movement. This upward hip action signals punt-blocking teams to start their charge and get a jump on the offense.

As the snap is made, the snapper must watch his target until the ball has left his hands. The palms of the hands finish upward as the follow-through is completed. The snapper must follow through with both arms; then, as the ball is released, snap them forward as the head is quickly lifted upward looking for someone to block.

The center blocks passively, as in a pass-protection block. Once this second responsibility is completed, he can release downfield toward the punt receiver. The other men in the punt-coverage wave set their lanes by where the center is moving.

Guards and tackles may line up with their heads at the snapper's number and in a two-point stance. At the snap, they can step back and absorb the charge of the defender or they can attack forward for two seconds, then get into their punt coverage responsibilities.

The field goal and extra point snap must be both fast and accurate. Since the kick must be away in 1.2 to 1.4 seconds, the snap should be in the holder's hands in .4 to .5 seconds. Accuracy is more important than speed, however.

The snap should be low, between 1 and 2 feet off the ground. One foot high is perfect. If possible, the laces should be pointed upward as they hit the holder's hands. Since the distance from the snapper to the holder is always the same, it is possible to put the laces where you want them most of the time.

It is quite simple to get the laces on top. Let the snapper take his normal grip and snap several times. Note where the laces land in the holder's hands. It should be nearly the same each time. Then adjust the laces for the center's grip. For example, if the laces continue to be on the bottom when the holder catches it, just rotate the ball 180 degrees from where the snapper had it originally. If the laces are off by 90 degrees, the snapper will have to turn the ball 90 degrees one way or the other in order to make them land high in the holder's hands.

Punting

The punter will set up at 10 yards in the tight punt formation, at 12 or 14 for a high school spread punt, and at 15 yards for a college spread punt.

The stance of the punter is leaning slightly forward with the feet parallel or the kicking foot slightly forward. The legs should be shoulder-width apart with the weight on the balls of the feet. The punter should be ready to move right or left—always expecting a bad snap. The hands should give the snapper a low target, just inside the kicking-leg knee (see Figure 18.2).

The punter should wear low-cut shoes and remove the tongue of the shoe and kick without a sock. He should tie his shoes on the inside of the shoe so that the knot will not contact the ball.

Figure 18.2 Punter's stance—giving a low target

The mechanics of the punt start with the punter moving in front of the ball. If the ball is snapped to his right, he steps right with his right foot, then moves his left foot to the right and reestablishes his stance. He should never reach for the ball, but always move his whole body in front of it. He looks the ball into his hands, then adjusts the laces to the right—to a "one o'clock" position, if right-footed—as he starts his first step with his kicking leg. Both the laces and the valve are "dead spots," which should not hit the foot. This is very important, because the punter's foot will drive halfway into the ball on contact and the ball will bounce faster off the foot the more it is compressed. Kicking a dead spot will reduce the reaction of the ball off the foot (see Figure 18.3).

If the ball is over his head, he should back up and reach up for it. If it is way over his head, he must turn and run back. The punter should then run away from the opponents and kick the ball. If it would be blocked, he should just run with it.

Figure 18.3 Holding the ball for the punt

The punter keeps the ball out away from his body from the catch to the kick. It should not be brought into the body. The punt can be a two- or three-step kick. The two-step kick is explained below.

The first step is with the kicking leg. It is a short step made as the ball is being adjusted.

The second step is a normal-length step. During this step the punter makes the final adjustments to the ball and prepares it for the drop.

Most punters angle the ball slightly inward and downward so that it will spiral better. The inward angle should have the front end of the ball over the big toe or slightly outside it. Experience will teach the punter the correct angle for him.

During this second step, the ball is brought up to chest height and held away from the body. The ball should not be lifted or lowered from this chest-height position. The head should be down with the eyes on the ball. At the finish of this step, the kicking leg starts forward.

The kicking movement begins as the ball is dropped during this forward whip of the kicking leg. The body must continue to lean forward. The drop is the most important part of the punt. The punter should experiment with several methods of holding the ball so that it drops consistently. One constant is that the distance the ball should be dropped should be as short as possible. The longer the ball is in the air, the greater any mistakes in the drop are magnified. Also, when there is a wind, errors are magnified.

The kicking-side hand is near the back of the ball and on top, with the other hand forward and on top. The ball should be dropped from a spot over where the kicking leg will swing; it should not be dropped in the center of the body.

A punter with a "quick" leg can drop the ball from a lower point. A punter with a slow leg must drop it from a higher position in order to get the ball to the foot at the proper spot. For a higher punt, hold the ball higher and closer to the body. For a lower punt, such as one into the wind, the ball should be held lower and farther from the body.

If the ball is dropped correctly, the nose will drop earlier than the rear of the ball. This allows the ball to be angled downward as it hits the instep. It should be at the same angle downward as the angle of the foot. A correct drop and foot contact will result in a spiraled kick.

If the nose of the ball is too far down or the toe is up at contact, the ball may be kicked end over end, with the front end going upward and backward. This results in a very ineffective punt, which will be short and which will probably bounce back toward the scrimmage line after it hits. If the ball is not angled downward sufficiently, the rear tip may be contacted first and another end-over-end kick, with the back end of the ball going up and forward, may result.

The kicking action starts with the kicking leg back. It is whipped forward through the ball. The kicking foot is extended so that the top of the foot continues in a straight line from the lower leg. For most punts, the ball should be contacted just below knee level. This should give the punt good height. In cold weather, the ball should be contacted higher because it will not compress as much so will leave the foot quicker.

The height at which the ball is contacted determines the trajectory of the ball. If the ball is being kicked high and short, it indicates that the ball is being met too far above the ground. Meeting it too high will also generally reduce the time that the ball is on the foot. The kicking leg may also be nearly fully extended if the ball is met too high. Both of these factors affect the amount of force imparted to the ball.

The follow-through should be as high as possible. If the kicking leg is stopped quickly, it means that the leg was slowing down as the ball is on the foot. This takes speed off the ball. The force of the kicking action tends to give the body a rotating motion, forcing the kicking leg to finish on the opposite side of the body. This must be eliminated or minimized for maximum efficiency.

A hang time of about 4 seconds is essential if you are covering the kick, rather than kicking it out of bounds. Some punters get hang times of over 5 seconds. An excellent hang time for high school is 3.8 seconds, for college kickers 4.3, for pros 4.5.

An acceptable hang time would be .1 of a second per yard from the line of scrimmage. So a 38-yard kick should have a hang time of 3.8 seconds. This would be acceptable for high school.

Individual differences will account for some variation in technique. A punter with shorter arms probably needs to hold the ball closer to its end. The long-armed player may hold it more in the middle. The punter with less ankle flexibility may need a greater angle of the ball to the foot so that the toe does not contact the ball and create an end-over-end punt.

Angling the punt to the "coffin corner" is done by turning the body toward the target after catching the snap. The point of aim is determined by whether the punt drifts after it is kicked. A good punt will go straight, but some punters get a drift. This drift is usually to the side of the punting leg, so a right-footed punter may get a drift to the right. If so, his target will not be in line with the arc of his kicking leg. If this drift is common for your punter, he can aim at the goal line if he is right footed. A lower punt will generally go straighter to the target and will vary less in the wind.

The pooch punt is aimed down the middle. It may be fair caught at the 10 or allowed to bounce by the receiver and downed by the punting team. The pooch punt is easier to teach. The punt is kicked high to allow the coverage to get down under the punt and force the fair catch or down the ball before it goes into the end zone. The ball should be held with the nose up and kicked with the toe up. This will increase the chances of the ball bouncing straight up after it hits the ground.

The time of the punt is dependent on the distance the punter is from the snapper. At 12 yards, the punt should be away in 2.0 seconds, at thirteen yards in 2.2, and at 15 yards in 2.3. If it takes .3 seconds longer than the above-noted times, there is a very good chance that the punt will be blocked if the opponents are rushing.

The Place Kick

The place kick is used to score extra points, field goals, and to kick off. The older style of place kicking was the straight-ahead kick. This is quite accurate but lacks the distance of the more popular soccer-style kick used most often today. The soccer-style kick allows the player to get a longer leg whip prior to the kick, increased power from the hip rotation, and more of the foot into the ball. These three factors allow for increased force to be imparted to the ball. In addition since more of the foot contacts the ball, there is greater margin for error than in the straight-ahead kicking technique, where a slight misplacement of the kicking toe may misdirect the ball.

The hold is done from a point 7 to 8 yards behind the snapper. Because rushers are much taller than they used to be, the traditional 7-yard depth is generally not far enough back. This is particularly true when kicking off the grass and for soccer-style kickers who don't get the quick lift of the ball. The lower trajectory of a long field goal also makes a deeper hold a real consideration.

The holder's down knee is closest to the center. The other leg is flexed and near the armpit closest to the kicker. The cleats under the toe should be on the ground so that the holder can stand up, if necessary, to handle a bad snap or to move out if a fake kick is called. The hand closest to the kicker may touch the target (tee or spot on the grass) with the other hand providing the target for the snapper about a foot off the ground and slightly in front of the knee on the ground (see Figure 18.4).

As the ball is caught, the holder must turn the laces forward so that they do not affect the flight of the ball after it is kicked. Laces at the side may make the ball drift in that direction. Laces at the rear may affect the kick if the kicker's foot contacts them. The hold is done with one finger of either hand.

In holding for a soccer-style kicker whose kicks drift, the holder and kicker can experiment with holding the ball at an angle. By holding the top of the ball in the direction opposite the drift of the

Figure 18.4 Holder

ball, the drift may be eliminated. So, for a right-footed kicker whose ball drifts left, the top of the ball can be held to the right. A properly kicked ball will not drift. You may notice some pro kickers whose holds are tilted as much as 3 or 4 inches off center.

If wind is a factor, the holder can tilt the top of the ball into the wind about an inch. This will help to offset the effect of the wind.

The European soccer-style or "sidewinder" kick has greater power and is recommended by the major kicking coaches. Since the ball is contacted higher and with the thick part of the foot, there is more lineal power but less rotary power imparted to the ball. This does not allow for as much quick height on the ball.

The kicker must experiment with the exact starting point for his stance. Most kickers walk three normal steps straight back from the ball then take two small steps (about 2 to $2\frac{1}{2}$ feet each) to the side (the side away from the kicking foot). This puts them at a 30-degree angle to the ball. From this point, the kicker may step up or back another foot in order to get to the precise spot where he will be able to feel the most comfortable in his approach to the ball.

If the kicker starts too far away from the ball, greater than a 30-degree angle, the ball will generally slice to the right. If the kicker isn't far enough over laterally, less than a 30-degree angle to the ball, the kick will generally hook to the left.

Most kickers take a stance with the kicking foot back. This gives them two long steps into the kick. Whatever stance is comfortable should be used, however. Keep the head down and the eyes on the target—the tee.

As the ball contacts the hands of the holder, the kicker starts forward with his kicking leg. This step can be as short as 6 inches or as long as a few feet. He then steps with the nonkicking leg, with the foot landing even with the ball. The exact spot is dependent on the kicker. Most kickers land with the instep to the heel of the foot even with the ball. It is essential that the nonkicking foot be aligned with the desired flight of the ball. The toes point at the target (the middle of the goalposts or a wider target if a crosswind is expected to affect the flight of the ball).

The foot plant of the nonkicking foot should be 6 to 8 inches to the side of the ball. If kicking off the grass, the toe should be 6 to 8 inches ahead of the ball. If kicking from a 2-inch tee, the toe should be 2 to 4 inches forward of the tee. This placement varies a bit from kicker to kicker.

The correct placement of the nonkicking foot is essential to an accurate kick. Right-footed kickers may look for mistakes in foot placement by following these cues: If the ball hooks left (to the right for left footers), it is probably an indication that the foot is too close to the ball. If it slices to the right (to the left for left footers), the anchored foot is too far from the ball. If the kick is too low, the planted foot is too far back or the body is leaning backwards. The correct placement of the nonkicking foot is essential for an accurate kick, so it must be practiced continually. Adjust the starting point and the angle of approach until the kicking foot's plant is perfect every time.

The kicking leg swings down through the ball, contacting it about $1\frac{1}{2}$ inches below the center. The toes must be pointed down (ankle extended) throughout the arc of the kicking leg's downward swing. The knee extends quickly, called a "fast knee" by the pros. To get greater distance, approach the ball as usual but make the leg whip quicker.

The body must remain forward to obtain maximum power. The eyes must be on the ball. The body must lean forward throughout the kicking action. Being straight up or leaning backward will cause a hook or a low kick.

To get more height when kicking off the grass, the kicker can bend the knee more forward and contact the ball with the outside part of the instep. This gives a "9-iron" effect and lifts the ball quicker than when the ball is contacted with the inside part of the instep.

The follow-through should be straight toward the goalposts.

The more the body turns, the greater the chance of error. The follow-through should be high; the shorter the follow-through, the greater the chance that the leg was losing power and speed while it was in contact with the ball.

The kicker will hop on the nonkicking foot as his body moves through the ball and as his leg follows through.

Kickoff

The objective is to kick the ball consistently inside the 10-yard line with a hang time of four seconds. In order to get the proper steps, the soccer-style kicker starts 10 yards back and 5 yards to the side. Then he runs forward and kicks an imaginary ball. The coach marks the spot. The kicker repeats this several times until the run at the ball seems comfortable. Some kickers feel comfortable with a few steps; others want several. Once the steps seem comfortable, they should be marked off with the traditional stepping method.

The ball is generally teed up as straight as possible. However, individual preferences as to tilt can be considered. As the kicker approaches the ball, he will generate more speed than he would with the field goal. Because of this his strides will be longer and the kicking leg will flow through a greater arc, thus generating more speed.

Figure 18.5 Kickoff follow-through

The kicking action is the same as described for the field goal—a quick leg snap. However, power is more important than accuracy in the kickoff. For this reason, the kicker must "attack" the ball with a very quick leg action. The whole body is used to kick. It is therefore not uncommon for a kickoff man to lift his body 2 feet off the ground. After the follow-through, the kicker lands on his kicking foot (see Figure 18.5).

For soccer-style kicks from a 2-inch tee, the kicker's foot plant should be 6 to 8 inches to the side of the tee and 2 to 4 inches behind it. From a 1-inch tee, the toe should be 2 to 4 inches in front of the ball. This varies slightly from kicker to kicker. The ball is kicked just below the center of the ball.

As the ball is kicked, the hips and shoulders should be parallel to the goal line. If the ball hooks to the left (for right footers), the planted foot is probably too close to the ball. If it slices to the right, the foot is probably too far from it.

If the kicker is told to aim toward a particular spot on the field (kicking away from an outstanding returner), he should follow through into that area. As the follow-through is completed, the kicker continues directly toward the ball and is the safetyman.

The squib kick is used when a team wants to change the timing of a return or to reduce the possi-bility of a long return. It can also be used when a team does not have an effective kickoff man. The kick will not be long—probably between the 20 and 30—but it should be difficult to control and may well be fumbled by the receiver. For the squib kick, the ball is placed on its side with the long axis parallel to the goal line. The ball should be kicked to the side of the center so that it will bounce unpredictably.

Onside Kickoff

The kickoff specialist must also know how to perform the onside kickoff. One method is simply to kick the ball softer straight downfield about 12 to 15 yards deep, then recover it.

A second method is to kick high on the ball—the "tipoff" kick. If properly done, this makes the ball take a short hop, then a high bounce, which should enable the cover men to get to the ball and outnumber the receivers at the point where the ball will come down. This should be aimed at the sideline about 12 to 15 yards deep.

Catching the Kicked Ball

The receiver must learn to adjust to the kicked ball, particularly the high-kicked ball. When catching the ball, the returner must keep his elbows in close to his body so that if he misses the catch with his hands, his elbows can still secure the ball. The ball should be caught in the hands, then brought down to the ball-carrying position. Then he can look up and start to run.

If fair-catching the ball, the receiver must wave his hand overhead. He should be clear in his intention. Occasionally a returner will put his hand up to shield his eyes from the sun and inadvertently signal for a fair catch.

DRILLS

For the Snapper

1. Pass the ball overhand (overhead) with both arms.
2. Snap at a target (a manager or a fence).
3. Snap the ball and quickly assume the blocking position.

For the Punter

1. Bad snap drills. Make the punter continuously aware of a high, low, right, or left snap. Even during full-team punting, the coach should occasionally (once each day) signal the snapper to snap high or low, left or right.
2. Timing the punt with a snapper (2.0 seconds or less if 12 yards back) and without a snapper (1.1 seconds or less).
3. Angle for sidelines. Aim at the goal line if a right-footed punter is punting to his right. Aim at the 12-yard line if a right-footed punter is kicking to the left "coffin corner."
4. "Pooch" punt to the 12-yard line.
5. Ball-drop drill. The punter drops the ball without kicking it. When it hits the ground, it should bounce back past the kicking foot to the outside. This will ensure that the ball has been angled in and that the nose was slightly lower than the back end.

For Place Kickers

1. Practice from a very sharp angle to the goal posts. This makes the target very small, and makes the kicker much more aware of the importance of his alignment and follow-through. Kicking from the intersection of the sideline and the goal line is a good place to use.
2. From a point 4 to 5 feet from a wall, kick a soccer ball continually into the wall to get the proper feeling of the foot on the ball.

For Returners

1. Catch punts and kickoffs as often as possible.

    a. Stand farther back than where you expect the kick to go and run into it, catching it on the run.
    b. Stand closer to the kicker than you expect the ball to land and run back to catch the kick. If a Jugs ball-throwing machine is available, use it as often as possible to catch as many kicks as possible.
    c. When it is windy, practice catching punts in the crosswind, into the wind, and with the wind.

CHAPTER

20

STRATEGY: DECIDING ON THE GAME PLAN

"Advance planning is the key to success."

Since each football team uses basically the same offensive and defensive theories throughout the year, opponents have a pretty good idea of what to expect in terms of formations, basic plays, and basic defensive alignments. Some high schools scout a team only once, but most major colleges and the pro teams scout many games. Generally, the opponent's last three games and the games they have played against your team give more than enough information to give you some insight into their basic theories and strategies, and it gives you a pretty good idea of which players will be playing in the game against you.

Percentages play a big part in developing the week-to-week strategy for an opponent. Do they have certain tendencies on third and one when the game is tied? Do those tendencies change if they are ahead or behind? Are they likely to pass from inside their own 20-yard line? Do they usually run to the wide side of the field or to the right side of their formation? When are they likely to blitz or stunt? The answers to these and hundreds of other questions help coaches develop their strategy for next week's opponent.

Developing the Offensive Strategy

Once the tendencies of the defense have been charted, the coach can begin to plan his own strategy of attack. If the opponent has shown marked tendencies against every team they have played, the coach has a good hint about what might work against that opponent.

Does the team nearly always stunt in a third-and-long situation? Do they often or always run a man-to-man defense against a short passing offense or when they are in a goal-line defense? Do they generally slant to the wide side of the field? Do they usually stay in the same pass coverage or do they vary it? What are we likely to see when we are faced with third and long? What is their goal-line defense? When do they go into their true goal-line defense? These are some of the questions that *must* be answered if an effective strategy is to be implemented for the next game.

If a team blitzes often, the quarterback should be taught to recognize the blitz before the snap. He might be able to "audible" a special play at the line of scrimmage to capitalize on the weakness of that defense. In addition, pass patterns might have to be adjusted in blitz situations. However, since a team might run only a certain blitz once or twice during a game, you will have to make certain that the quarterback and receivers can recognize special blitzes the instant they are evident.

Strategy to Beat the Defense

Offensively, you should first try to beat the opponent's basic defensive alignment, its theory of defense, and its basic pass coverage. Does the team generally run a 4-3 or a 3-4? Do the linemen charge hard, or do they play more of a "hit-and-react" technique? Are they primarily a man-to-man team, or are they basically zone?

Next, try to create a mismatch. In developing your passing strategy, perhaps you can put your best receiver on their poorest defender. Or, if they run a lot of zone defense, you might try to get two men into one defender's zone. If they play a lot of man-to-man defense, try to get your fastest receiver on their slowest defender, such as a running back against a linebacker.

In developing your running strategy you might try to create a mismatch by bringing your tight end to the side toward which you want to run so that he can double-team a tough defensive end. Or you might motion a slotback to help block at a certain hole. Maybe he could trap a lineman from the outside or perhaps help out on a double team. If a team plays a lot of zone defense and doesn't adjust well to strength when you motion a man from one side of the field to the other, you might motion your flanker to the play side and thus gain an additional blocker.

At the higher levels of football, many teams like to have at least two ways to block every problem defender. The outstanding players just can't be handled on every play with a one-on-one basic block. They have to be hit by different people, both linemen and backs, and they may have to be double- or triple-teamed if you expect your quarterback to survive until halftime.

Hall of Fame coach Hank Stram was outstanding on scouting personnel and coming up with ways to beat certain individuals. He would look for the two or three best people, the ones that had to be controlled to win, then devise ways to beat them. He didn't want a person or a team to be able to effectively do what they had been able to do best.

Against a quick-reacting linebacker, you might run play-action passes to keep him out of his zone, or a draw play might go if he reacted back very quickly to the quarterback's drop.

Coaches are cautioned not to make major changes in offense or defense. Adjustments should be made depending on personnel; whether your team or the opponent has injured players who won't play; particular weaknesses or strengths of an opponent's offense, defense, or kicking games; or tendencies such as sideline, down and distance, and so on. Will a play or a defense work because of a technical weakness of the opponent or a weakness of one of their players?

Self-scouting will tell you what you likely will do in each situation. So if you come up with a third and three and have been running your tailback most of the time, you might decide to throw deep, or let the tailback throw the running pass.

Running Game Strategy

First the coach must determine whether the opponent's running defense is based on a "hit-and-pursue" or an "attacking-and-penetrating" type of defense. Versus the strong-pursuit teams, the offense might well think first of quick plays and counters. Versus the attacking defense, the offense might think of using wide plays (especially the quick pitch) and trapping plays.

Next, the coach has to look at the basic alignment used by the opponent's defense. How many "down linemen" does he use—three, four, five, or six? Do they stay in that set or do they over- or undershift it often? Does the opponent use multiple defensive sets? If so, which of the coach's players will have to learn more than one assignment?

Is the defense balanced? Draw a line through the center, then count the number of offensive players and defenders on each side of the ball. Does the offense have an advantage to either side? If so, does the defense cover the unbalance with a slant or backfield rotation?

Does the team blitz or stunt? If so, when is it most likely to do so—on obvious passing downs, on long yardage, on short yardage, or on first down? If the team stunts, who is most likely to stunt—a middle backer, an outside backer, a safety, a corner? Or do they prefer to "twist" the linemen when rushing a pass, while keeping their backers free to pursue the run or drop for the pass?

What are the linebackers' keys? Does the team pursue too quickly? Recently a pro team that didn't run many reverses was playing against a team that pursued very quickly. For that week, they worked on a reverse. It scored.

The next week, knowing that the opponents knew about the reverse, the team faked the reverse and threw a pass for a touchdown.

A way to work on a good defensive lineman who reacts well is to influence him. In an influence block, one man false-blocks a defender, then releases on a linebacker or defensive back. A trapper then comes to take the defender in the same way he is reacting.

What is the action of the defensive backs? If they are a four-deep team, do they get their run support mainly from the safeties or from the corners? Do they play a lot of man to man? If so perhaps a wide run at a cornerback who is watching his man run deep rather than watching for the run might work.

Next, the offensive strategist must look for weaknesses in individual linemen and linebackers. Are there any injuries to the starters that must be filled by second-stringers? Is one player adept at going to his right but not to his left? Or, is one player relatively slow? Does one linebacker react too slowly to a run, or does he commit so quickly that he might be vulnerable to a play-action pass, a counter, or a special blocking technique?

Developing the Passing Strategy

Some teams, such as the Raiders, always want the threat of the deep pass. If it's there—great! If not, it opens up other things, like 20-yard curls or outs. Often those 20-yard patterns go all the way. While a "big-play" team may actually call only six or eight long passes in which the deep man is the prime receiver, it will have potential receivers running deep patterns quite often—even if the quarterback isn't paying any attention to them.

Do the opponents always use a 4-3 or a 5-2 zone? Do they always use a tight man-for-man defense? If either of these is true, the types of pass patterns, which works well against man-to-man or zone, can be put into the game plan.

On the goal line, are the opponents always in a man-to-man defense? If so, crossing patterns, hooks, or fade patterns can be put into the game plan.

In creating the mismatch, you might look for a weak defender against which you can put your best receiver. How can this best be accomplished? Perhaps he is a cornerback. If so, you can motion your best receiver toward him or flank your best receiver on his side.

When developing the passing strategy for the game, the coach should look at how he can match up his best receiver with the weakest defender. Every game plan should have the potential of hitting quick with big-play potential for each receiver.

Developing the Overall Strategy for the Game: The Game Plan

Two questions must always be on your mind in planning for a game. How can we win the take-a-way battle and how can we win the kicking game? Does the quarterback hold his arms wide when he drops? If so, you can work on a blindside strip with the blitzer driving his hands inside the passer's elbows and ripping down. Does a ball carrier always carry the ball in his right arm? Then when he runs to your right, you have a better chance for a strip. Practice it; get the players aware of when and how to emphasize the strip.

In preparing for a team, you must think of the overall theories of the opposing coach. What does he like to do? Is he conservative or is he a gambler? If he has been in the league a long time, the other coaches know a lot about him. But what about the new coach in the league?

You can use a computer analysis that records a team's tendencies over several years to give an idea as to the coach's thinking on such concerns as when he likes to block punts, if he often uses an "onsides" kickoff, when he is likely to blitz, what types of plays he likes on third-and-long yardage, what his favorite goal-line plays are. In football, it is the coach who directs the team.

Another consideration is, "How have they played a team similar to ours?" If your opponents were successful against teams similar to yours, they may use a similar strategy against you.

Most coaches call certain plays early in the game to see how the defense adjusts. The coach may look for defensive adjustments to such things as stretch motion (running a back farther out to the same side on which he started), crossing motion (having the back go across the formation therefore, changing formation strength), motion to a slot or flanker set, a formation with an unbalanced line, or the reaction of the linebackers on a play-action pass. You will also want to know what the team does in short-yardage situations.

Years ago Sid Gilman, one of the finest coaches the game has ever seen, got credit for using the first quarter to analyze the opponent's defense—then attacking that defense for the next three quarters. Many coaches have followed his lead. Bill Walsh, after working with Paul Brown (who wanted three opening plays), increased his openers to ten when he was with the Chargers, then went to about twenty when at Stanford, and finally settled for twenty-five when he was with the 49ers. Other situations you should plan for are: third and 3, third and short, short-yardage passes, red-zone offenses (from the 20 to 25 yard lines—the red zone may vary week to week), from the 10 to the 3 or 4, and from the 4-yard line to the goal line. Football is a game of varying situations; you must plan for the major situations that may occur.

Another factor that might change a team's strategy is the injury factor. If a team's best passer or receiver is out of the game, the running attack might become more important in the game plan. If the best runner or pulling guard is hurt, it might mean another type of change for the game plan.

The weather is another factor to consider. If the weather is expected to be very cold or wet, the running game might become the dominant part of the game plan. Power plays, quick plays, or counters might have a better chance of working than long passes. Or perhaps the coach might decide to punt on early downs and wait for the opponents to make mistakes, which result in turnovers.

The Offensive Game Plan

Most coaches develop a "ready list" of plays for each situation. Both the head coach, on the field, and the offensive coordinator, in the press box, will have copies of this list (see Figure 20.1).

As the game has advanced, ready lists have become even more specific for today's pro and college games (see Figure 20.2).

Developing the Defensive Strategy

Your first consideration is to take away their bread-and-butter plays, whether it is the off tackle, the isolation series, or the short passing game. You must stop what they do best and get them to try to beat you with their secondary attack.

Second, you want to know when you might get a big play. When are they likely to pass long or run a screen? If you can get a sack at this time, they lose a lot of yardage and their down. You should work a great deal on getting the big defensive play.

Look for the big defensive play, the sack or the interception, when your opponents have been forced into an obvious passing situation. In these situations, you may want to gamble in order to get the "big play."

Look for the big play on both offense and defense. Remember that when you go for the big

READY LIST

VS. _____

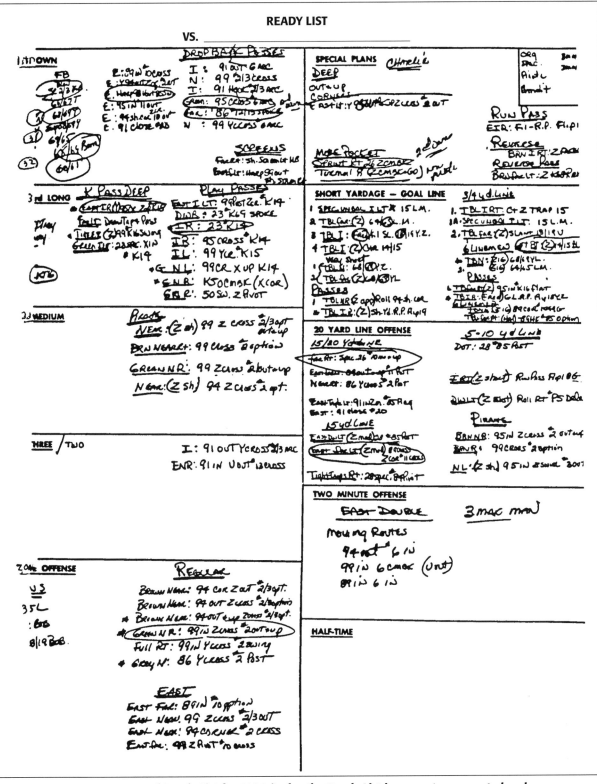

20.1 Super Bowl Ready List for 1984 (today the Ready List is computer-generated and includes more situations than this handwritten list).

Openers	Play Action	Long Yardage
1.	1.	1.
2.	2.	2.
3.	3.	3.
4.	4.	4.
5.		5.
6.	**Short Yardage**	6.
7.	*Runs*	
8.	1.	**Action**
9.	2.	1.
10.	3.	2.
	4.	3.
Base Runs	*Passes*	4.
1.	1.	
2.	2.	**Goal Line**
3.	3.	*(3-Yard Line)*
4.	4.	1.
5.		2.
6.	**Third and 3**	3.
7.	*Runs*	4.
8.	1.	*Passes*
9.	2.	1.
10.	3.	2.
	4.	3.
Base Passes	*Passes*	4.
1.	1.	
2.	2.	**+5-Yard Line**
3.	3.	*Runs*
4.	4.	1.
5.		2.
6.	**Third and 6**	3.
7.	*Runs*	4.
8.	1.	*Passes*
9.	2.	1.
10.	3.	2.
11.	4.	3.
12.	*Passes*	4.
13.	1.	
14.	2.	**+10-Yard Line**
15.	3.	*Runs*
16.	4.	1.
17.		2.
18.		3.
		4.
		Passes

Figure 20.2. Game Plan Call Sheet

1.
2.
3.
4.

+20-Yard Line
1.
2.
3.
4.
5.
6.

Attacking Blitz
1.
2.
3.
4.

Nickel
Runs
1.
2.
3.
Passes
1.
2.
3.
4.

Prevent
1.
2.
3.
4.

Last Six Plays
1.
2.
3.
4.
5.
6.

Attacking Stunts
1.
2.
3.
4.

Attacking Fronts
1.
2.
3.
4.

Attacking Coverages
1.
2.
3.
4.
5.
6.

Audibles
1.
2.
3.
4.

4-Minute Offense
Runs
1.
2.
3.
4.
Passes
1.
2.
3.
4.

Backed Up
Runs
1.
2.
3.
4.

Passes
1.
2.
3.
4.

Notes

2-Minute Offense
(3-Play Sequences)
1.
2.
3.

1.
2.
3.

2nd-Half Considerations
1.
2.
3.
4.
5.
6.
7.
8.
9.
10.

Screens
1.
2.
3.
4.

Specials
1.
2.
3.
4.

Figure 20.2. Game Plan Call Sheet, *continued*

play, you must gamble—but it's not like Las Vegas. Gamble when the odds are in your favor.

You will want to know how to get to the opponent's quarterback. Does he always drop back? Does he scramble a lot? When he does, is it usually to his right? Does he look for a hole in the middle to run through if his receivers are covered? You will certainly prepare differently for a pure drop-back passer than for one who runs often. Keep in mind the old coach's maxim to "rush to a good passer and drop back defenders against the poor passer."

Against a team with one outstanding receiver, you might decide to double-cover him all the time (or perhaps only in certain passing situations). Or you might plan to just cover him with your best defender. Against a team with a good short passing attack, you might decide to go man to man often.

The scouting report may reveal that the team plays very conservatively inside its own 30. This means that the defense can become more aggressive and perhaps downplay the possibility of a pass. The report may show that the team favors running to its right or to the wide side of the field. This could signal the defensive coordinator to slant the line or stunt a linebacker into the expected flow of the play.

Perhaps your linebackers have been taught to key the guards, but the opponents never pull the guards or double-team with them—so a better key might be found for that game. Or maybe your defensive backs have been taught to key the offside tackle and end to determine whether it is a run or pass play. But if the tackle never releases immediately downfield, a new key may have to be found for your backs.

Perhaps you can shake up the offense with a change of pace, or something the opponents have not seen before. In the 1985 Citrus Bowl game, Ohio State started rushing Robbie Bosco of BYU with only two men while dropping back 9. This confused BYU. As BYU began to make adjustments, Ohio State began rushing three, four, or more and blitzing others. The strategy was highly effective in that BYU scored only one touchdown in its 10-7 defeat.

Kicking Game Strategy

The kicking game is a highly scouted aspect of football. It is an area in which many "breaks" can be made, especially if they are planned.

Among the things to consider when the other team is kicking off are the average distance of its kicks, the average hang time, the type of kick coverage, and the speed of the kickoff team. If your opponent's kickoff is generally short, you may emphasize the return that week. If the kicking team coverage stays in lanes like they are supposed to do (about 3 to 5 yards apart) a middle return will probably work best. If they converge quickly on the ball, a wide return will be best. If most of them converge but those responsible for the wide plays stay wide, then a trap return will probably work best. If the kicking team crosses its widest men to make it more difficult to trap, this must be considered in setting up the blocking rules.

When you are kicking, you must consider the best return man for the opponents and kick away from him. You must know whether your opponents are likely to wedge, cross-block, or trap in order to prepare your coverage people for blocks from the side or from the front (such as occurs in a wedge return).

If the other team peels back quickly on the kickoff, you might consider an "onsides" kick. In the 1966 Rose Bowl game, UCLA pulled off what might have been the biggest upset in this traditional game. Top-ranked undefeated Michigan State was favored by two touchdowns. After a fumbled punt, UCLA scored. They kicked onsides and recovered, then quickly marched 42 yards to score. The Bruins got all of their 14 points without the Spartans touching the ball. Then they held on to win 14-12. Tommy Prothro, the UCLA coach, was a championship bridge player as well as a highly successful coach. His strategic and tactical decisions won a good many games for him—at the card table and on the gridiron.

When the other team is punting, you must know how many seconds it takes for the center to snap the ball to the kicker and how long it takes the punter to get the ball off. (Taking more than 2.2 seconds is usually a signal that the punt may be blocked.) Does the punter take long steps? Is the center likely to snap high or on the ground? If so, you can work on a block.

While the rules no longer allow the defensive players to hit the snapper, you may still bother him a bit if you put a man or two in the A gaps. He may snap extra hard so that he can quickly set himself to protect. This hard snap makes it more likely that he will snap high, thus increasing the time it takes to punt and increasing the likelihood of a blocked punt.

As the punting team, you want to make certain that you get the punt off. But if a team never rushes your punter, you might have him hold the ball for a second before he kicks it—in order to give your coverage people a chance to get further downfield. If they hit and peel back to set up a return, you might fake the punt and pass or run. If they always rush the punter, the fake punt might work. Should you decide to use a fake, maybe a pass into the area vacated by their rushers might work. For the punt return, coaches generally don't make any personnel changes. However, if the other team has had a personnel change it might affect who and how you would double-team to slow up their punt coverage.

The Challenge of Making Strategic Decisions

Some teams stay very basic with their offense and defense. The idea is to minimize their own mistakes. Other teams look for technical advantages and vary their attack and defense somewhat from week to week.

Sometimes the strategy hinges on pregame publicity. In 1904, Coach Fielding Yost at Michigan publicized the fact that his 265-pound lineman, Babe Carter, would carry the ball near the goal line. In the game, he inserted Carter as a back when his team got near the goal line. Carter faked, and another back scored.

The coaching staff generally sees more things they can do than the team has time to practice. The major question is whether the time spent teaching changes in offense, defense, or kicking will be more productive than spending time polishing the basic plays and defenses.

Most coaching staffs will not go "out of character" for a big play. They won't change a basic run or pass play just to gain a small advantage, because the practice time it would take to perfect the changes would not be worth the expected result. When they do make changes, it is more likely to be in the passing game than in the running attack, because passing changes are easier to install. Passes usually involve only two or three people, while a running change requires the whole offensive unit to be involved in the learning process.

Defensively, you not only must be prepared for what an opponent has done, but also for what it might do. The "what if" part of the preparation can drive you crazy. What if the players have their reverse man throw a pass? What if they run a hook and lateral? What if they try a reverse on the kickoff?

For many coaches, the week-to-week strategic adjustments are the most interesting and challenging aspects of the season. This is, perhaps, the major factor in the "violent chess match" of football.

To effectively plan your strategy for the next game, you must understand your opponents' mentality. Why do they use a certain formation? Why do they use a certain personnel grouping? What are they thinking in each down and distance situation when tied, ahead, behind? Why do they use motion or shifting? When behind late in the half or at the end of a game, does their mentality change (i.e., in their two-minute offense)?

Here are some questions you might answer when analyzing your opponent's videos, both during the season and in the post season analysis:

- If your opponent uses personnel groupings, what is the purpose of each group and who is the most productive member of the group?

- Does each grouping bring with it one or two formations—or are nearly all formations possible no matter what the personnel grouping?
- Is shifting or motion a pattern with certain groupings?
- When is the strength of the formation put into the boundary?
- Does motion by a specific player indicate a particular type of play or pass pattern?
- Does any type of motion or shift tip off a certain type of play?
- How effective is the tight end—as a blocker or receiver?
- Does the tight end flex or split—and if so, is he a deep threat?
- If two tight ends are used, do they have different strengths that should be accounted for?
- Is the tight end shifted or motioned—and if so, is it to gain a route or protection advantage or to lead a ball carrier?
- Is there a rotation of running backs—and if so, does each back have tendencies?
- Are the running backs used in patterns—and if so, what patterns?
- Does the quarterback have particular strengths and weaknesses? How does he handle a strong rush? Is he mobile? Are his elbows carried wide (where he can be stripped) or inside the line of the torso? Is he sturdy?
- What areas and receivers does the QB favor? What throws can he make consistently? Where is he likely to be intercepted? Does he look off the defense—and if so, when?
- How broad is the basic run package? How many draws, traps, options, counters?

- From shotgun, what is the run game? What is the ratio of runs by the QB and the running back?
- If boots are used, when are they most likely to be run?
- What is the base pass protection scheme (man, zone, slide, and so on)? Do they vary from it? If so when? How many players are committed to their base protection (linemen only, one back, tight end)? Is there a weak man or a weak area in the protection?
- How do opponents handle blitzes? What is their hot package? Who is the hot receiver keying?
- Is the speed option a significant part of the one-back or shotgun package?
- Is sprintout an integral part of their offense or is it used for pressure adjustments?
- How do they screen? Who are the most likely receivers? Where are the screens thrown?
- Who is the "go-to" guy on critical passing downs?
- What is their red zone and goal-line mentality? How does it vary from their open-field mentality?
- When do they use one-back or empty sets? What routes are most likely to be used?
- Do they have a bunch formation, or do they motion to a bunch formation? What do they do from this?
- How do their big plays come about—on their skill or their opponent's ineptitude?
- Is their offense patient?
- What defenses, blitzes, or stunts have been giving them the most trouble?
- Can we create a defensive look that will be effective?

CHAPTER

22

TACTICS: THE ADJUSTMENTS DURING A GAME

"Sound, quick thinking is essential."

Perhaps the toughest part of coaching is making the necessary tactical adjustments during a game. Seeing an unexpected defense, a substitute starting in place of a regular, being hurt by new plays, different formations, or new types of motion—all can force quick adjustments in the game. Also, seeing how opponents adjust to things you have done can force some quick thinking on the coach's part.

Information on the new "wrinkles" of an opponent usually comes first from the coaches in the press box. Each one is responsible for charting and diagnosing some aspect of the opponent's offense or defense. They are usually quick to make suggestions for adjustments. Perhaps you hadn't practiced these adjustments since the early part of the preseason, but they are still in your playbook. Sometimes you even must make an adjustment that you haven't practiced.

Intelligent tactical decisions play the percentages. Going for a first down on fourth and 2 on your opponent's 45 is generally not as good a percentage play as a punt. However, if it is late in the game and you are behind, your chances of winning are much better if you try for the first down.

Another tactical concern is the emotional factor. This is why coaches often go for the "sure" field goal on fourth and 1 on the 1-yard line. If the defense holds you scoreless, they get high and the offense feels bad. Even a field goal makes the offense feel good and the defense feel that it has failed.

There is also the control-of-time factor. When you want the game to speed up, you run and keep the ball in bounds. When you want to extend the game, such as in the "two-minute offense" at the end of a half, you throw the ball and get out of bounds.

Tactical Adjustments on Offense

At the professional level, some tactics relate to making substitutions based on the other team's subs; most teams do this. While in the huddle, the linemen will peek at the incoming subs and alert the quarterback to a possible audible call.

One time when Dallas played the Bears, every time Dallas sent in seven defensive backs on third and long, Mike Ditka called for a draw play. When the Cowboys made their adjustment and started going for running the back, the quarterback faked the draw and threw long to set up a key touchdown.

Some years ago Kansas City planned to stop the Raiders' running attack with five defensive linemen rather than their normal four-man front. It took the Raiders by surprise. But they soon realized that in playing a 5-2 alignment up front that they had to play man to man in the secondary. The Raiders split Cliff Branch as an end and put one back outside the tackles in a double wing. This forced the Chief safeties to "lock up" on the wingbacks and left no free safety to help on Branch. He faked out and went to the post, which, of course, was wide open. The 50-yard touchdown forced the Chiefs out of their five-man line and allowed the Raiders to revert to their game plan, which was primarily a running attack.

Are the backs playing man to man or zone? Are they challenging you in a "bump and run" or are they playing loose? Are they doing what you expected? Do they change coverages with changes in the down and distance situations? One of your prime concerns should be the depth that their corners are playing. This can change the types of patterns you might call.

You may want to go deep early to see how they are covering your receivers. If they are too deep, maybe you can break off your patterns at 20 yards, catch the ball, and still score.

You must quickly find your opponents' strengths and weaknesses, then attack them where they are weak. Darrell Royal, the former Texas coach, may have said it best when he said "No use fartin' against thunder," and another time, "Don't get in a pissin' contest with a skunk." Both ideas emphasize the obvious—that you don't want to go at your opponent's strengths.

When it was revealed that Bill Walsh had a list of twenty or thirty plays that he was going to call at the beginning of the game, people thought he was a genius: he was going to have his coaches quickly analyze the opponents' strategy in terms of formation, down, and distance tendencies. Then he was going to attack them where they were weak. The problem was that, as other coaches heard what he was doing, they just sent in defenses without any strategic reasons—then after twenty or thirty plays they began to use what they had worked on all week.

Sometimes tactical adjustments involve nothing more than going at a substitute or an injured player. Throwing to your best receiver when he is covered by a weak defensive back or running at a weak defensive lineman are obvious tactics that are often overlooked by coaches.

One of the first adjustments that power teams look for is of the defensive tackle's play. When a "power I" team double-teams the defensive tackle over and over

again, you might expect that he will start to fight to the outside. Once this is observed, the play that hits the next hole in is called and the tackle who is now fighting to get outside is trapped out.

One of the simplest checks for defensive coverage is to run a man in motion across the formation. If he is followed by a defender, they are probably in a man-to-man defense. If the defense just shifts a bit to compensate for the change in offensive strength, they are most likely in a zone. Only the most sophisticated teams can totally disguise their coverage until the ball is snapped.

Another quick check can be done by shifting the backs. Does the defense adjust to the new strength, and if so, how do they do it? Do they shift linemen or linebackers, or do they rotate their backs? Do they slant into the shift? Once the adjustment is found, the weakness can be attacked. For example, if they slant their linemen toward the shift, you might shift, then run a quick motion back to a balanced set and run the other direction—the direction toward which you looked weak.

You might design key-breaker plays for an opponent to quickly see the defensive adjustments. If you normally pull your guards, you might pull them one way and run a sweep the opposite way to see how the inside backers and tackles react. You might run a play-action pass early to see the aggressiveness of the backers and DBs.

If the defense is stunting linebackers often, you might alert your quarterback and ends to the "hot-receiver" technique (in which the quarterback and the receivers both watch the backers). When a backer rushes, the receiver yells "hot" and goes to the zone vacated by the backer. The QB throws quickly—before the backer can make the sack.

You can use a form in the press box to analyze your opponent's defensive tendencies. As you run an offensive set or play, the press box coaches can note the various movements of the defense so that you can take advantage of any weaknesses the defense has exhibited.

Defensive Tactical Adjustments

Some teams will have several defensive teams ready depending on the tactical situation. There might be a regular defense, a nickel (five defensive backs), a dime (six defensive backs), a short-yardage (elephant) defense, and a goal-line defense. The offensive coordinator or the quarterback might wait until the defense is on the field before calling a play.

If there is a 70 percent chance of a run, you might substitute the short-yardage "elephant" defense. If there is a 70 percent chance of a pass, you would probably put in the nickel or dime defense and rush the passer hard.

Some coaches just count the number of wide receivers in the game to determine their defensive adjustment. Since a team can have from 0 to five wide receivers in on any given play, it is often a good key as to the type of play that they have in mind— the more wide receivers, the better the chance that the play will be a pass.

A weak or inexperienced player might be just the one to stunt against. He is less likely to pick up the stunt and more likely to give you the big defensive play.

Early in the regular season you have to be ready for anything. Some teams that pass a great deal may not show much of their passing attack because they don't want the scouts to see what they will be doing during the league season. Other teams may show a lot during the preseason in order to drive the scouts crazy; then in the regular season be quite basic in most of their attack.

The following two figures will help the press box coaches to note any change in the expected tendencies of your opponent's offense (see Figures 22.1 and 22.2).

Tactics in the Kicking Game

In the 1986 Rose Bowl Game, Iowa won the toss and elected to kick off. In the second half, UCLA also elected to kick off. Both teams felt that their defenses could overpower the other's offense.

Sometimes a team will give up the option of receiving the kickoff in order to take the wind at their backs. Or they may choose to go on defense because they have a strong defensive unit, or because the field is wet or the stadium is windy.

In the 1985 Ram-Bear NFC championship game, John Robinson second-guessed himself after the game when he said that he should have taken the wind rather than kicked off when he had the chance. Former Ram coach and Bear assistant George Allen said after the game that when you play in Chicago, you always take the wind, if it is blowing more than 20 miles an hour.

Many people are not aware that in high school after a fair catch the receiving team has the option of taking a regular "scrimmage down" or a "free kick down." A "scrimmage down" occurs automatically when a team takes a first and 10 option. This happens after all kickoffs, turnovers, and punts in which there is no fair catch. A kickoff is an example of a free kick down—where the opponents are not allowed to rush a kick. While it is not allowed to score points for a field goal on a kickoff, it is allowed on other free kick downs. So if a team fair-catches a ball on its opponent's 30- or 40-yard line it has the option of sending in its kickoff team, and if the kicker kicks it through the uprights, three points are scored. While this option is seldom used, it does win some games—for coaches who know the rules (see Figure 22.3).

Making the Adjustments

Some people think the quarterbacks ought to call all the plays—and a few do. But generally it is the coaches who call the plays, with the quarterback having the option of changing it (calling an "audible"). Some coaches let the quarterback call the play but have him signal the play back to the bench. The coaches must know the play so that they can concentrate on the defensive adjustments.

1. Safeties

    Quickness to zone, quickness to support run _____

    How do they cover off side receiver? _____

    Who do they key? End, WB, off End, off WB _____

    Safety responsibility? _____

    M-4-M on whom? _____

    Zones—which used _____

    Suggested formations? _____

    Suggested patterns? _____

2. Corners and outside backers (reaction to flow, to reverse) _____

    Corner responsibility on pass, M-4-M or Zone _____

      on runs to him_____

    Speed mismatches we can get _____

    Suggested formations, patterns, wide plays _____

3. Line (height of charge of each lineman) _____

    Line charge _____

    Who always plays high—wedge _____

    Who knifes in low, when—trap _____

    Nose _____

    Tackles _____

    Do any follow the pull ? _____ Influence trap? _____

4. Ends _____

    Who can be wedged _____

    Who can be trapped _____

    Suggested formations? _____

    Plays? _____

Figure 22.1. Game day analysis of opponent's defensive tendencies

5. Inside backers _____

    Key FB, TB, guards? _____

    Reaction to inside and outside plays _____

    Reaction to reverse _____

    Reaction to counter _____

    Reaction to draw _____

    Reaction to drop back _____

    Reaction to play action _____

    Reaction to screen _____

    Suggested formations? _____

    Plays? _____

Figure 22.1 Game day analysis of opponent's defensive tendencies, *continued*

Down and Distance Expected ratio Run/Pass Defenses Actual ratio R/P

1–10

1–5

2–10

2–7 to 9

2–5 to 6

2–3 to 4

2–1 to 2

3–10

3–7 to 9

3–5 to 6 Tendencies here very important

3–3 to 4 Tendencies here very important

3–1 to 2

4–3 to 10+

4–1 to 2

Figure 22.2 Down and Distance Changes from Expected Run/Pass Ratio

Versus Our Punt

Opponent's 1st man down _____ 2nd man down _____ 3rd man down _____

Punt return who is held up? _____

Punt return safety weakness—should we directional kick? _____

Versus Opponent's Punt

Punt line weakness (area we can block their punt)

Their punt: *time/distance/direction* _/_/_ _/_/_ _/_/_ _/_/_ _/_/_ _/_/_

_/_/_ _/_/_ _/_/_ _/_/_ _/_/_ _/_/_ _/_/_ _/_/_ _/_/_

Punt block spot _____

Punt return return type we might use (wall, trap)? _____

Personnel changes _____

Our Kickoff Return

Who made the tackle? _____

Who was not effectively blocked? _____

Our Kickoff

Who made tackles? _____

Who was blocked? _____

Who was out of rushing lane? _____

Were our safeties in position? _____

Our Field Goal—Extra Point

Who missed assignment? _____

Our Field Goal—Block

Their personnel changes? _____

Where is weakness in their blocking? _____

Time of kick? _____ _____ _____ _____

Figure 22.3 Kicking Game Analysis

Generally the coaches in the press box are responsible for varying aspects of the opponent's offense and defense. It is typical for a pro team on offense to have three coaches watching the defense—one looking at the defensive linemen, another at the linebackers, and another at the secondary.

If the coach responsible for the defensive backs knows that a play is to be run wide to the right from a set with two tight ends and that the offensive left end is to release downfield but the right end is to block, he might be able to pick up the way the defensive backs are keying the ends. If the safety on our right end starts playing for the pass, he is probably keying the release of the opposite end. If he comes up quick, he is probably keying the end near him. If he is keying the end near him, you might release that end rather than have him block on the next running play to that side.

Perhaps you find that the linebackers are well drilled in keying the guards. If a guard fires out at the linebacker, the backer comes up hard to hit him. But if the guard sets up to pass block, the backer drops quickly. You might then call a lot of draw plays with the guards setting to pass. If the backers come up fast, you might call play-action passes and throw just behind the backers. Maybe the linebacker on your tight end drops as the end releases.

If so, you might run a delayed play at the spot that he vacated.

When Ray Perkins was the coach at Alabama, he was asked what adjustment he made at the halftime of the Aloha Bowl against USC. He said, "We told them to stop making mistakes. Second, we told them not to lose their concentration and composure over the officials' bad calls. Third, we told them to get physical with USC." Hardly a gigantic change in strategy—but it worked. So tactical adjustments may need to be more psychological than technical. It is the coach's job to determine what is needed to win—then do it.

One of the real challenges of the game is making the tactical adjustments during a game. At the lower levels of play, including some high school games, there may be little need to make adjustments if your strategic game plan is complete. But at the more advanced high school levels and in college and pro games, adjustments are always a part of the game. The adjustments you make during a game, whether technical or psychological, may make the difference between winning and losing. You must be knowledgeable about the game, have your players prepared to make adjustments, and make the proper adjustments quickly.

CHAPTER

23

COACHING: IT'S MORE THAN Xs AND Os

While a coach must be concerned with his theory of the game and his knowledge of teaching fundamentals, there are other concerns of primary importance. The complete football program is much more than Xs and Os. The coach must relate well with his staff, his players, the parents, and the community. He must set goals, organize, and evaluate his team's progress. And, he must keep up with the game. The real crux of coaching can be seen in how the coach develops and handles the goals, organization, and evaluation of the total program.

Because of the nature of the game of football (the opportunity to regroup after every play), the game can be controlled by the coach more than can any other game. In games that have a continuous flow, such as soccer and basketball, major adjustments can be made only during timeouts. In football, a major adjustment can be made on the next play. How will you plan for this to happen?

Football, more than any other sport, is a game that is generally decided on the mistakes and errors of the teams. The number of mistakes must be reduced in order to decrease the chances of losing. The emphasis on "not losing" rather than "winning" has long been the major concern of coaches. Coaches have continually admonished themselves to "not beat ourselves" in the game. This requires that mistakes be minimized. Close games are usually "lost" by one team rather than being "won" by the other. A muffed punt, a blocked kick, a clipping penalty, a bad snap—all are errors that can be reduced or eliminated if practice is sufficient. What

practice goals will you adopt to minimize these occurrences?

One of the great advantages an experienced coach possesses is that he has seen and made so many mistakes that he probably plans his practices to minimize or eliminate the most costly game-losing types of errors. The offside penalty, the blocked punt, the unsportsmanlike conduct penalties, and the fumble are the types of mistakes that can be reduced. There is never enough time to eliminate all mistakes, but the coach can go a long way to reduce his chances of losing a game because of the "breaks." How do you plan to do this?

The coach must select goals to accomplish the most desirable outcomes for each important learning period, whether that is beating next week's opponent or preparing for the year ahead. Consequently, both long-term and short-term goals and objectives are essential to developing the most effective program.

The annual football season does not provide enough time to practice sufficiently to eliminate all errors. It is therefore essential that the coach sets goals that can be accomplished. One coach may decide that the passing offense is the most important aspect of the game. Another coach may believe that defense or kicking is most important. These are decisions based on their theories of how best to win the game. The goals you set for the year and the season must reflect your basic theories.

Goals and objectives must be set for the year, the playing season, the upcoming week, the current day, and for each drill. Without goals, the coaching staff and the players do not know where they are heading. Some goals must be set by the staff, some can be set by the players. There should be goals and objectives for every aspect of the program—from how much money is needed through fund-raising to how much contact there should be in practices.

Let's take a quick look at the area of establishing goals for full-team-contact practices. There will be great differences in the goals set depending on the level of play. For youth coaches, goals should revolve around enjoying the game. While some emphasis on conditioning and fundamentals is essential, there should be a great deal of scrimmaging—because that's what is fun.

There is little chance of injuries when 70-pounders bounce into each other. But the higher the level, the more chance there is for injury. If you run a practice for ten-year-olds the same way that Jon Gruden runs a practice, they wouldn't have a lot of fun. At the frosh level of high school, winning becomes more important. There can still be a great deal of scrimmaging because the boys aren't usually so big and fast that they can hurt each other very much. Some coaches want the frosh level to be fun so that everyone can play. This is more likely to bring them back next year. Other coaches are concerned only with teaching the system and developing a winning attitude at this level.

By the time they get to the varsity the boys range from 220 to 300 pounds and run 4.5 to 5.0 40s, so the chance of injuries increases greatly. Many coaches therefore reduce their full-contact scrimmages, opting more for thud contact. It is always a question of whether the team will be stronger with more scrimmaging or with fewer injuries to the starters. At the Division 1 level of college play, there will be a great deal of contact in the spring, with some eleven-on-eleven full-team contact during the preseason weeks in the fall. And by the time you conduct pro practices, you will find very little, if any, full contact during the season. At the highest level, the weekly goals are more likely to be recover-

ing from the bruises of the last game, working on mismatches, and perfecting the small things that may win the game—like who and how will a take-away be best accomplished, what passes will work best against the expected coverages, what blitz pickup will most likely be effective. So the overall goals and the week-to-week goals will be quite different at each level of the game.

Coaches can also help their players to set both short-term and long-term goals concerning such things as studying, attending college, preparing for a job, and so on. The effective coach up through the college level should be concerned with the total development of his players. The boy with goals and accomplishments outside of football is more likely to be the kind of boy who will be a real credit to the program. Real "pride" comes from the whole player, not just that aspect of him that plays football.

Setting conduct goals is often best done by the team members. What are the goals for living more effectively and performing better on the field? Particularly at the high school level, the players will generally be more strict than the coach would be. They should, of course, be prepared by the coach for whatever rules he would like to see. He is more likely to be an expert on the effects of smoking, alcohol, and other drugs. He should be more aware of other values that ought to be considered such as academic progress, a weeknight or weekend curfew, hair length, absence from practice or meetings, and so on.

Setting performance goals can be done solely by the coaches or in cooperation with the individual team members—making them aware of how they can be more effective players and team members. Some teams set very specific goals for such things as the number of first downs per game the team should make, the number of interceptions the team is expected to make, the amount of return yardage on each type of kick, and so on. Generally these performance goals are set by the coaches—but if the players are involved, they are given more "ownership" of the goals and are more likely to be intrinsically motivated to achieve them.

The goals should be realistic and attainable. Setting a goal of holding the opponent to minus yardage on offense or of blocking three punts during the game is probably unrealistic.

Examples of Offensive Goals

- Make 20 first downs a game.
- Average 350 yards per game.
- Have a 60/40 run-to-pass ratio in yards gained.
- Have a 75 percent 3rd down conversion percentage.

Examples of Defensive Goals

- Hold opponents to 200 yards per game.
- Intercept one of every seven passes.
- Force four turnovers per game.
- No eight-play drives.

Examples of Kicking-Game Goals

- Limit opponents' punt returns to a four-yard average.
- Average 35 yards per punt.
- Block one in ten punts.

Performance goals will be specific for each coach, opponent, and team. One coach may want a 90/10 ratio of run to pass while another may want a 50/50 ratio. If you have performance goals, you must practice effectively to meet them, or your goal setting is meaningless. Looking at the above goals, how much practice time in a week would be necessary to accomplish all those goals? You have to be realistic.

Organization and motivation are required to make certain that goals are achieved. As with goals, the organizational plans will include the long-range goals for the year, the week-to-week goals for the upcoming opponent, and the day-to-day objectives.

Effective coaches can get more done in less time, so their teams are further ahead. While some coaches practice four to six hours daily in order to be successful, others can accomplish as much in two to two and a half hours. The motivation of the players will be a major determinant in how well the skills necessary to accomplish the goals are learned.

Evaluations

Evaluation is vital to determine whether the goals are being achieved and whether the organization is effective in achieving the stated goals.

Week-to-Week Evaluations

Team members and coaches should be apprised of the accomplishment of each goal every week. This can usually be done by looking at the statistics. Individual goals can be evaluated by looking at the grades of the players for each play after the film analysis.

George O'Leary, of Central Florida, grades not only the individual plays on offense, defense, and kicking, but he looks for the big-play production of the player.

On defense he grades for tackles, tackles for loss, sacks, hurrying the passer, causing fumbles, recovering fumbles, interceptions, and deflected passes. If a player does one of these things in 20 percent of his plays, he is a very productive player; you can win with such playmakers. George has found that a player may grade out well on a play-for-play basis because he doesn't make many mistakes, but the important thing is whether he was a productive defender.

While coaches are generally well aware why they lost a game, they may not be as concerned about analyzing why they won a game. It is imperative to know what you are doing well and continue to work on these strong points.

Season-Ending Evaluations

Evaluations with all players about their progress as football players, students, and human beings is essential if the individual is to improve in each of these areas. The coach must realize that in all probability he is one of the most important people in his players' lives—often the most important person. His loving and concerned advice may well make major changes in their lives.

Every player and every coach should also be evaluated and asked for evaluations. You may find that the players have lost faith in a coach and that he is no longer effective. You may find a rotten apple among the players—a negative leader. If he can't be turned around in the off-season, you may be better without him.

Team Leadership Is Essential

Drawing out the leadership on your team is essential to making your program the most effective. While the head coach and his assistants are the major leaders, it is critical to have leadership from the team. Some leaders are verbal; others lead only by example. The effective coach will work to make certain that as many leaders as possible will emerge from the team. A major factor of leadership is wanting to succeed as an individual and working as hard as possible for that to happen. In a team game such as football where a number of players may have the same goal, one or a few players may light a fire under several others to get each to work harder and more effectively. So the true leaders tend to emerge rather than be voted in. As the players work toward team goals, the "team" begins to emerge as something more important than the self and the esprit de corps of the group reaches new highs.

It is obviously a requirement that the head coach be an outstanding leader. Mike Bellotti states that in order to be a leader, you must earn the trust of your players and their respect. You earn their trust by showing that you care about them and are willing to help them achieve their goals. You earn their respect by showing that you are fair, willing to work hard, are good at what you do, and are a person who is consistent and practices what he preaches.

Keeping Up with the Game

Since the game of football is continually evolving, the coach must keep up with changing theories. There are associations, clinics, books, and periodicals that the coach can use to keep himself updated on the game.

The American Football Coaches Association (AFCA) is the best way to keep current in the field. Coaches from every major university as well as high school and youth coaches and former coaches make up this association. Other members include foreign coaches and some of professional team coaches.

AFCA dues are inexpensive. They entitle the member entry to the annual four-day meeting in January each year, the clinic notes from the meeting, a special summer manual, and directory of members. It is the best money a coach can spend. (American Football Coaches Association, 100 Legends Lane, Waco, TX 76706; phone 254-754-9900, info@afca.com)

Local and state coaching associations often hold their own clinics. They also work to advance the profession in their area. They can be influential in developing laws or rules that are essential in the conduct of higher-level physical education and athletics.

The American Association for Health, Physical Education, Recreation, and Dance (AAHPERD) is the primary physical education organization in the country. Athletics is becoming an increasingly important aspect of this national association. State associations connected with AAHPERD are also important areas for the physical educator–coach. (1900 Association Drive, Reston, VA 22091; phone 703-476-3430)

The Football Coaches Professional Growth Association (FCPGA), provides clinics, camps, and thousands of videos and films that can be borrowed and copied. (FCPGA, 13868 Olive Mill Way, Poway, CA 92064 619-748-7566 billwilliamsfcpga.com).

The rules for your level of play must be studied. There are over two-hundred rule differences between high school and college rules and another two-hundred-plus from college to pro rules. Generally you will be provided with a rulebook and a casebook for your level of play. If you have the chance, it is a good idea to attend officials' meetings, and possibly join their association to really understand the nuances of the very complicated rules of our game.

Books and Magazines

Scholastic Coach and Athletic Director is a major magazine for coaches. *Scholastic Coach* not only presents timely articles on football and other sports but also covers other areas such as weight lifting, administration, and facilities. In addition, it can keep the coach current on available equipment. (Scholastic Coach, Box 54490, Boulder, CO 80322-4490)

Videos

Coaches Choice is the major publisher of football coaching videos and books. Check their Web site, coacheschoice.com.

Unless you can attend all of the "Coach of the Year" clinics, you will want to buy the annual publication that gives you the printed speeches of every coach at every clinic; it is definitely worth the money. If you don't have the whole set already, you can purchase previous editions.

So Onward!

Football is the greatest game ever invented. Coaching it can be the most rewarding experience of your life. There is so much to learn and to do to be an effective coach. But don't you enjoy nearly every contact with a player? Aren't you excited every time you step into the weight room or onto the practice field? As coaches we know that we must keep up with an ever-changing game and that there is always something else we can do to make our program better. It's exciting. It's invigorating. Heck, yes! It's football!

Good luck to you all. And may the only "downs" in your life be first downs and touchdowns!

GLOSSARY

Angle block: Blocking a player inside or outside who is not "on" or "shading" the blocker.

Arc block: A block on the defensive end or corner by a running back with the back attempting to block the defender in. The blocker starts wide for a few steps then attacks the defender.

Audible: Calling the offensive play at the line of scrimmage.

Back numbering: QB is 1, LH or TB is 2, FB is 3, RH or WB is 4.

Backpedal: Running directly backward; a technique used by defensive backs and linebackers.

Blitz: A defensive play in which a linebacker or defensive back attacks past the LOS.

Bomb: A long pass.

Boot or bootleg: Quarterback fakes to backs going one way while he goes the opposite way to run or pass.

Bump and run: A technique in which the defensive back hits the potential receiver on the line of scrimmage then, to slow his route, runs with the receiver.

Chop block: A block in which one player stands up a defender and another blocker hits the defender at the knees with the intent to injure the defender's knee. It is illegal.

Chucking: Hitting a receiver before the pass is thrown.

Clip: A block in which the defender is hit from behind. It is illegal.

Cloud: A commonly used term indicating the cornerback will cover the outside flat zone on a pass.

Combo or combination block: A block in which linemen exchange responsibilities.

Corners or corner backs: The widest secondary players in an umbrella (four deep) defense.

Counter: A play that ends going a different direction than the initial flow of the backs would indicate.

Crackback block: A block by an offensive player who has lined up more than 2 yards outside of the tackle and is blocking a man inside him. It is illegal.

Crossover step: A step by a lineman or back in which, when moving laterally, the player steps first with the foot away from the direction toward which he is traveling.

Curl: A pass pattern in which the receiver runs 12 to 20 yards downfield then comes back toward the passer in an open area of the defensive coverage.

Cut back: The movement of a ball carrier away from the direction he was originally running so that he can run behind the tacklers.

Cut block: A block aimed at the ankles or knees of the defender. It is illegal at some levels of play.

Cut off: A block in which a player blocks a player who is closer to the hole than is the offensive player.

Dash: A planned passing action in which the passer drops back then moves to his right or left in a planned action. The blockers move with him.

Defense: The team which is not in control of the ball.

Dime defense: A defense in which six defensive backs are in the game in order to stop a likely pass.

Dive: A quick straight-ahead play with the halfback carrying the ball.

Dog or red dog: A linebacker attacking past the LOS at the snap of the ball.

Double cover: Two defenders covering one offensive receiver.

Double option: Two players involved in the option, the QB and a running back.

Double team: A block in which two offensive players block one defender.

Down: A play which begins after the ball is stopped. There are two types of downs, a scrimmage down and a free kick down.

Down block: Linemen block down toward center.

Down lineman: A defensive lineman.

Drag: A delayed pattern in which a tight end or a wide out runs a shallow pattern across the center.

Draw: A fake pass that ends with one of the backs carrying the ball after the defensive linemen are "drawn" in on the pass rush.

Drive block: A straight-ahead block done with the hands or shoulder.

Drop: The action of the passer as he moves away from the line of scrimmage. 3-, 5-, 7-, and 9-step drops are common.

Eagle: A 5-2 defensive alignment with the tackles outside of the offensive guards and the linebackers on the ends.

Encroachment: Entering the neutral zone (the line of scrimmage bounded by both ends of the ball) before the ball is snapped. It is a penalty in high school football. At the college and pro level, it is a penalty only if contact is made with the other team.

End around: A reverse play in which a tight end or a wide out carries the ball.

End zone: The 10-yard area between the goal line and the end line.

Even defense: A defensive alignment in which there is no defensive lineman over the center.

Extra point: See *point after touchdown.*

Fade: A pass pattern used generally against a man-for-man coverage in which the receiver runs deep and fades away from the defender.

Fair catch: The opportunity for a receiving player to catch a kicked ball and not be tackled. It is signaled by waving one arm overhead. The ball cannot be advanced after making a fair catch. The team has an opportunity to put the ball in play by a scrimmage down or a free kick down.

False block: Hitting an opposing lineman on the same side as you wish him to move, used against good reacting defensive lineman.

Far: A player who is aligned away from where the ball will be run or passed. The "far" guard may trap block or the "far" back may be the ball carrier.

Field goal: A ball place- or drop-kicked over the goal posts. It scores 3 points.

Flanker: A back split wider than a wingback.

Flipper: A forearm shiver; the elbow is flexed at 90 degrees and the forearm is lifted by the shoulder muscles.

Flood: A pass pattern in which the offense sends more receivers into an area than there are defenders. It uses both a horizontal and a vertical stretch.

Flow: The apparent direction of the ball during a scrimmage play. Most plays attack in the direction of the flow. Counters, reverses, and throwback passes go against the flow.

Fold: A block in which an offensive lineman blocks the next defender on the line while the offensive lineman nearest that defender moves behind the blocker and blocks the near backer.

Forearm shiver (forearm lift or rip): A block protection technique in which the defender wards off the blocker by hitting and lifting him with his forearm.

Formation: The alignment of the offensive team. At least seven players must be within a foot of the line of scrimmage.

Forward pass: A pass thrown forward from behind the line of scrimmage. College and pro teams are allowed only one forward pass per play. High schools are allowed multiple forward passes on one play.

Free kick down: A down in which the kicking team can tee up the ball to kick (as in a kickoff) or can place kick or punt the ball after a safety. The defensive team must stay at least 10 yards from the ball. Free kick downs occur after a touchdown or field goal. They can also occur after a safety under high school rules (when the team scored against can have one scrimmage down or a free kick down in which it can kick the ball in any manner) or after a fair catch (in which the receiving team has the choice of a set of scrimmage downs or one free kick down in which it can score a field goal.)

Free safety: The safety man opposite the power side of the offensive line (the tight end). He is usually free to cover deep zones.

Freeze option: A play in which an inside fake to one back running up the middle should freeze the linebackers. The play then ends as an option play between the quarterback and another runner.

Front: The alignment of the defensive linemen.

Game plan: The offensive, defensive, and kicking strategy for an opponent.

Gap: Space between offensive or defensive linemen.

Gap defense: A defensive front with the defensive linemen in the offensive gaps.

Gap lettering: Center-guard gap is A, G-T gap is B, T-E gap is C, Outside end is D.

Goal line: The area over the inside edge of the chalk mark that marks the end of the playing field. The 10-yard end zone is beyond the goal line.

Guards: The offensive linemen on either side of the center.

Hand shiver: A defensive block protection in which the defender hits the blocker with his hands and extends his arms to keep the blocker away from his body.

Hang time: The amount of time a kick stays in the air.

Hash marks: Short lines parallel with the sidelines, which intersect each 5-yard mark on the field. They are $\frac{1}{3}$ of the way in from the sideline ($18\frac{2}{3}$ yards) for high school and college and even with the goal posts for the pro game. Every play starts from a point on or between the hashmarks.

Hitch: A quick pattern to a wide receiver in which he drives off the line then stops.

Hitting position: A balanced "ready position" in which the weight is on the balls of the feet, the knees are flexed, the torso is flexed forward, and the head is up.

Hook block: A block in which the offensive blocker must get outside of a defender who is outside of him, then block that defender in.

Hook pattern: A pass pattern in which the receiver runs downfield, stops, then comes back toward the passer.

Horizontal stretch: Forcing the pass defenders to cover the entire width of the field on a pass.

Horn block: See **Fold Block.**

Hot receiver: A receiver who becomes open because the defender who would have covered him has stunted into the offensive backfield. The receiver yells "hot" when he sees he will be open, and the passer passes quickly to him.

I formation: A formation in which the quarterback, fullback, and tailback are in a line. Maryland I has four backs in a line.

Influence: Getting an opponent to move in the direction desired through finesse.

Inside slot: A slotback aligned close to the tight lineman.

Invert: A four-deep defensive alignment in which the safeties are closer to the LOS than are the corners. They are expected to quickly assist in run support.

Jam: Hitting a potential receiver before the ball is released by the passer. It may also mean the position of the pass defender on a wide out, either up on the line or back 2 yards.

Key: Watching an opponent to determine what he or his team will be doing.

Lateral pass: A pass thrown parallel with the LOS or backward. It can be thrown overhand or underhand.

Lead: An offensive player goes through the hole and leads the ball carrier, usually looking to the inside to pick up a backer.

Lead step: A step with the foot closest to the direction toward which the player is moving.

Line of Scrimmage: An area approximately a foot wide (the width of the ball) that stretches from sideline to sideline.

Load: A block in which an offensive player coming from the inside blocks a wide defender on a wide play. The blocker will have his head and shoulders on the offensive side of the defender, and the play is designed to go around him.

Log: A block on a wide defender, which stops him from penetrating.

Loop: A defensive lineman's move from a gap to a man, a man to a gap, or sometimes from a man to another man.

LOS: Line of scrimmage.

M4M: An abbreviation for man-for-man pass defense.

Mac: Middle linebacker ("mac" means "middle back").

Match-up zone: A zone coverage in which the defenders are responsible to play man to man on various receivers, depending on the receiver's route.

Mike: Middle guard or "nose man" (Mike means "middle in").

Misdirection: A play that goes against the flow of the play, such as a bootleg, reverse, or throwback.

Muff: A mistake in catching the ball on a kicking play.

Near: The player aligned close to the point of attack. So the "near" guard may trap or the near back may be the ball carrier.

Neutral zone: The area bounded by each end of the ball, which extends from sideline to sideline and from the ground to the sky. Only the snapper can be in that zone before the ball is snapped.

Nickle defense: A defense with five defensive backs.

Nose guard or nose tackle: A defensive lineman playing on the offensive center.

Numbers defense: Defenders are given a number that tells them where to play on the offensive lineman: 0 = over center, 2 = head up on guard, 4 = head up on tackle, 6 = head up on tight end, 8 = wide; 1 = inside shade of guard, 3 = inside shade on tackle, 5 = outside shade on tackle, 7 = inside shade on end, 9 = outside shade on end. Not all coaches use all of these numbers and some will add an (i) to mean inside shade.

Odd defense: A defense that has a man on the offensive snapper. This will result in a defensive line with an odd number of players on it.

Off side: Side of the line away from where the play will attack.

Off tackle play: A play that hits in the area of the offensive tackle and end.

Offense: The team controlling the ball.

Okie: The Oklahoma 5-2 defense (Linebackers over the offensive guards).

On side: Side of the line to that the play will attack

On side kick: A short kickoff that travels at least 10 yards, which can then be recovered by either team.

Option play: A play in which the quarterback runs at a wide defender forcing the defender to either tackle him or stop the pitch to a trailing back. QB can keep or pitch.

Overshift: The alignment of the defensive linemen one man closer to the strength of the formation. This is normal for that defense.

Pass pattern: The path or route that a receiver runs in attempting to get open.

Passing tree: The potential routes that a receiver can run. When drawn together, they resemble a tree.

Penetration: The movement across the line of scrimmage by the defenders.

Pick: A pass pattern in which one of the potential receivers hits or screens off a defender, allowing his teammate to be free. It is used primarily against a man-to-man defense. It is illegal to hit a defensive back before the ball is caught, but it is legal to create a screen by stopping (as in a hook pattern) or having the receivers cross close to each other.

Place kick: A kick in which the ball is either held by a player or held by a tee. It is used for kickoffs, field goals, and points after touchdowns.

Play action: A pass off of a run fake.

Pocket: The area surrounding a passer that is being protected by his blockers.

Point after touchdown (PAT): An extra play allowed after a touchdown in which the team has an opportunity to make one point by kicking the ball through the goal posts or 2 points by running or passing the ball over the goal line (high school and college game only). Ball is spotted at the 3-yard line for this play.

Presnap read: A read by the quarterback or receivers based on the alignment of the pass defenders before the ball is snapped.

Press: A tight alignment on a wide receiver. For some coaches it means very tight, for others it means a position off about 2 yards.

Prevent defense: A defense sometimes used by a team that is ahead late in a half. It uses extra defensive backs playing deeper than usual and fewer-than-normal pass rushers.

Primary receiver: The first choice of the passer in a pass pattern.

Pull: The movement of an offensive lineman behind the line as he leads the play.

Punt: A kick made on a scrimmage down, which is designed to make the most yardage when possession is changed.

Pursuit: The movement of the defensive players to get them to a spot where they can make the tackle.

Quick count: A snap count that gets the ball in play quicker than normal, hoping to catch the defensive team unprepared.

Quick side: The side of the offensive line away from the strong side.

Reach block: An offensive lineman blocking a defender who is closer to the point of attack than himself or a tight end getting outside position on a backer who is slightly outside of him. Some coaches use the term *reach block* when a blocker is blocking down.

Read: Getting an idea of what the opponents are doing by looking at one or more of them as the play develops. It can be done by defenders watching offensive linemen or backs or by passers and receivers watching pass-coverage defenders.

Red zone: The area from the 20- to 25-yard line to the goal line. The most critical area for both the offense and the defense.

Reduced front: A defensive lineman playing closer to the center than normal. An example would be a tackle playing on the guard rather than on the offensive tackle.

Release: The movement of a receiver in leaving the line of scrimmage.

Reverse: A play in which a wide player on one side runs the ball against the flow of the other backs.

Rollout: A deep, generally wide path of the quarterback behind the other backs.

Rotation: The movement of the defensive backs to either a predetermined spot or to areas dictated by the movement of the ball.

Rove: See **Dash**.

Rover: A defensive back who can be given various assignments. He is usually playing in a defense that has a 5-2 front and three defensive backs.

Run force: The responsibility of a defender to make the runner commit to an inside or outside path once he has passed the offensive end.

Sack: The tackling of the passer before he has a chance to pass.

Safety: A 2-point play that occurs when an offensive player is tackled behind his own end zone.

Safetyman: The defensive back or backs with the deepest responsibility.

Scoop: A block in which a lineman blocks the next defensive man to the play side; this releases the next lineman out to block a backer.

Scramble: The running of the quarterback after he has been forced out of the pocket on a pass play.

Scrape: The path of a linebacker who is moving into the offensive line, usually on a key.

Screen: A pass, usually behind the LOS, after a deep drop by the quarterback. Some linemen pull to lead the receiver.

Scrimmage down: One of four attempts of the offense to advance the ball 10 yards and make another first down.

Seams: The areas between the defensive zones that are more likely to be open to complete passes.

Secondary: The safetymen and cornerbacks.

Set: The offensive or defensive alignment.

Setup: The last step of a quarterback's drop—the spot from which he would like to pass.

Shading: The defender is not head up on the blocker but part of his body overlaps the body of the offensive player.

Shift: A change of alignment from one set to another before the snap of the ball. It can be used by the offensive or the defensive team.

Shiver: A defensive technique used to protect the defender from the block. It can be done with the hands or the forearms contacting the blocker.

Short list: The list of plays most likely to be used in a game with plays listed according to each situation.

Shotgun: A formation in which the quarterback sets several yards behind the center to be able to see the field better on a pass play. More wide receivers are also used. Some runs will be made from this formation to keep the defense honest.

Shuffle: The path of a linebacker who is moving nearly parallel with the LOS as he diagnoses the play and determines how he will attack the ball carrier.

Signals: Offensive or defensive code words that tell the team which alignment and which play to use. Also the cadence called by the quarterback to get the play started.

Sky: A term used in pass coverage to indicate that a safety will cover a short flat zone.

Slant: As a defensive term it is a hard move, usually from an offensive lineman into a gap; as an offensive term it is a pass pattern, usually by a wide receiver, angling in toward the center of the field.

Slip block: See **Scoop**.

Slot: A back lined up in the area between a split end and the tackle.

Snap: The act of putting the ball in play. It can be handed to the quarterback or thrown (between the legs or to the side) to a back.

Snapper: The offensive lineman who puts the ball in play, usually the center.

Spearing: An illegal action in which a player drives his head into a player, usually a player on the ground.

Speed option: An option play in which there is no inside fake. All backs run wide immediately.

Sprint draw: A draw play off of a sprint-out move by the quarterback.

Sprint out: A fast and shallow path of the quarterback.

Spy: Keeping a defender near the line of scrimmage on pass plays in order to stop a draw play or a run by the quarterback.

Squib kick: A low, flat kickoff that is difficult to handle. It is often used when the receiving team has an effective kick returner or when the kicking team does not have a long-ball kicker.

Stack: Playing a linebacker directly behind a defensive lineman.

Streak: A pass pattern in which the receiver runs long and fast.

Stretch: To widen the defense by placing offensive men in wide positions.

Strong safety: The safety on the strong side (tight end) of the offense.

Strong side: The side of the offensive line that blocks for the power plays. Usually the side of the tight end is designated the strong side.

Stunt: A defensive maneuver in which linemen create a hole for a backer to move through the line, or a movement between defensive linemen that will allow at least one to penetrate the LOS.

Sweep: A wide offensive power running play.

Tight end: A receiver playing close to the offensive tackle.

Touchback: A play that ends behind the receiver's goal line but in which the impetus of the ball was generated by the other team. There is no score. The ball is moved to the 20-yard line for the first down.

Trap: Blocking a defensive lineman by an offensive player who did not line up close to him originally. In a trap block, the blocker will have his head on the defensive (downfield) side of the opponent, and the play is designed to go inside the block.

Triangle: Triple key for a defensive player. A blocking triangle involves the three most dangerous blockers who could attack him. For a linebacker, it would involve one or two linemen and one or two backs.

Triple option: Three people involved in two options, usually the QB and fullback or a halfback on the first option; then if the QB still has the ball, the QB and another running back involved in the second option.

Twist: A movement between defensive linemen, especially in a pass situation, in which the linemen cross hoping that at least one will get clear into the backfield.

Two-minute offense or two-minute drill: The attack used by a team late in a half when they are behind and attempting to score while conserving time.

Umbrella: A secondary four-deep alignment, usually with the corners closer to the LOS than the safeties.

Unbalanced line: An offensive alignment in which four or more linemen are set on one side of the line of scrimmage.

Undershift: A defensive alignment in which the defensive linemen have moved a man away from their normal position away from the strength of the offensive formation.

Uprights: The vertical poles that hold up the crossbar of the goal posts.

Vertical stretch: Forcing the pass defenders to cover deep even if the pass is in the short or intermediate zones.

Waggle: A pass action off a running play in which the quarterback moves wide and deep after faking to a back. Some coaches call it a *waggle* if the quarterback moves in the direction of the flow behind the backs to whom he has faked. Others call it a *waggle* if he moves opposite the flow and is protected by a pulling lineman. Most would call this a *bootleg*.

Walkaway: A position taken by a linebacker or defensive back between a wide receiver and the offensive linemen. It allows the defender to be in position to stop the quick slant pass and still be able to play a wide run.

Weak side: The side of the offense away from the tight end.

Wedge: A block in which three or more players block an area.

Wide out: A split end or flanker.

Wide receiver: See **Wide out**.

Wing: A back lined up outside a tight end (usually a yard outside and a yard back).

X: The split end.

Y: The tight end.

Z: The flanker.

Zone area pass protection: Pass-protection blockers protect an area rather than blocking a specific man. It is used against stunting defenses.

Zone blocking: Two adjacent offensive linemen double-team a down lineman, while both watch the backer. Whichever side the blocker moves, that lineman releases and blocks him. The rule is "Four hands on the lineman, four eyes on the backer."

Zone defense: A pass coverage in which the linebackers and defensive backs protect areas and play the ball rather than watch specific men.

INDEX

"A" formation, 25
Actual alignment, 34
Aiming point, 30
Air Force, 47
Air Force flex bone, 41
Alignment(s)
    defensive, 69–73
    of offensive line, 103
    secondary, 78–79
All-curl pattern, 64
Allen, George, 199
Allen, Marcus, 26, 45
"Alumni zone," 13
American Association for Health,
        Physical Education,
        Recreation, and Dance
        (AAHPERD), 208
American Football Association, 9
American Football Coaches
        Association (AFCA), xiii, 1,
        108, 208
Amos Alonzo Stagg Award, 1
Angle block, 130
Arc block, 146
Arm lift, 128
Arm lift and charge technique, 136
Army, 49
Assignment defense, 22
Assumed on inside man, 34
Assumed on outside man, 34
Attitude, xiii, 8
Auburn University, 26
Automatics, 37

Back in motion, 46–48
Backer and safety blitz, 52
Backfield shift, 45
Backpedaling, 94, 121, 151–52
Backs, placement of, 44–45
Balague, Gloria, 9

Balance, 81, 96
Balanced line, 43
Balanced wing T, 41
Ball
    carrying the, xiv, 118–19
    passing the, 121–23
    path of, xiv
    pursuit to the, 137
    raking the, 98
    receiving the, 123–25
    stripping the, 98
Ball control theory, 13–14
Ball shape, 49
"Base blocking" rules, 34, 38
Beamer, Frank, 12, 83
Bellotti, Mike, 208
"Big on big," 52
"Big play" approach, 14–15
BlisScout, 170, 171, 173
Blitz, forward pass against the,
        67–68
Blitzing, 77
Block protection, 128
Blocking angles, creating, 43
Blocking for the running play,
        29–38
    and adjusting to unexpected
        defenses, 37
    code words used in, 35–37
    defensive calls for, 35
    designing schemes for, 32, 33
    downfield, 38
    individual assignments in,
        30–32
    rules of, 32–35
    selecting schemes for, 38
    techniques of, 29–30
Blocking near man, 35
Blocking rules, 32–35
Blocking schemes, 32

Blocks and blocking, 104–11
    basic techniques of, 106–11
    drive block, 104–6
    in offensive backfield, 119
    and offensive line, 104–11
    playing the block, 142–43
    and protecting the passer, 51–53
    punt, 89–91
    punt-protection, 87
    scramble block, 106
    teaching, 30
    use of hands in, 14
Body position, 30
Bootleg, 51, 68
Bosco, Robbie, 186
Bowden, Bobby, 1, 10
"Box," 48
Branch, Cliff, 197
Brodie, John, 44
Brown, Paul, 6, 182
Bruce, Earl, 9
Bryant, Bear, 73
Buck lateral series, 24, 25
Buck lateral system, 21
Bull rush, 134, 135–36
Bump-and-run approach, 60, 66
Bump-and-run players, 149
Bunched four point, 30
Butt and control, 129
Buttonhook pattern, 54
BYU, 50, 186

Cadence, 103–4
Cadigan, Dave, 105
Call blocking, 35–37, 37
Calling out defense, 35
Camp, Walter, 49
Canadian rules, 46
Carroll College, 49
Carrying the ball, 118–19

Carter, Babe, 187
Catching the ball, 123–25, 153
    See also Receiving
Center, 34, 69
Center snap, 102–3
Character development, 5–6
Charge, varying the, 129–34
Cheating, 1
"Cheating" the backs, 44
"Cherry pick," 65
Chicago Bears, 73, 197
Chop block, 108
City block, 36
Clear defense, 35
Cloud coverage, 62
Club and spin technique, 136
Coaching, 1–3, 205–9
    books and magazines on, 209
    elements of successful, 8–10
    and evaluations, 207–8
    fascination of, 7
    joy of, 3, 7
    and keeping up with the game,
        208–9
    philosophy of, 2
    and planning strategy, 3
    and setting goals, 206–7
    and tactical situations, 3
    and team leadership, 208
    and theory of game, 2
    videos on, 209
Cochems, Eddie, 49
Code words, 35, 36
College football statistics, 12
College 4-3 alignment, 33, 70
"Color" block, 36
Colors, field-position, 13
Combination blocks, 109–10
Complementary patterns, 55, 56
Compusports, 170, 174
Contact, 95–96
"Corner" route, 54
Cornerbacks, xiv, 72
Coryell, Don, 19, 50, 59
Counter trey, 25
Counters for passing attack, 66–67
Courage, 5
Cross block, 31, 35, 110, 143, 145–46
Cross reads, 140–41
Cross-block return, 85
Crossbuck, 18, 21, 24, 25
Crossing motion, 47
Crossing patterns, 60

Curtice, Jack, 66, 67
Cut block, 145
Cutoff block, 107

Dallas Cowboys, 197
Davies, Bob, 9
Davis, Al, 7
Davis, Mouse, 50, 64
Decision making, 187–88
Decleating, 105
Deep curl patterns, 56
Deep pattern, 62
Defense and defensive plays, 69
    attacking with defense, 74
    balance in, 81
    blitzing, 77, 80–81
    and defensive backs, 78
    goal-line defense, 81
    keying, 76
    and linebackers, 75–76
    line-play techniques, 74–75
    offense vs., xiii
    reading, 76–77
    scouting report, analysis in,
        171–72
    secondary alignment, theory of,
        78–79
    stemming, 77
    stunting, 77
    and taking away specific areas, 80
    using two gap stacks, 33
    and zone coverage, 79–80
Defensive alignment, 69–73, 78–79
Defensive back, 78, 94
Defensive halfback, xiv
Defensive line, 127–37
    and block protection, 128–29
    and blocking progressions,
        132–34
    drills for improving, 137
    goal line charge from, 130
    loop charge from, 130
    and pass rush techniques,
        134–36
    and pursuit to the ball, 137
    slant charge from, 129–30
    stunts, use of, 136–37
    theory of, 73–74
    and varying the charge,
        129–34
Defensive lineman, xiv
Defensive line-play techniques,
    74–75

Defensive secondary, 149–59
    drills for improving, 159
    and goal line, 158
    man-for-man coverage, 153–58
    zone techniques, 151–53
Defensive strategy, 182, 186, 192–93
Defensive tactical adjustments,
    199–203
Delayed pattern, 68
Dent, Richard, 73
Digital Scout (computer
    program), 169, 170, 173
Directional punting, 88
Ditka, Mike, 197
Dive, 25
"Dive and drive" drill, 85
Dodd, Bobby, 27
Double cut, 56–57
Double defense, 35
Double options, 22, 24
Double tight and double flanker, 42
Double-wing T, 40
Double-team blocks, 17, 31, 108,
    131–32
Double-wedge return, 85
Double-wide slot, 42
Down block, 30, 143
Downfield block, 37–38, 108
Drive block, 104–6, 145
Driving block, 108
Dropback passes, 50

Eagle alignment, 71, 73
Eagle 5-2, 33
Edwards, LaVell, 50, 59
Ellison, Glenn "Tiger," 50, 64
End trapping on reverse, 37
Ends, 70
Evaluations, 207–8
Evashevski, Forest, 21, 28
"Even" defense, 35

"Fade" route, 66
Fake handoff, xiv
Fake punts, 88
Faking, 118–19, 124–25
Faurot, Don, 27
Field goals, 91–92
Field position theory, 11–13
Finesse game, 17–18, 21–24
5-3 alignment, 33, 34, 69, 74
5-2 Oklahoma defense, 27
Five-under, two-deep zones, 54

Five-under man, two-deep
  safeties, 54
"Flag" route, 54
Flanker set motioned to set slot, 47
Flip-flopping teams, 43–44
Flood pattern, 56, 62
Flores, Tom, xi, 6–7
Florida-type double option, 24
Fly series, 25
Fold block, 31, 35, 110, 143
Foot placement, 44–45
Football Coaches Professional
  Growth Association
  (FCPGA), 209
Footwork, 30
Ford, Gerald, 8
Forearm block, 129
Forearm rip, 129
46 defense, 73
Forward pass, 59–68
  attacking defense with, 60
  against blitz, 67–68
  counters for, 66–67
  designs of, 59
  factors in, 59
  goal-line, 68
  against man-to-man coverage,
    60–61, 65–67
  as mental game, 68
  and planning scramble, 68
  and "reading" concepts, 63–64
  run-and-shoot, 64–65
  against zone coverage, 61–62
"Four down territory," 13
"Four Horsemen," 29
Four-point stance, 102, 127
4-3 defense, 71
Freeze option, 22
Fry, Hayden, 102
Full house, 27, 41
Fullback, 69
Fullback buck, 17, 18
Fullback counter from the I, 25
Fullback threat, plays starting with
  the, 24–25
Fumbling, 118

Gagliardi, John, 1
Galloping ghost, 45
"Gangster pass right" series, 64
Gap 8, 33
Gap control, 73
Gap placement, 32

Gap responsibility, 129–31
Gap stack, 32–34
Garrett, Mike, 26, 45
Gibbs, Joe, 8, 25
Gilman, Sid, 59, 182
"Go" call, 36
Goal line charge, 130
Goal-line defense, 81
Goal-line passing attack, 68
Goals, setting, 6, 206–7
Graham, Otto, 6, 7
Grange, Red, 45
Graves, Ray, 77
Green Bay sweep, 20
Grosscup, Lee, 66
Gruden, Jon, 206
Guard to playside, 34

Halfback threat, plays starting with
  the, 25–26
Hand shiver, 128
Handoffs, xiv, 117
Harvard's short punt, 39
Hayes, Woody, 2, 64
Head bob, 124
Head-and-shoulder fake, 124
Hefflefinger, Pudge, 8
Heisman, John, 49
Heisman Trophy, 49
Hendricks, Ted, 73
High-form tackling, 96
Hip roll, 30
Hitting position, 95, 96
Hitting surface, 30
Holtz, Lou, 9
"Hook and go," 65
Hook block, 107, 143, 146
Hook pattern, 54
Horizontal stretch, 50, 55, 61
"Hot" yell, 62–63
Houston veer, 23
Huff, Sam, 6

I formation, 19, 20, 41
I fullback counter trap, 20
Illinois preshift position, 45
"In and out," 65
Incomplete passes, 15, 49
Influence, 1
Inside belly series, 25, 27
Inside linebackers, 139–42
Inside veer at guard, 26
Inside zone block, 31

Inside-out block, 146
Inside-out trap, 37
Interceptions, 15
Iowa, 199
Isolation block, 143

Jackson, Bo, 26
Jerk, the, 134
Jitterbugging, 77
Johnson, Jimmy, 11–12
Johnson, John, 44

Kansas City Chiefs, 197–198
Keeping up with the game, 208–9
Kemp, Jack, 8
Kennedy, John, 8
Kentucky, 60
Key man, 35, 36
Keying, 76, 78, 139–40
Keys, 22
Kicked ball, catching the, 167
Kicking, 163–70
  drills for improving, 168
  long snap, 161–62
  place kick, 165–66
  punt, 162–64
Kicking game
  strategy for, 186–87, 194–95
  tactical adjustments in, 199, 203
Kickoff, 83–86, 166–67
  basic play, 83
  covering the, 84–85
  onside, 167
  onside kick, 84
  return strategies, 85–86
  two-kicker, 83
KISS approach, 28
Knute Rockne, All American
  (film), 49

Landry, Tom, 8, 45–46
Lateral holes, creating, 28
Lead block, 31, 107, 132
Leadership, team, 208
LeBaron, Eddie, 27
Legal chipping zone, 108
Line of scrimmage (LOS), 43
Line shifts, 45, 46
Line splits, 43
Linebacker(s)
  blocking a, 107
  and blocking progressions,
    143–45, 146

Linebackers, *continued*
  in blocking schemes, 32
  and defense, 69–73, 75–76,
      139–50
  diagram key for, xiv
  drills for, 148
  inside, 139–42
  man-for-man pass defense
      by, 147–48
  outside backers, 144–46
  and playing the block, 142–43
  responsibilities of, 146–48
  zone defense by, 147
Linemen, placement of, 43–44
Liszt, Franz, 5
Load block, 109, 146
Lombardi, Vince, 8, 20
Long snap, 89, 161–62
Loop, 74, 77
Loop charge, 130
LOS (line of scrimmage), 43
Louisiana State's formation, 40
Low-form tackle, 97
Lubick, Sonny, 9

"Mac," 72
MacArthur, Douglas, 7
McClendon, Charlie, 1
McKay, John, 19, 26, 28, 44–45
McKissick, John, 1
Mad dogs, 85
Madden, John, 7
"Man" blocking, 52
Man in motion, path of, xiv
"Man" rules, 33
"Man stack," 33
Man under, three-deep zones, 54
Man-for-man (M4M) coverage,
      54, 57, 60–61, 65–67, 153–58
Man-for-man pass defense, 147–48
Man-to-man defense, 79, 150
Marino, Dan, 50, 68
Maryland I formation, 19
"Me" call, 36
Melosky, Andy, 6
Meyer, Urban, 9, 24
Michelangelo, 8
Middle guard, 71–72
"Mike," 72
Millan, Matt, 6
Minnesota's spread, 40
Mismatches, 42, 56
Monster, 78–79

Montana, Joe, 93
Moore, Bud, 22
Motion, use of, 47–48
Motivation, 9
Movement, 93–95
Moving pocket, 51
Multiple formation, 47–48
Multiple offense, 28
Munn, Biggie, 28
Muscle contractions, 95

Narleski, Ted, 19
Neale, Earl "Greasy," 71
Nelson, Dave, 21, 28
Nelson, Karl, 29
Neyland, Robert, 69
"Nickel" defense, 39
90-degree angle cut, 56–57
Nixon, Richard, 8
Nose guard, 75
Notre Dame, 49
Notre Dame box, 39
Nugent, Tom, 19
Number blocking, 30, 33, 34
"Numbers" defense, 73, 74

Oakland Raiders, 73, 197
O'Connor, Bob, 29
"Odd" defense, 35
Off tackle, 18, 19
Offense
  advantages of, 69
  defense vs., xiii
  drills for improving, 115
  scouting report, analysis in,
      173–75
  strategy for, 179–85, 189–90
  tactical adjustments on,
      197–198
Offensive backfield, 115–20
  blocking in, 119
  and carrying the ball, 118–19
  center-quarterback exchange in,
      115–16
  drills for improving, 120
  handoffs in, 117
  and pitch plays, 117–118
  and power running, 119–20
  running back, stance of, 116
  and timing plays, 116–17
Offensive formation(s), 39–49
  back placement in, 44–45
  evolution of, 39–40

linemen placement in, 43–44
  motion, use of, 47–48
  selecting, 40
  shifting, 45–47
  spread, 48
  T-, 40–42
Offensive line, 101–14
  alignment of, 103
  and blocking, 104–11
  and center snap, 102–3
  importance of, 29
  and pass protection, 111–13
  and snap count, 103–4
  stance on, 101–2
  and the start, 103
Offensive linemen, 37
Offensive player, diagram key for,
      xiv
Offside guard, 35
Offside tackle, 35
Ohio State, 11
Okie defense, 72–73, 76, 78
Oklahoma 5-2, 33, 34, 36, 52
O'Leary, George, 12, 207
One-hand snap, 103
One-on-one block, 29, 30, 36
Onside guard traps, 35
Onside kick, 84
Onside kickoff, 167
"Option" football, 22–24
Orbit pattern, 61
"Out and up," 65
"Out" pattern, 54
Outside backers, 144–46
Outside belly series, 25, 27
Outside veer, 25–26
Outside zone block, 32
Overhand spiral, 49
Owens, Steve, 70, 72

Parcells, Bill, 97
Parent involvement, 9
Partial rollout, 50, 51
Pass patterns, 53–54, 59
Pass protection, 111–13
Pass rush, 134–36
Pass rusher, countering the, 113
Passer, 50–53
Passing, 49–57, 121–23
  action of passer in, 50–51
  calling routes in, 54–56
  development of, 49
  drills for improving, 125

early rules of, 49
    getting receiver open in, 56–57
    protecting passer in, 53–55
Passing game, 14–15, 50, 181, 190–91
Passing tree, 54–55, 57
Paterno, Joe, 1
Penn State's formation, 40
Perkins, Ray, 203
Philosophy, 2, 5–10
"Pick" play, 60–65
Pitch plays, 117–18
Place kick, 165–66
Planning strategy, 3
Plato, 5
Play series, selecting, 24
Play-action passes, 50, 51, 68
Player(s)
    character essentials for, 10
    contact with, 95–96
    movement of, 93–95
    path of, xiv
    tackling, 96–97
Playing the block, 142–43
Playing the Offensive Line (Nelson and O'Connor), 29–30
Playside end, 35
Playside tackle, 34
Plyometrics, 95
Pooch punt, 164
Pool, Hamp, 20
Portland State, 50
"Post" pattern, 54–55
Post-and-pivot block, 108
"Post-read" pattern, 62, 63
Power game, 17–20
Power I double tight, 41
Power I formation, 19–20
Power running, 119–20
Presnap cues, 127–28
Presnap read, 50
Princeton's formation, 40
Priorities, 2
Priority rule, 34
Pro football statistics, 11–12
Pro punt, 87
Probabilities of scoring, 11–13
Pro 4-3, 33, 52
Pro-I formation, 19, 28
Prothro, Tommy, 186
Prowling, 77
Pull and swim technique, 136
Punch, the, 98

Punt and punting, xiii, 12, 86–91, 162–64
    blocking, 89–91
    coverage, 87, 88
    direction of punt, 88
    distance of punt, 88
    fake punts, 88
    height of punt, 88
    pro punt, 87
    return strategies, 88–89
    spread and semispread punts, 87
    "tight punt" formation, 86–87
Pure man, loose coverage, 54
Pure man, tight coverage, 54
Pursuit to the ball, 137

Quarterback, 72, 79–80, 115–16
    eyes of, 147
    and zone defense by linebacker, 147
Quarterback sneak, 27
Quick kicks, 12
Quick pitch, 20, 21, 25
Quick-feet drills, 97
Quickness game, 17, 20–21
Quickness plays, 33
"Quick-side" linemen, 44

Raiders, 62
Raking the ball, 98
Reach block, 30, 107, 143, 145
Reading, 60, 63–64, 76
Reagan, Ronald, 8
Receivers, opening the, 56–57
Receiving, 123–25
Red zone, 13
Reducing formation from flanker to wing, 47
Responsibility, 1, 5
Return, punt, 88–89
Return strategies (kickoff), 85–86
Reverse club and slip technique, 136
Reverse shoulder block, 30
Reverse to wide receiver from pro-set T, 21
Reynolds, Jack "Hacksaw," 8
Rice, Homer, 22
Rice, Jerry, 93
"Riding," 25
Rip and run technique, 134–35
Robinson, Bradbury, 49
Robinson, Eddie, 1
Robinson, John, 7, 44–45, 199

Rockne, Knute, 1, 13, 29, 39, 40, 45
Rockne's box left, 45
Rockne's box right, 45
Rockne's Notre Dame box, 39
Rockne's T formation, 45
Rollout action, 50
Rounded cut, 57
Rover, 78–79
Rovering, 77
Royal, Darrell, 13, 22, 198
Rule blocking, 30
Run-and-shoot approach, 50, 59, 64–65
Running attack, 17–28
    basic series of, 26–28
    combinations in, 28
    developing, 24
    finesse game in, 21–24
    fullback threat starting the, 24–25
    halfback threat starting the, 25–26
    inside belly series, 27
    outside belly series, 27
    power game in, 18–20
    pro-I, 28
    quickness game in, 20–21
    split-T dive-option series, 27–28
    tailback threat starting the, 26
    traditional tight T/full house, 27
    wing T, 28
Running backs, 116, 118
Running game, 14–15, 180–81

Safeties, xiv, 85
St. Louis University, 49
San Diego Chargers, 50
San Francisco 49ers, 50, 59
Scholastic Coach and Athletic Director, 209
Scoop block, 31, 110, 132, 143
Scoring, probabilities of, 11–13
Scoring percentage chart, 12
Scouting, 169–71
Scouting report, 170–78
    collecting data for, 170–71, 176
    data input for, 171
    defensive analysis of, 171–72
    forms for, 176–78
    offensive analysis of, 173–75
Scramble, planning for the, 68
Scramble block, 29, 106
Scrapes, 144

Screen passes, 66, 67
Seal block, 107
Secondary alignment, theory of, 78–79
Semispread punts, 87
"Seven Mules," 29
Seven-diamond alignment, 69
Shift to eight-man line, 43, 46
Shift to unbalanced line, 43, 45, 46
Shifting offense, 45–47
Shiver, 75
"Short motion," 47, 48
Short passes, 59
Short punt, 39
Shoulder block, 105–6
Shoulder club and swim technique, 135
Shovel pass, 66, 67
Shuffles, 144
Shula, Don, 68
Sideline pattern, 54
Sideways, moving, 95
Sidewinder kick, 165
Simple sentence rule, 33–34
Simpson, O. J., 26, 45
Singletary, Mike, 1, 73
6-1 defense, 71
Six-shallow and three-deep zones, 53
Size of player, 30
Sky coverage, 62
Slant charge, 74, 129–30
Slant play, 25
Slants, 77
Slide protection, 52
Slip block, 143
Slot set motioned to flanker, 47
Snap count, 103–4
Snapper, diagram key for, xiv
Snapping the ball, 102
Soccer-style kicks, 165, 167
"Solid" defense, 35
Specialized defense, 46
Speed, developing, 93–95
"Speed" option, 22
Split ends, 42
Split left, quads right, 42
Split 4 alignment, 70
Split 6 alignment, 70
Split 6 attack, 33
Split-T attack, 20, 76
Split-T dive, 17, 27–28
Split-T option, 22

Split-T series, 25
"Spot" pass, 54
Spread attack, 26
Spread formation, 48–49
Spread punt, 87
Sprint out pass, 51
Sprinting, 93–94
Square cut, 57
Squib-kicking, 84
"Stack" defense, 35
Stack 4 alignment, 70
Stagg, Amos Alonzo, 1
Stance, 30, 101–2, 149
Stand block, 107
Standard 6, 33
Stanford, 44–45
Start, the, 103
Stemming, 77
Stevenson, Robert Lewis, 5
Stram, Hank, 180
Strategy
    to beat defense, 179–80
    checklists for, 190–95
    and decision making, 187–88
    defensive, 182, 186, 191–93
    kicking game, 186–87, 194–95
    offensive, 179–85, 189–90
    overall, 181–82
    passing game, 181, 190–91
    running game, 180–81
Stretch blocking, 32
Stretching formation from wing to flanker, 47
Stripping the ball, 98
"Strongside" linemen, 44
Stunts and stunting, 53, 75, 77, 136–37
Surface, hitting, 30

T formation, 20, 26, 40–42, 116
Tackle trapping on crossbuck, 37
Tackling, 96–97
Tactical adjustments, 197–203
    defensive, 199
    in kicking game, 199, 203
    making, 199, 203
    on offense, 197–98
Tactical situations, 3
Tailback counter, 21
Tailback threat, plays starting with the, 26
Tatum, Jim, 27
TCU, 22

Teaffs, Grant, 1
Team, chemistry of, 7
Team leadership, 208
Tennessee single wing, 17, 26
Texas Tech, 62
T-formation snap, 102
Three-step and turn drill, 94
Three-deep, four-shallow zones, 54
3-4 defense, 27
Three-point stance, 101
Tight end, 102
Tight end right, trips left, 42
Tight formation, 40–42
Tight man under, single safety, 54
"Tight punt" formation, 86–87
Tight 6 alignment, 70
Timed patterns, 59
Timing plays, 116–17
Tipoff kick, 167
Total educational program, 5
Traditional "tight T," 27
Trap block, 31, 35, 37, 109, 130–31, 143
Tressel, Jim, 11
Triangle, 142, 145
Triple option, 22–23
Turnovers, 97–98
Twists, 53, 137
Two-hand snap, 103
Two-kicker, 83
Two-point stance, 44, 102

UCLA, 19, 44–45, 186, 199
Umbrella defense, 70–72, 78
Unbalanced line right, 43

Values, 9
Van Brocklin, Norm, 7
Veers, 23, 25–26, 41
Vertical holes, creating, 28
Vertical stretch, 50, 61, 62

Waggle, 51
"Walkaway" number 4 man, 64–65
Walsh, Bill, 7, 50, 59, 93, 198
Warner, Glenn "Pop," 1
Warner's double wing, 39
Warner's single wing, 39
Weather, 15
Weave and rounded cut, 57
Wedge block, 31, 32, 85–86, 109–10
Wedge on offensive center, 18

West Coast offense, 33, 50, 59
Wet fields, 13
Wide formations, 42
Wide plays, 34
Wide slot left, bunch right, 42
"Wide tackle 6," 69–70
Wilkinson, Bud, 27, 72
Wind, 13
Wingback reverse, 18
Wing-T, 21, 28
Winning, theories of, 11–15

Wishbone formation, 41, 117
Wishbone teams, 34–35
Wishbone triple option, 18, 23
Wrap-around tackling, 96, 97
Wrist club and swim technique, 135

Yale's formation, 40
Yeoman, Bill, 23
Yost, Fielding, 187
"You" call, 36
Youth football, 5, 7

Zampese, Ernie, 59
Zone blitz, 80
Zone block, 30, 32, 53, 104, 110, 111
Zone coverage, 61–62, 79–80
Zone defense, 57, 147
Zone teams, 78
Zone techniques, 151–53
Zones of field, 12, 13
Z-out pattern, 60, 65
Zuppke, Bob, 45